Vicesimus Knox

The spirit of despotism

Vicesimus Knox

The spirit of despotism

ISBN/EAN: 9783742859273

Manufactured in Europe, USA, Canada, Australia, Japa

Cover: Foto ©ninafisch / pixelio.de

Manufactured and distributed by brebook publishing software (www.brebook.com)

Vicesimus Knox

The spirit of despotism

THE
SPIRIT
OF
DESPOTISM.

BY

VICESIMUS KNOX, D.D.

Divitias comitatur Luxus, et Luxus, exit in Tyrannidem.
                                                    ERASMUS.
Ex Regum immoderati libidine *injusta* bella temerd plerumque suscipiuntur, scelerate geruntur, turpiter deponuntur.
                                                    BUCHANAN.

LONDON:

PAINTED IN THE TEAR MDCCXCV:

REPRINTED FOR WILLIAM HONE,
45, LUDGATE HILL.

1822.

ADVERTISEMENT

BY THE EDITOR.

THE Public are informed, that this Work, was written at the end of the year 1794, or the beginning of 1795, by the learned and excellent person, whose name now appears in the title page, and whose death the nation has recently had occasion to deplore. The confederacy to crush the rising liberties of France, that originated with the continental Despots, had not only received the active co-operation of this government, but was countenanced by associations formed by ministerial agents, and openly favoured by a powerful party in England. That a war, directed against the best interests of mankind, should be supported by England, the Author attributed alone to the influence of that pernicious spirit, which he has designated the ᴹ *Spirit of Despotism*a spirit always found arrayed against all political improvement, and which was then making an alarming progress in this kingdom. Under that persuasion he composed this treatise.

It was, however, among the various admirable qualities of the writer, that although, from a peculiar sensibility and fervour of feeling, he frequently gave expression to his opinions with less reserve than is the practice of men with colder natures, he rarely *acted* with precipitation; and never hesitated to retrace his steps, if his deliberate judgment pronounced them, in any respect, questionable. Upon a calm review of this work, notwithstanding every sentiment in it is founded upon humanity, truth, and justice; upon the principles of the British constitution, and upon the precepts of the Christian Religion; still he was apprehensive, that in his ardent manner of treating the subject, he might, perhaps, be considered as occasionally employing language too glowing and enthusiastic, and as' having been too much under the influence of strong indignation, when excited by a subject to which he was ever tremulously alive,—a ruinous, sanguinary, and wicked war:—he therefore ultimately determined TO SUPPRESS THE PUBLICATION ALTOGETHER, AND NOT A SOLITARY COPY HAS BEEN, AT ANY TIME, CIRCULATED WITH HIS CONSENT.

However the Editor may lament, that the world should so long have been deprived of the benefit of a production so highly conducive to the happiness of the human race, at the distance of nearly thirty years from the formation of the Author's decision he respectfully abstains from any comment upon it. He proceeds to detail the circumstances under which he caused the work to be printed anonymously, in another form, at the commencement of the last year.

It seems, notwithstanding the directions given for the total suppression of the work, that three [1] copies, by some means, were preserved; from one of them an edition had been printed in America without a name, the author having been there also unknown; another fell accidentally into the hands of a private gentleman; and a third was as

accidentally purchased at a bookseller's in London, by the Editor. Struck with the extraordinary importance of the matter—the pure benevolence of the sentiments—the warm love of civil liberty—the sublime views of Christianity *
which it exhibits—and the forcible and polished style in which it is written; feeling also that the revival and assertion of strongly despotic pretensions, on the part of Austria, in the affairs of Italy, and the connivance those pretensions met with from other powers, as well as that certain measures of this government gave the work a peculiar interest at the present day/the Editor determined to cause it to be published. He made fruitless inquiries after the name of the author, and it was not until a large impression was in circulation, that he discovered it. During his lifetime it would have been improper to have divulged it, the book having been made public without his permission, or even knowledge; but now, the Editor cannot refrain from adding, to the effect that the patriotic and virtuous sentiments contained in it must of themselves produce, the sanction and auth

In closing this brief notice, the Editor has the satisfaction of adding, that, at an interview which he solicited last spring, for the purpose Of apologizing for the unauthorized publication of this work, and explaining the cause of it; he found, that the interval which had elapsed since its composition, had only tended to confirm the writer in the constitutional principles of English liberty that in the following pages are so forcibly maintained.

Purity of heart, integrity of principle, profound erudition, powerful eloquence, a reputation equally high in theology, as in the belles lettres, together with singular simplicity of manners and sincerity of disposition, pre-eminently distinguished Dr. Knox, and should have raised him to the most elevated station in the establishment. He looked, however, above the world; and, if in an age, when public virtue leads not to court favour, and apostacy, sycophantic subserviency, and parliamentary interest, are the surest, if not the only passports to ministerial patronage, he descended to his tomb, unmitred and unrewarded; yet the successful labours of a life (of no short duration) unremittingly continued to its close, in the advancement of knowledge, morality, and religion, and the promotion of the happiness of mankind, will ever rank him among the brightest ornaments of our country, and enrol his name with the benefactors of the Human Race.

PREFACE

BY THE AUTHOR.

THE heart is deceitful above all things; who can know it? As far as I know my own, it feels an anxious desire to serve my fellow-creatures, during the short period of my continuance among them, by stopping the effusion of human blood, by diminishing or softening the miseries which man creates for himself, by promoting peace, and by endeavouring to secure and extend civil liberty.

I attribute War, and most of the artificial evils of life, to the *Spirit of Despotism>* a rank, poison* ous weed, which grows and flourishes even in the soil of liberty, when over-run with corruption. I have attempted to eradicate it, that the salutary and pleasant plants may have room to strike root and expand their foliage.

There is one circumstance which induces me to think that, in this instance, my heart does not deceive me. I am certain, that in attempting to promote the general happiness of man, without serving any party, or paying court to any individual, I am not studying my own interest. On the contrary, I am well aware that my very subject must give offence to those who are possessed of power and patronage. I have no personal enmities, and therefore am truly concerned that I could not treat the Spirit of Despotism, without advancing opinions that must displease the *nominal great*. I certainly sacrifice all view of personal advantage to what appears to me the public good; and flatter myself 'that this alone evinces the purity of my motive.

Men of feeling and good minds, whose hearts, as the phrase is, lie in the right place, will, I think, agree with me in most points; especially when a little time, and the events, now taking place, shall have dissipated the mist of passion and prejudice. Hard-hearted, proud worldlings, who love themselves only, and know no good but money and pageantry, will scarcely agree with me in any. They will be angry; but, consistently with their general haughtiness, affect contempt to hide their choler.

I pretend not to aspire at the honour of martyrdom: yet some inconveniences I am ready to bear patiently, in promoting a cause which deeply concerns the whole of the present race, and ages yet unborn. I am ready to bear patiently the proud man's contumely, the insult of rude ignorance, the sarcasm of malice, the hired censure of the sycophantic critic, (whose preferment depends on the prostitution both of knowledge and conscience,) and the virulence of the venal newspaper. It would be a disgrace to an honest man not to incur the abuse of those who have sold their integrity and abilities to the enemies of their country and the human race. *Strike, but hear,* said a noble ancient. Truth will ultimately prevail, even though he who uttered it should be destroyed. Columbus was despised, rejected, persecuted; but America was discovered. Men very inconsiderable in the eye of pride, have had the honour to discover, divulge, and disseminate doctrines that have promoted the liberty and happiness of the human race. All that was rich and *great*, in the common acceptation of that epithet, combined against Luther; yet when pontiffs, kings, and lords had displayed an impotent rage, and sunk into that oblivion which their personal insignificance naturally led to, Luther prevailed, and his glory is immortal. He broke the chain of superstition, and weakened the bonds of despotism.

I have frequently, and from the first commencement of our present unfortunate and disgraceful hostilities, lifted up my voice—a feeble one indeed—against War, that great promoter of despotism; and while I have liberty to write, I will write for Liberty. I plead weakly, indeed, but sincerely, the cause of mankind; and on them, under Goo, I rely for protection against that merciless SPIRIT which I attempt to explode.

CONTENTS.

SECTION
- I. INTRODUCTORY   page 1
- II. Oriental Manners, and the Ideas imbibed in Youth, both in the West and East Indies, favourable to the Spirit of Despotism   12
- III. Certain Circumstances in Education, which promote the Spirit of Despotism   19
- IV. Corruption of Manners has a natural Tendency to promote the Spirit of Despotism   26
- V. An Abhorrence of Despotism and an ardent Love of Liberty perfectly consistent with Order and Tranquillity; and the natural Consequence of well-formed Understandings and benevolent Dispositions   32
- VI. On the Venality of the Press under the Influence of the despotic Spirit, and its effects in diffusing that Spirit   39
- VII. The fashionable Invectives against Philosophy and Reason, a Proof of the Spirit of Despotism   46
- VIII. Of Loyalty, and certain mistaken Ideas of it   52
- IX. On taking Advantage of popular Commotions, accidental Excesses, and foreign Revolutions, to extend Prerogative and Power, and encroach on the Liberties of the People   59
- X. When Human Life is held cheap, it is a Symptom of a prevailing Spirit of Despotism   69
- XI. Indifference of the middle and lower Classes of the People to public Affairs, highly favourable to the Encroachments of the Tory Principle, and therefore to the Spirit of Despotism   76
- XII. The despotic Spirit is inclined to discourage Commerce, as unfavourable to its Purposes   84

SECTION	
XIII.	*The Spirit of Despotism displaying itself in private Life, and proceeding thence to avail itself of the Church and the Military* page 92
XIV,	*, The despotic Spirit inclined to avail itself of Spies, Informers, false Witnesses, pretended Conspiracies, and self-interested Associations affecting Patriotism* 106
XV.	*The Manners of Tory Courtiers, and of those who ape them, as People of Fashion, inconsistent with Manliness, Truth, and Honesty; and their Prevalence injurious to a free Constitution, and the Happiness of Human Nature* 114
XVI.	*The Spirit of Truth, Liberty, and Virtue, public as well as private, chiefly to be found in the middle Ranks of the People* 125
XVII.	*On debauching the Minds of the rising Generation, and a whole People, by giving them military Notions in a free and commercial Country* 132
XVIII.	*Levity, Effeminacy, Ignorance, and Want of Principle in private Life, inimical to all public Virtue, and favourable to the Spirit of Despotism* 139
XIX.	*Certain Passages in Dr. Brown's " Estimate" which deserve the serious Consideration of all who oppose the Subversion of a free Constitution by Corruption of Manners and Principles, and by* undue INfluence 146
XX.	*On several Subjects suggested by Lord* Melcombe's *" Diary !" particularly the Practice of bartering the Cure of Souls for the Corruption of Parliament* 154
XXL	*On choosing rich Men, without Parts, Spirit, or Liberality, as Representatives in the National Council* 162
XXII.	*Of the despotic Influence of great Merchants over their Subalterns, of* Customers *over their Tradesmen, and rich trading Companies over their vari-*

SECTION	
	ous Dependents, in compelling them to vote for Court Candidates for Seats in Parliament, merely to serve private Interest, without the smallest Regard for public liberty and Happiness, or the Fitness or Unfitness of the Candidate..................page 169
XXIII.	Of the Pageantry of Life; that it originates in the Spirit of Despotism; and contributes to it, without advancing private, any more than public felicity....................
XXIV.	Insolence of the higher Orders to the middle Ranks and the Poor; with their affected Condescension, in certain Circumstances, to the lowest if the People................ 184
XXV.	Of a Natural Aristocracy.................igj
XXVI.	The excessive Love of Distinction and Power which prevails wherever the Spirit of Despotism exists, deadens some of the finest Feelings of the Heart, and counteracts the Laws of Nature 199
XXVII.	On the Opinion that the People are annihilated or absorbed in Parliament; that the Poice of the People is no where to be heard but in Parliament; and on similar Doctrines, tending to depreciate the People..................205
XXVIII.	The fashionable Contempt thrown on Mr. Locke, and his Writings in Favour of Liberty; and on other Authors and Books espousing the same *fawse ....
XXIX.	Of the Despotism of Influence, while the Forms of a free Constitution are preserved 819
XXX.	The Spirit of Despotism delights in War or systematic Murder 227
XXXI.	On the Idea that we have arrived at Perfection *** Politics, though all other Sciences are in a progressive State..................285
XXXII.	On Political Ethics; their chief Object is

SECTION

to throw *Power into the Hands of the worst Part of Mankind, and to render Government an Institution calculated to enrich and aggrandize a few, at the Expense of the Liberty, Property, and Lives of the many*........................ page 242

XXXIII. *On trafficking with the* Cure of Souls (Cura Animarum) *for the Purposes of political,* i. e. moral *Corruption*.. 249

XXXIV. *Of Mr.* Hume's *Idea, That* absolute Monarchy *is the easiest Death, the true* Euthanasia *of the British Constitution*   256

XXXV. *The Permission of* Lawyers *by Profession, aspiring at Honours in the Gift of the Crown, to hape the greatest Influence in the Legislature, a Circumstance unfavourable to Liberty.*   269

XXXVI. *Poverty, when not extreme, favourable to all Virtue, public and private, and consequently to the Happiness of Human Nature; and* enormous *Riches, without Virtue, the general Bane.* 269

XXXVII. *On the natural Tendency of making Judges and Crown Lawyers Peers; of translating Bishops, and annexing Preferments to Bishopricks, in, what is called,* commendam............................ 276

XXXVIII. *That all Opposition to the Spirit of Despotism should be conducted with the most scrupulous Regard to the existing Laws, and to the Preserva'tion of public Peace and good Order..* 287

XXXIX. *The Christian Religion favourable to Civil Liberty, and likewise to* Equality *rightly understood.* 294

XL. *The Pride which produces the Spirit of Despotism conspicuous even on the Tombstone. It might be treated with total Neglect, if it did not tend to the Oppression of the Poor, and to Bloodshed and Plunder.*

XLI. Conclusion   v\........................... 308

THE SPIRIT OF DESPOTISM.

SECTION I.

INTRODUCTORY.

MAN in a state of simplicity, uncorrupted by the influence of bad education, bad examples, and bad government, possesses a taste for all that is good and beautiful. He is capable of a degree of moral and intellectual improvement, which advances his nature to a participation with the divine. The world, in all its magnificence, appears to him one vast theatre, richly adorned and illuminated, into which he is freely admitted, to enjoy the glorious spectacle. Acknowledging no *natural* superior but the great architect of the whole fabric, he partakes the delight with conscious dignity, and glows with gratitude. Pleased with himself and all around him, his heart dilates with benevolence, as well as piety; and he finds his joys augmented by communication. His countenance cheerful, his mien erect, he rejoices in existence. Life is a continual feast to him, highly seasoned by virtue, by liberty, by mutual affection. God formed him to be happy, and he becomes so, thus fortunately unmolested by false policy and oppression. Religion, reason, nature, are his guides through the whole of his existence, and the whole is happy. VIRTUOUS INDEPENDENCE, the sun, which irradiates the morning of his day, and warms its noon, tinges the serene evening with every beautiful variety of colour, and, on the pillow of religious hope, he sinks to repose in the bosom of Providence.

But where is man to be found, thus noble, thus innocent, thus happy? Not, indeed, in so many parts of the terraqueous globe as he ought to be; but still he is to be found wherever the rights of nature and the virtues of simplicity are not violated^ or banished by the false refinements, the base artifices of corrupted government.

Unhappily for man, society has been almost universally corrupted, even by the arts intended for its improvement; and human nature is gradually de? praved in its very progress to civilization. Metamorphosed by the tampering of unskilful or dishonest politicians, and the craft of interested priests, co-operating with politicians, man at present appears, in many countries, a diminutive and distorted anim&l> compared with what he was in his primaeval state. He is become the dwarf and the cripple of courts and cities, instead of the well-formed, beautiful creature, who once bounded, in the glory of, health and strength, over the forest and the mountain, glowing with the warmth of virtue, and breathing the spirit of independence.

Various are the causes which contribute to the factitious depravity of man. Defective and erroneous education corrupts him; the prevalent examples of a degenerate community corrupt him; but bad *government* corrupts him more than all other causes combined. The grand adversary of human virtue and happiness is DESPOTISM. Look over the surface of the whole earth, and behold man, the glory and deputed lord of the creation, withering under the influence of despotism, like the plant of temperate climes scorched by the sun of a torrid zone. The leaf is sickly, the blossom dares not expand its beauty, and no fruit arrives at its just size and maturity.

' Turkey, Jtaly,./Egypt! how changed from what ye were when inhabited by antient Greeks, Romans, Egyptians! Nature, indeed, still smiles upon them with unaltered favour. The blue mantle of the skies is still spread over them in all its luminous magnificence. There is no reason to suppose the earth less fertile. The corn laughs in the vallies. The tree aspires to Heaveu with all its original verdure and majesty. But MAN decays; withered, shrunk, enervated; a form without spirit, an animal less happy than the beasts of the field, and more ignoble, inasmuch as degeneracy is baser than native, original, created inferiority. Fallen with the columnar ruins of better times, over which, in these countries, he often tramples, MAN himself appears little better than a ruin, displaying all the deformity of the

■mouldering pile, with scarcely any vestige of its former magnificence. It would equally contradict philosophy and experience to attribute this moral degeneracy to the decay of nature's vigour. There is no reason to conclude that the natural faculties of men who inhabit countries once free, but now enslaved, are produced in a state of less perfection at this hour, than in the days of their illustrious forefathers. Anatomy discovers no defect in the fibres of the heart or the brain; yet the degeneracy remains uncontested. In truth, *government* has counterapted the beneficence of nature, The men are fallen; while the *human figures,* with their internal and external organization, continue similar, or the same. They are inactive and pusillanimous. They aspire at no extraordinary excellence or achievements; but crouch beneath their despot, glad of the poor privilege allowed them by a fellow-creature, as weak and more wicked than themselves, to eat, drink, sleep, and die. Any pre-eminent degree of merit among them would render the distinguished possessor of it fatally illustrious, the certain object of a tyrant's vengeance; and they find their best security in their want of virtue. By a voluntary submission to contempt, they retain and transmit the privilege of breathing, and build the bulwark of their safety on their personal insignificance.

FEAR must of necessity become the predominant passion in all countries subject to the uncontrolled dominion of an individual and his ministers: but fear chills the blood, and freezes the faculties. Under its icy influence there can arise no generous emu-

OF DESPOTISM.

lation, no daring spirit of adventure. Enterprize is considered as dangerous, not merely from the general casualty of all human affairs, but because it excites notice, and alarms the jealousy of selfish power. Under a despotic government, to steal through life unobserved, to creep, with timid caution, through the vale of obscurity, is the first wisdom; and to be suffered to die in old age, without the prison, the chain, the dagger, or the poisoned bowl, the highest pitch of human felicity.

IGNORANCE of the grossest kind, ignorance of man's nature and rights, ignorance of all that tends to make and keep us happy, disgraces and renders wretched more than half the earth, at this moment, in consequence of its subjugation to despotic power. Ignorance, robed in imperial purple, with Pride and Cruelty by her side, sways an iron sceptre over more than one hemisphere. In the finest and largest regions of this planet which we inhabit, are no liberal pursuits and professions, no contemplative delights, nothing of that pure, intellectual employment which raises man from the mire of sensuality and sordid care, to a degree of excellence and dignity, which we conceive to be angelic and celestial. Without knowledge or the means of obtaining it, without exercise or excitements, the mind falls into, a state of infantine imbecility and dotage; or acquires a low cunning, intent only on selfish and[1] mean pursuits, such as is visible in the more ignoble of the irrational creatures, in foxes, apes, and monkies. Among nations so corrupted, the utmost effort of genius is a court intrigue or a ministerial cabal;.

; A degradation of the understanding, like this, is usually accompanied with depravity of heart. From an inability to find pleasure and honourable employment in the energies of thought, in noble and virtuous action, in refined conversation, in arts, in commerce, in learning, arises a mischievous activity in trifles, a perversion of nature, a wantonness of wickedness, productive of flagitious habits, which render the partaker of reason the most despicable and detestable animal in the whole circle of existence. Thus sunk under the pressure of despotism, who can recognize, notwithstanding the human shape they bear, the lineal descendants of ^Egyptian, Grecian, Roman worthies, the glory of their times, the luminaries of their own country and the world, the instructors and benefactors of human nature? Thus the image of the Deity, stamped on man at his creation, is defiled or utterly effaced by government, instituted and exercised by man over his fellow-man; and his kindred to Heaven is known no more by the divine resemblance. A bad government is therefore the curse of the earth, the scourge of man, the grand obstacle to the divine will, the most copious source of all moral evil, and for that reason, of all misery; but of bad governments, none are comparable, in their mischievous effects, to the despotic.

But if despotism in its *extreme* produces consequences thus malignant, reason will infer, and experience will justify the inference, that all the *subordinate degrees* of despotism are proportionally destructive. However it may be disguised by forms, it is ever seeking its own increase and aggrandizement* by'opeiily crushing, or secretly undermining, the OFabric of liberty: it is ever encroaching on the privi*leges and enjoyments of those who are subjected to it;- greedily, though foolishly, wishing to engross every good of every kind in this sublunary state, ex*cept the good of virtue.

POWER, though *limited* by written laws, in the hands of mortal men, poorly educated, and surrounded by sycophants and flatterers, who wish, by partaking tbe power, to partake also of its profits and distinctions, and thus gratify at once their pride and avarice, is always endeavouring to extend itself *beyond the limitations*,* and requires to be watched with the most jealous eye, by all who are subject to it, and to be restrained within its bounds by tbe manliest efforts, and the most determined resolution of virtue. Every engine of artifice and terror will be used to suppress such virtue: but tbe friend of man and of his country will defy persecution, fines, imprisonment, and death, in attempting, by every lawful and rational means, to push back the gigantic strides of encroaching despotism, more destructive of happiness than an earthquake or a pestilence. A country deserves no love, when it ceases to be a country of liberty. Human beings constitute a country; not a soil in a certain latitude; and an attachment to liberty is the truest loyalty.

It is therefore highly expedient, whenever a people, free by law and constitution, appear in the *smallest degree* to remit their attention to tbe preservation of freedom, to urge them, by the most serious admonition, to an immediate resumption of their vigilance.

While they slumber and sleep, lulled by the Circeari cup of corruption, the enemy is awake, and busily making his insidious approaches to the citadel. Every inch of ground, they carelessly relinquish, is > eagerly seized by the covetous possessor of dominion; the love of which, like the love of money, increases by accession. Nor are there ever wanting numbers of artful men who stimulate a weak or a wicked prince in his encroachments; sensible as they are, that their own power and privileges will be augmented with those of the prince, whose exclusive favour they have gained by sycophantic arts and by co-operation in the fallacious service of enlarging his prerogative. The more the power of the prince is augmented, the greater will be the emoluments, the more brilliant the distinctions of the courtier. *A -star shines with higher lustre, a riband displays a brighter hue, a title soothes the ear with sweeter music, when conferred by a mighty potentate far exalted above vulgar control, and who holds his crown in contempt of his people.* If kings can be once elevated to the rank of Heaven's vicegerents, how must admiring plebeians idolize their choice favours and their prime favourites ? There is always, therefore, a set of men (to whom pomp and vanity are the chief good) who are continually endeavouring to add glory and greatness to the orb from which they derive their own lustre. Moons and satellites would shine faintly indeed, unless the sun of the system glittered with intolerable efful-, gence. If the sun were shorn of its beams, their native opaqueness would pass without notice*

OF DESPOTISM. 9

So many advantages do the professors of power enjoy for its extension, in all countries where courts have influence, that the people, however great their numbers, are scarcely a match for its subtle contrivances, its false alarms, its bribes, its spies, its informers, its constructive treasons, its military force, its superstitious terrors, invented and diffused by a policy, which often laughs in secret at the religion which it enforces with solemn hypocrisy. A court has an opportunity of gratifying, in a thousand different ways, both secretly and openly, the most prevalent and violent passions of human nature. When the mass of the people are artfully seduced to throw their weight into the same scale with the court, liberty in the other must kick the beam. When the aristocracy of rank and riches unite hand in hand, to seduce the people, the delusion may for a time be successful, and advantages may be taken, during the temporary delirium, to rifle the castle of liberty, to weaken its foundations, to break down its battlements, or to lull its watchmen asleep with a powerful opiate.

It has indeed been said in antient times, and often repeated, that if the *people will be deceived, let them be deceived;* but they have no choice, no chance to escape deception, unless the truth be fairly and publickly exhibited to them, and their minds duly enlightened. When dust is thrown into their eyes, more especially gold dust, the political ophthalmist must honestly endeavour to clear away the obstruction. It becomes every lover of his country, especially a country like England, where even the throne itself is fixed on liberty as on a corner stone, to •warn his countrymen of the danger, wherever he observes the smallest encroachment on their rights, and the spirit of the times tending but remotely to despotism.

If there be a time, in which the senate of a free country has declared that the influence of the crown *has increased, is increasing, and ought to be diminished;* and if, instead of a consequent diminution, there be an evident increase of that influence; if acts, like the *habeas corpus,* highly favourable to liberty,.be s benevolences be encouraged; if places and pensions be multiplied; if juries be censured by great men for honest verdicts in favour of freedom; if endeavours be made to restrain the press by sycophantic associations; if spies and informers be kept in pay for the purpose of prosecuting innocent men who espouse-the cause of their country; if the press be hired to calumniate both liberty and the people; if wars, neither just nor necessary, be undertaken tb divert the public mind from domestic reformation; if a party prevail by artifice, who hate the name of liberty, who are continually employed in aggrandizing monarchy, aristocracy, and in depreciating the people; in such a time, and in such a conjuncture; it becomes every honest man, not yet drawn into the whirlpool of political corruption, to warn his fellow-citizens against an *encroaching spirit of despotism.*

In tbe following pages, I offer some suggestions on the subject. I have indeed few qualifications for the task besides sincerity, an earnest desire to promote public aud private happiness, and an independence of spirit; but these I certainly have, and profess to maintain. I wish the rising generation may be awakened, and learn to place a due value on the liberty handed down to them by their ancestors. I would inspire them with a generosity of mind, which should scorn dissimulation; which should neither practise the arts of corruption, nor become their dupe. I am desirous of discrediting the whole system of corruption, and of rendering all civil government fair, just, open, and honourable. All government, founded on insincerity and injustice, debases the morals and injures the happiness, while it infringes on the civil rights of the people. I wish to revive in the people a due sense of their native and constitutional importance. I endeavour, in this book; to plead the cause of man; firmly convinced that the cause of man is the cause of GOD.

SECTION II.

Oriental Manners, and the Ideas imbibed in Youth, both in the West and East Indies, favourable to the Spirit of Despotism.

THE foundations of the fair fabric of liberty in Europe were laid in ages when there was but little intercourse, commercial or political, with the remote countries of Asia and America. A hardy race, in ungenial climates, with nerves strung, by the northern blast, though little refined by knowledge, felt in an early age, the sentiments of manly virtue, and spurned the baseness of slavery. Luxury had not emasculated their minds; and they threw off, with native elasticity, the burden of unjust dominion. While they submitted, with graceful acquiescence, to all lawful authority, established by their own consent, for the general good; they preserved a noble consciousness of native dignity, and maintained a personal grandeur, a proud independence, a greatness unindebted to the morbid tumour of rank and riches.

In later times the facility of navigation and the improvements of science have brought into close connexion the extremes of the habitable globe. The asperity of manners which sometimes disgraced the virtues of our forefathers, has indeed been softened by various and constant intercourse; the manly spirit has exchanged ferocity for gentleness,

OF DESPOTISM. 13

and rendered the energetic character consistent with the amiable. It was a happy change; for why should manly virtue assume a forbidding aspect, and lose the recommendation of engaging manners, the happiness of loving and being loved, wbile it commands, by deserving, cordial reverence?

But from the intercourse of England with the East and West Indies, it is to be feared that something of a more servile spirit has been derived, than was known among those who established the free constitutions of Europe, and than would have been adopted, or patiently borne, in ages of virtuous simplicity.

A very numerous part of our countrymen spend their most susceptible age, in those countries, where despotic manners remarkably prevail. They are themselves, when invested with office, treated by, the natives with an idolatrous degree of reverence, which teaches them to expect a similar submission to their will, on their return to their own country. They have beeu accustomed to look up to personages greatly their superiors in rank and riches, with awe; and to look dowu on their inferiors in property, with supreme contempt, as slaves of their will and ministers of their luxury. Equal laws and equal liberty at home appear to them saucy claims of the poor and the vulgar, which tend to, divest riches of one of the greatest charms, overbearing dominion.

We do indeed import gorgeous silks and luscious sweets from the Indies, but we import, at the same time, the spirit of despotism, which adds deformity to the purple robe, and bitterness to the honied beverage.

The vassals of the feudal times, it is true, were abject slaves; but their slavery was freedom compared to the slavery of the negro. They were not driven by the whip to work in a torrid zone. They were not wanted to administer to personal luxury; for personal luxury did not exist. But the negro is rendered a two-legged beast of burden; and looks up to the infant son of his lord, as to a superior being, whoni he is bound to obey, however vicious, whimsical, or cruel the command. Cradled in despotism, the young planter comes to England for education, and brings with him the early impressions which a few years residence in the land of freedom can seldom obliterate. He returns; grows rich by the labour of slaves, over whom, for the sake of personal safety, the most arbitrary government is exercised, and then perhaps retires to England to spend his age and his acquirements'in the capita), the seat of pleasure, the theatre,of commercial splendor and courtly magnificence. He mixes much in society, and inevitably communicates his ideas, which have now taken deep root, on the necessity of keeping -the vulgar in a state of depression,' and strengthening the hands of the rich and 'the[1] powerful. In the virtuous struggles of the lower and middle ranks for constitutional liberty, is it likely that he should join the contest, on the side of the people? Is it nof most probable, that he wilt throw all his weight, which, considering the *weight of money,* is often great, in opposition to the popular side? A long succession of such men, personally respectable, but, from. peculiar circumstances, favouring the extension of power, and disposed, by habits and principles sucked in with the mother's milk, to repel tbe claims of their inferiors, must contribute greatly to diffuse, in a free country, the spirit of despotism.

That *oriental* manners are unfavourable to liberty* is, I believe, universally conceded. The natives of tbe East Indies entertain not the idea of independence. They treatthe Europeans, who go among them to acquire their riches, with a respect similar to the abject submission which they pay to their native despots. Young men, who in England scarcely possessed the rank of the gentry, are waited upon in India, with more attentive servility than is paid or required iu many courts of Europe. Kings of England seldom assume the state enjoyed by an East India governor, or even by subordinate officers.

Enriched at an early age, the adventurer returns to England. His property admits him to the higher eircles of fashionable life. He aims at rivalling or exceeding all the old nobility in the splendor of his mansions, the finery of his carriages, the number of his liveried train,, the profusion of his table, in every unmanly indulgence, which an empty vanity can covet, and a full purse procure. Such a man, when he looks from the window of his superb mansion, and sees the people pass, cannot endure the idea, that they are of as much consequence as himself, in the eye of the law; and that he dares not insult or oppress the unfortunate beiug who. rakes his kennel or sweeps his chimney. He must wish' to increase the power of the rich and great, thdt the saucy vulgar maybe kept at a due distance, that they may know their station, and submit their necks to the foot of pride.

The property of such a man will give him great weight in parliamentary elections. He probably purchases a borough. He sides with the court party on all questions; and is a great stickler for the extension of prerogative. In his neighbourhood, and as a voter for representatives, he uses all his interest in supporting such men as are likely to promote his views of aggrandizing the great, among whom he hopes to be associated, and in depressing the little, whom he despises and shuns. Having money sufficient, his present object is a title. This he knows can only come from the possessors of power, to whom therefore he pays such a submission as he has seen paid to himself in India by oriental, slaves.; His whole conduct tends to increase the influence' of riches, from which alone, he is conscious, he derives his own importance. What is his eloquence ? What his learning ? What his beneficence to mankind ? Little; perhaps none. But his estate, is large, his house large, his park large, his manors many, his equipage, on a birth-day, the most splendid in St. James's street. Long-Acre gives him a passport to court favour. With a seat in the house, and an.unrivalled equipage and mansion, he deems, himself justly entitled to be made, in due time, a. baronet at least, if uot an hereditary lawgiver of his: country.

' By a constantly successive influx of such men from the eastern climes, furnished with the means of corruption, and inclined to promote arbitrary principles of government, it cannot be doubted, that much is contributed to the spirit of despotism. Who among them would not add to the mass of that power and splendor, to possess a large share of which has been the first object of a life spent in unceasing cares, at the risque of health, and in a torrid zone?

And what is left to oppose the spirit of despotism thus animated in its progress by enormous opulence? Is it the virtue of the honest country gentleman, who lives on his estate, possessing nothing and hoping nothing from the favour of courts ? Is it the independence of the middle and the lower ranks, too numerous to be bribed either by gifts or expectations? Both, it is to be feared, will be too slow in their opposition to the gigantic monster, if not too feeble. They will not often risque their repose in a dangerous contest with opulence and power. They stand in awe of the sword and the law; which, in bad times, have been equally used as instruments of injustice. Contented with tlie enjoyment of plenty, or the amusemeuts of rural sports, they siuk into a state of indifference to public affairs, and thus leave the field open to those who have no right to occupy it. at all, much less exclusively.

Thus the community becomes divided into two descriptions of men; the corruptors and the indifferent; those who seek wealth and honours without virtue, and those who seek only their own ease, regardless of the public.

This indifference is scarcely leSs culpable than corruption. It must be laid aside. The independent country gentleman, seconded by the people, is the character, on whom Liberty must rely, as oil her firmest supporter, against the incursion of oriental pride.. Let him preserve[1] his independence by frugality. Let him beware of emulating either the brierital Or occidental upstart, in expences which he cannot equal, without diminishing his patrimony and losing his independence. Let him cultivate every social virtue, reside on his estate, and become popular by exhibiting superior excellence both of heart and' understanding. He will then do right to offer himself a candidate in his vicinity for a seat in the senate; beCause, as a senator, he will gain a power to act with effect against the increasing weight of corrupt influence. The truly WHIG PARTY, the lovers of liberty and the people, is not only the most favourable to human happiness, but certainly most congenial to the constitution of.England, and ought to be strengthened by the junction of all independent men, lovers of peace, liberty, and human nature.

The TORY AND JACOBITE SPIRIT, under other more plausihle names, is still alive, and has increased of late. AH who have a just idea of the British constitution, and of the value of liberty, will oppose it, by cultivating manliness of spirit, by illuminating the minds of the people, and by inspiring them with a regard to truth, justice, and independence, together with a love of order and of peace, both internal and external.

SECTION III.

Certain Circumstances in Education which promote the Spirit of Despotism.

MANY who have arisen to high elevation of rank or fortune seem to think that their nature has undergone a real metamorphosis; that they are refined by a kind of chemical process, sublimed by the sunshine of royal favour, and separated from the feces, the dross, and the dregs of ordinary humanity; that humanity, of which the mass of mankind partake, and which, imperfect as it is, God created. They seem to themselves raised to a pinnacle; from which they behold, with sentiments of indifference or contempt, all twb-legged and unfeathered beings of inferior order, placed in the vale, as ministers of their pride, and slaves of their luxury, or else burdens of the earth, and *superfluous sharers* of existence.^

T?he great endeavour of their lives, never employed in the essential service of society, is to keep the vulgar at a distance, lest their own purer nature should be contaminated by the foul contagion. Their offspring must be taught, in the first instance, to kno w aiid revere, ndt God, not man, but their own rank in life. • The infants are scarcely suffered to breathe the common air, to feel the common sun, or to walk 6n the common earth. Immured in nurseries till the time for instruction arrives, they are then surrounded by a variety of domestic tutors. And what is tbe first object in their education? Is it the improvement of their minds, the acquisition of manly sentiment, useful knowledge, expanded ideas, piety, philanthropy? No; it is the embellishment of their persons, an accurate attention to dress, to their teeth, to grace in dancing, attitude in standing, uprightness, not the uprightness of the heart, but the formal and unnatural perpendicularity of a soldier drilled on the parade. If a master of learned languages and philosophy be admitted at all, he feels himself in less estimation with the family than the dancing-master; and if possessed of the spirit, which the nature of his studies has a tendency to inspire, he will soon depart from a house, where he is considered in the light of an upper servant, paid less wages, and subjected to the caprice of the child, whom he ought to control with the natural authority of superior wisdom. To assume over his pupil the rights of that natural superiority, would be to oppose the favourite ideas of the family, *"that all real pre-emi-* *"nence is founded on Birth, fortune, and court fa-* *"vour."* The first object with the pupil, and the last, the' lesson to be got by heart, and to be repeated by night and by day, is an adequate conception of his own native consequence, a disposition to extend the influence of rank and riches, and to depress and discourage the natural tendency of personal merit to rise to distinction by its own elastic force.,

If the boy be allowed to go to any school at all, which is not always deemed prudent, because schools in general have a few plebeians who raise themselves there, to some degree of superiority, by merit only,

OF DESPOTISM. 21

it is only to schools, which fashion recommends, which abound with titled persons, and where the expences are so great, as to keep ingenious poverty, or, even mediocrity of fortune, at a respectful distance. Here he is instructed to form connexions with his superiors. The principal point is to acquire the haughty air of nobility. Learning and virtue may be added, if peradventure they come easily; but the. formation of connexions, and the assumption of insolence, is indispensable. To promote this purpose, pocket-money is bestowed on the pupil with.a lavish hand by his parents, and all his cousins who court his favour. He must shew his consequence,, and.be outdone by no lord of them all, in the profusion of his expences, in the variety of his pleasures, and, if his great companions should happen to be vicious, in the enormity of his vice. Insults and injuries may be shewn to poor people who attend the school, or live near it, as marks of present spirit and future heroism. A little money makes a full compensation, and the glorious action, on one side, and the'pusillanimous acquiescence under it, on, the other, evinces the great doctrine, that the poor are by: nature creatures of other mold, *earth-born perhaps*, and made for the pastime of those who have had the good fortune to be born to opulence or title. The masters themselves are to be kept in due order by the illustrious pupils, or a rebellion may ensue. Such an event indeed is sometimes devoutly wished, as it affords opportunities for *embryo heroes* to shew their prowess and their *noble* pride. Every ebullition of spirits, as it is candidly called, displaying itself in insolence or ill-usage of the inferior ranks, defenceless old men or women, and the poor in general, is remembered and cherished with cane, as a flattering prognostic of future eminence in the Cabinet, the senate, at the bar, or in the field. Justice, generosity, humility, are words indeed in the dictionary, and may adorn a declamation; but insolence, extravagance, and pride, must mark the conduct of those who are sent, rather to support the dignity of native grandeur by the spirit of arrogance, than to seek wisdom and virtue with the docility of modest and ingenuous disciples. Practical oppression of inferiors is one of the first elements of eristic cratical education; and the order of *Faggs* (as they are called) contributes much to familiarize the exercise of future despotism. Mean submissions prepare the mind, in its turn, to tyrannize.

Let us now suppose the stripling grown too tall for school, and entered at an university. The English universities are admirably well adapted to flatter the pride of wealth and title. There is a dress for the distinction of the higher orders extremely pleasing to aristocratical vanity. in the world at large the dress of all gentlemen is so similar, that nothing is left to point opt those who think themselves hf a superior order; unless indeed they ride in their coaches, and exhibit their splendid liveries behind, and armorial ensigns on the sides; but at Oxford, they never walk the streets, on the commonest occasions, without displaying their proud pre-eminence by gowns of silk and tufts of gold.

As noblemen, or gentlemen commoners, they not

only enjoy the privilege of splendid vestments, but of neglecting, if they please, both learning and religion. They are not required, like vulgar scholars, to attend regularly to the instruction, or to the discipline of the colleges; and they are allowed a frequent absence from daily prayer. They are thus taught to believe, that a silken gown and a velvet cap are substitutes for knowledge; and that the rank of gentlemen commoners dispenses with the necessity of that devotion which others are com* polled to profess in the college chapels. High privileges these! and they usually fill those who enjoy jtifaetn with that attachment to rank, which leads directly to the spirit of despotism. They are flattered in the seats of wisdom, where science and liberality are supposed to dwell, with an idea of some inherent virtue in mere rank, independently of merit; and after having learned a lesson so pleasing to self-love and idleness, they go out into the world with confidence, fully resolved to practise the proud theories they have imbibed, and to demand respect without 'endeavouring to deserve it.

Without public or private virtue, and without even the desire of it; without knowledge, and without even a thirst for it; many of them, on leaving college, enlist under the banners of the minister for the time being, or in a self-interested opposition to him* and boldly stand forth candidates to represent boroughs and counties, on the strength of aristocrat tical influence. Though they appear to ask favours of the people, tjiey pay no respect to. the people, but rely on rahk, riches, and powerful connexions. Eva-

inclined to favour and promote the old principles of jacobitism, toryism, and unlimited; prerogative, they hope to be rewarded.by places, pensions, titles; and then to trample on the *wretches* by whose venal votes they rose to eminence.   >

The ideas acquired and cherished at school, and at the university are confirmed in the world by as* sociation with persons of a similar turn, with Oriental adventurers, with pensioners and courtiers, with all who, sunk in the frivolity of a dissipated, vain, and useless life, are glad to find a succedaneum for every real virtue, in the privileges of titular honour, in splendid equipage, in luxurious tables, in magnificent houses, in all that gives distinction without merit, and notoriety without excellence. Their number and their influence increase by an union of similar views and ^principles; and a formidable phalanx is formed against those liberties, for: which the most virtuous part of mankind have lived and died. Under the auspices of multitudes, thus corrupted and united, it is not to be wondered, that the spirit of despotism should increase.. Despotism is indeed an Asiatic plant; but brought over by those.who have long lived in Asia, and nursed in a hot-house with indefatigable care, it is found to vegetate, bloom, and bear fruit, even in our cold, ungenial climate.

It might; then be worthy a wise legislator to reform the modes of education, to explode the effeminacy of private and superficial nurture,, to promote an; *equality of. rank* in schools and universities, and to suffer, in the immature age, no other distinctions than those, which may be adjudged by grave and virtuous instructors, to distinguished improvement, exemplary conduct, goodness of heart, and a *regard to the happiness of inferiors.*

The constitution of England is founded on liberty, and the people are warmly attached to liberty; then why is it ever in danger, and why is a constant struggle necessary to preserve it uninfringed? Many causes combine,-and perhaps none is more operative* than • a corrupt education, in which pride is nourished at the tenderest: period, and the possession or expectation of wealth and civil honours is tacitly re*, presented, even in the schools of virtue, as superseding the necessity of personal excellence.

SECTION IV.

Corruption of Manners has a natural Tendency to promote the Spirit of Despotism.

WHEN man ceases to venerate virtue in himself, he soon loses all sense of moral beauty in tbe human species. His taste becomes gross; and he learns to consider all that is good and great, as the illusion Of simple minds, the unsubstantial phantom of a young imagination. Exlretne selfishness is his ruling principle, and he is far from scrupulous in following its dictates. Luxury, vanity, avarice, are his characteristics. Ambition indeed takes its turn; yet, not that noble ambition, which seeks praise and honours by deserving them, but the low spirit of intrigue and cunning, which teaches to secure high appointments, titular distinctions, or whatever else can flatter avarice and pride, by petty stratagem, unmanly compliance, the violation of truth and consistency, and at last the sacrifice of a country's interest and safety.

In nations enriched by commerce, and among families loaded with opulence by the avarice of their forefathers, the mere. wantonness of unbounded plenty will occasion a corruption of manners, dangerous to all that renders society happy, but favourable to the despotic principle. Pleasure of the meanest kind will be the first and the last pursuit. Splendor, external show, the ostentation of riches, will be deemed objects of prime consequence. A COURT will be the place of exhibition; not of great merits, but of hue garments, graceful attitudes, and gaudy equipagesj every frivolous distinction, which boldly claims the notice due to virtue, and assumes die dignity which public services ought solely to appropriate. :

The mind of man, still wanting in the midst of external abundance, an object iii futurity; and satiated even to lothing with the continual banquej; of plenty, longs to add titular honours, or official importance, to the possession of superfluous property, But these, if. they mean any thing, are naturally the rewards of virtuous and useful exertion; and such exertion.is incompatible with the habitual indolence, the ignorance, the dissipation, the vice of exorbitant wealth, gained only by mean avarice, and expended in enjoyments that degrade, while they enervate. Men, distinguished by riches prdy, possess not, amidst all their acquirements, the proper price that should purchase civil distinctions, if they were disposed of only to *merit.* There they are bankrupts. They have no claims on society; for their purposes have been selfish, and their conduct injurious: yet the distinction must be obtained, or they sicken in the midst of healthy and starve, though surrounded with plenty. How then shall they he obtained ? They must be bought with money; but how bought ? Not directly, not in the market-place, not atpuhlic sale, But is there a borough hitherto auti-ministerial, and to convert which from the error of ite ways, a very expensive election must be engaged ini The ambi* tious aspirant at honours is ready with his purse. By money he triumphs over opposition, and adds the weight of his wealth to ministerial preponderance. He assists others in the same noble and generous services of his country. Though covetous, he perseveres,, regardless of expence, and at last richly merits, from bis patron, the glittering bauble which hung on high, and led him patiently through those dark and dirty paths which terminate in the temple of prostituted honour. His brilliant success excites others to tread in his steps with eager emulation; and though many fail of the glorious prize, yet all contribute, in the selfish pursuit, to increase and to diffuse the spirit of despotism.

Men destitute of personal merit, and unrecommended by the plea of public services, can never obtain illustrious honours, where the people possess a due share of power, where liberty flourishes, unblighted by corruption; and therefore such men will ever be opposed to the people, and determined enemies to liberty. The atmosphere of liberty is too pure and defecated for their lungs to inhale. Gentles and other vermin can exist only in filth and putrefaction. Such animals, if they possessed reason, would therefore endeavour to contaminate every healthy climate, to destroy the vital salubrity of the liberal air, and diffuse corruption with systematic industry. Are there not political phaenomena, which would almost justify a belief in the existence of such animals in the human form; and is not mankind interested, as they value their health, in impeding the progress of infectious pollution ?.

OF DESPOTISM.

Corruption does not operate, in the increase of the despotic spirit, on the highest; orders only,' and the aspirants at political distinction and consequence, but also on tbe crouded ranks of commercial life. In a great and rich nation, an immense quantity and variety of articles is ever wanted to supply the army and the navy. No customers are so valuable as the public. The pay is sure and liberal,.the demand enormous, and a very scrupulous vigilance against fraud and extortion seldom maintained with rigid uniformity. Happy the mercantile men who can procure a contract! The hope of it will' cause an obsequious acquiescence in the measures of the ruling minister. But it happens that such acquiescence, in such men, is peculiarly dangerous, in a commercial country, to the cause of freedom. The mercantile orders constitute corporate bodies, rich, powerful, influential; they therefore have great weight in elections. Juries are chiefly chosen from mercantile life. In state trials, ministers are anxious to obtain verdicts favourable to their retention of emolument and place. If the hope of contracts and other douceurs should ever overcome the sanctity of oaths, in an age when religion has lost much of its influence, then will the firmest pillar of freedom' be undermined, and courts of justice become mere registers of ministerial edicts. Thus both senatorial and judicial proceedings will be vitiated by the same means; and LIBERTY left to deplore a declining cause, while CORRUPTION laughs from a Lord Mayor's coach, as she rides in triumph to Court, to present, on her knees, the address of sycophancy.

When the public mind is so- debauched * as[1] to consideh titles and mbhey as the chief good of iban, weighed with which honesty and conscience ate but as fidst in the balance, can it be Supposed that a due teverence will be paid tb the obsolete parchments of a *tnagna ckartu*, to bills of rights, or to revolutions which banished the principles of the Stuarts together with their families, which broke their despotism 111 pieces together with their sceptres, and trampled their pride under foot with their crowns and robes of purple? The prevalence of corruption can call back to life the race *Ofjacobites* and *tones*, and place oh the thrOne of li berty au imaginary Stuart. It was not the person, hilt the principles which rendered the old family detestable to a people who deserved liberty, because they dared to claim it. The revival of those principles might render a *successor,* though *crowned* by Liberty herself, equally detestable.

To avoid such principles, the corruption that infallibly leads to them must be repelled. The people should be tinctured with philosophy and religion; and learn, under their divine instruction, not to consider titular distinction and enormous riches as the chief good, and indispensably requisite to the happiness of life. A noble spirit of personal virtue should be encouraged in the rising race; They should be taught to seek and find resources in themselves, in an honest independence, in the possession of knowledge, in conscious integrity* in manliness of sentiment, in contemplation and study, in every thing which adds vigour to the nerves of the mind, and teaches it to deem all honours disgraceful, and all profits vile, which accrue, as the reward of base compliance, and of a dastardly desertion from tbe upright standard of truth, the unspotted banner of justice;. -

SECTION V.

An Abhorrence of Despotism and an ardent Love of Liberty perfectly consistent with Order and Tranquillity; and the natural Consequence of well-informed Understandings and benevolent Dispositions.

THOSE who are possessed of exorbitant power, who pant for its extension, and tremble at the apprehension of losing it, are always sufficiently artful to dwell with emphasis, on the evils of licentiousness; under which opprobrious name, they wish to stigmatize liberty. They describe the horrors of anarchy and confusion, in the blackest colours; and boldly affirm that they are the necessary consequences of *entrusting* the people with power. Indeed, they hardly condescend to recognize the idea of a PEOPLE; but whenever they speak of the mass of the community, denominate them the mob, the rabble, or the swinish multitude. Language is at a loss for appellatives, significant of their contempt for those, who are undistinguished by wealth or titles, and is pbliged to content itself with such words as reptiles, scum, dregs, or the many-headed monster.

Man, that noble animal, formed with powers capable of the sublimest virtues, possessed of reason, and tremulously alive to every finer feeling, is degraded by his fellow man, when drest in a little brief authority, to a rank below that of the beasts of the field; for the beasts of the field are not treated with epithets of.contumely, but regarded with a degree of esteem. The proud grandee views the horses in his stable and the dog's in his kennel with affection, pampers them with food, lodges them in habitations, not only commodious, but luxurious; and,, at the same time, despises his fellOw-creatures, scarcely fed, wretchedly cloathed, and barely sheltered in the neighbouring cottage. And if this fellow-creature dares to remonstrate, his complaint is contumacy and sedition, and his endeavour to meliorate his own state and that of his peers, by the most lawful means, downright treason and rebellion.

Villainous oppression on one hand, and on the other, contemptible submission. If such acquiescence, under the most iniquitous inequality; such wretchedness, without the privilege of complaint, is the peace, the order, and the tranquillity of despotism; then peace, order, and tranquillity change their nature, and become the curse and bane of human nature.' Welcome, in comparison, all the feuds, animosities, and revolutions attributed to a state of freedom; for they are symptoms of life and robust health, while the repose of despotism is the deadness of a palsy. Life, active, enterprising life, with all its tumult, disaster, and disappointment, is;to be preferred to the silence of death, the stillness of desolation.

But I deny that a love of liberty, or a state of liberty, is of necessity productive of injurious or fatal disorder. I presuppose that the minds of the people, even the lowest of the people, are duly enlightened; that the savageness of gross ignorance is mitigated by culture; by that culture, which alt well-regulated states are solicitous to bestow on every partaker of the rational faculty.

In a state of liberty, every man learns to value himSelf as man; to consider himself as of importance in the system which himself has approved and contributed to establish; and therefore resolves to regulate his own behaviour consistently with its safety and preservation. He feels as a proprietor, not as a tenant. He loves the state because he participates in it. His obedience is not the cold, reluctant result of terror; but the lively, chearful, and spontaneous effect of love. The violation of laws, formed on the pure principle of general beneficence, and to which he has given his full assent, by a just and perfect representation, he considers as a crime of tbe deepest die. He will think freely, and speak freely, of the constitution. He will incessantly endeavour to improve it; and enter seriously into all political debate. In the collision of agitated minds, sparks will sometimes be omitted; but they will only give a favourable light and. a genial warmth. They will never produce an injurious conflagration.

What employment, in the busy scene in which man engages from the cradle to the tomb, is more worthy of him than political discussion? It affords a field for intellectual energy,- and all the finest feelings of benevolence. It exercises and strengthens every faculty. It calls forth latent virtues, which else had slept in.the bosom, like the diamond in the mine.; And is this employment, thus useful and honourable, to be confined to a few among the race of mortals? Is there to be a monopoly of political action and speculation ? Why then did Heaven bestow reason and speech, powers of activity, and a spirit of enterprize, in as great perfection on the lowest among the people, as on those who, by no merit of their own, inherit wealth and high station ? Heaven has declared its will by its acts.. Man contravenes it; but time, and the progressive improvement of tbe understanding, will reduce the' anomaly to its natural rectitude. And if a few irregularities should sometimes arise in the process, they are of no importance when weighed with the happy result; the return of distorted systems to truth, to reason, and the will of God. Occasional ferments, with all their inconveniencies, are infinitely preferable to the putrescence of stagnation. They are symptoms of health and vigour; and though they may be attended with transient pain, yet while they continue to appear at intervals, there is no danger, of mortification. Good hearts, accompanied with good understandings, seldom produce, even where mistaken, lasting evil. They repair and Compensate.

But I repeat that the people should be enlighten-. ed, in every rank, the highest as well as the lowest, to render them Capable of perfect liberty, without danger of those evils which its enemies are always asserting to be its unavoidable consequences. The vulgar must be instructed not merely in the arts which tend to the acquisition, increase, and preservation of. money, but -in a generous philosophy^ They must be liberalized. They must early learn to view human life and society in their just light;- to consider themselves as essential parts of a whole,: the integrity of which is desirable to every compo-' nent member. Their taste will improve with their understanding; and they will see the beauty. of order, while they are convinced, of its utility.. Thus principled by virtue, and illuminated with know-' ledge, they will eagerly return, after every deviation,' which even a warmth of virtue.may cause, to regular obedience, and to all the functions of citizens;' valuing the public peace and prosperity, because they understand clearly that the public happiness is[1] intimately combined', with their own. They may infringe laws, from the imperfection of their nature;' but they will return to their obedience without force;: having been convinced that no laws are made, but such as are necessary to their well-being in society.; They will consider laws, not as chains and fetters, but as helmets and shields fOr their protection!. The light of the understanding will correct the eccentricities of the heart; and all deviations/however rapid at their commencement, will be short, itt ex-; tent and transitory in duration.

. Such would be the effect of enlightening the people with political knowledge, and enlarging their'; minds by pure philosophy. But what say the des-> pots? Like the tyrannical son of Philip, when'he; reprimanded Aristotle for publishing his Discoveries, they whisper to their myrmidons, "Let us diffuse

OF DESPOTISM. 37

darkness round the land. * Let the people be kept in a brutal state. Let their conduct, when assembled, be riotous and irrational as ignorance and *our* SPIES can make it, that they may be brought into discredit, and deemed unfit for the management of their own affairs. Let power be rendered dangerrous in their hands, that it may continue unmolested inourowu. Let them not taste the.fruit of the tree ofknowledge, lest they become as we are, and learu to know good and evil," •

V- That such are the sentiments of the men who wish for the extension of royalism and the depression of the people, is evident from the uneasiness they have shewn at all benevolent attempts to diffuse knowledge among the poor. They have expressed, in terms of anger and mortification, their dislike of Sunday schools. The very newspapers which they have engaged in the service of falsehood aud toryism, have endeavoured to discountenance, by malignant paragraphs, the progress of those patriotic institutions. Scribblers of books and pamphlets, in the same vile cause, have intimated their apprehensions that the poor may learn to read political books in learning to read their Bible; and that the reading of political books must unavoidably produce discontent. A wretched compliment to the cause which they mean to defend! It is impossible not to infer from their apprehensions, that as men increase in understanding and knowledge, they must see reason to disapprove the systems established. These

* XtoTim, ntrmi, *darken your doctrines,* said the despot, Alexander, to the great philosopher.

men breathe the very spirit of despotism* and wish to commupicate it. But their conduct, in this in-
stance, is an argument against the spirit which they endeavour to diffuse. Their conduct seems to say, The spirit of despotism is so unreasonable, that it can never be approved by the mass of the people, when their reason is suffered to receive its proper cultivation. Their conduct seems to say, Let there be light, and the deformity of despotism will create abhorrence. ∎

Be the consequence what it may, let the light of knowledge be diffused among all who partake of reason; aud let us remember that it was THE LORD GOD ALMIGHTY who first said: LET THERE BE LIGHT.

SECTION VI.

On the Venality of the Press under the Influence of the despotic Spirit, and its Effects in diffusing that Spirit,

THE most successful, as well as the most iusidious mode of abolishing an institution which favours liberty, and, for. that reason, alarms the jealousy of encroaching power, is to leave the form untouched, and gradually to annihilate the essence. The voracious worm eats out the kernel completely, while the husk continues fair to the eye, and apparently entire. The gardener would crush the insect, if it commenced the attack on the external tegument; but it carries on the work of destruction with effir cacy and safety, while it corrodes the unseen fruit, and spares the outside shell.

The liberty of the press in England is not openly infringed, ft is our happiness and our glory. No man or set of men, whatever be their power or their wishes, dares to violate this sacred privilege. But in the heathen mythology we learn, that when Jupiter himself could not force certain obstacles by his thunderbolt, he found an easy admission, in the shape of a golden shower.

In times when. the jacobitical, tory, selfish, and despotic principles rear their heads, and think opportunities favour their efforts.for revival, the press is bought up as a powerful engine of oppression-

The people must be deceived, or the despots have no chance to prevail in the dissemination of doctrines, unnatural, nonsensical, and injurious to the rights of human nature. The only channel, through which the knowledge of what it most imports them to know, next to morality and religion, devolves upon the mass of the community, is a newspaper. This channel must therefore be secured. The people's money must be employed to pollute the waters of truth, to divert'their course, and, if occasion require, to stop them with dams, locks, and floodgates. The press, that grand battery, erected by the people to defend the citadel of liberty, must be turned against it. Pamphlets are transient, and confined in their operation. Nothing will satisfy the zeal of the assailant but the *diurnal* papers of intelligence. They keep up a daily attack, and reach every part of the assaulted edifice.

' Newspapers, thus bought with the people's -money, for the purpose of deceiving the people, are, in the uext place, circulated with all the industry of zealous partizans, and all the success, that must attend the full exertion of ministerial influence. Public houses in great towns, are frequently the property of overgrown traders, who supply them with the commodities they vend; and who dictate the choice of the papers, which they shall purchase for the perusal of their customers. Whoever" frequents such houses; -ruled as they are- by petty despots, must swallow the false politics, together with, the adulterated beverage, of the lordly manufacturer. A distress for rent, or an arrest for debt, might follow the rash choice of a paper favourable to truth, justice, and humanity. If any conversation should arise among the customers, friendly to liberty, in consequence of perusing an interdicted print of this kind, the licence of the house might be in danger, and an honest tradesman with his family turned out of doors to starve. Spies are sent to his house to mix with the guests, that in'the moment of convivial exhilaration, when prudence sleeps, some incautious comment-on the newspaper may be seized and carried to the agent of despotism, who, like the tyger, thirsting for human blood, lies watching for his prey in the covert of obscurity. The host, therefore, for the sake of safety, gladly rejects all papers.of intelligence, which are free to speak the truth, and. becomes a useful instrument, in the hands.of.selfish placemen, in the dissemination of doctrines subversive of liberty, and therefore of the constitution which is founded upon it as a corner stone..

. So far as such venal papers are diffused, under influence thus arbitrary, the liberty of the press is, in effect, destroyed. It is made to serve the purposes of slavery, by propagating principles unfavourable to the people's rights, by palliating. public abuses, varnishing ministerial misconduct, and concealing facts in which the people are most deeply interested. Perhaps there is nothing which contributes so much to diffuse the spirit of despotism as venal newspapers, hired by the possessors of power, for the purrpose of defending and prolonging their possession. The more ignorant classes have a wonderful pro?pensity to be credulous in all that they see in print, and. will obstinately continue to believe a newspaper, to which they have been accustomed, even when notorious facts give it the lie. They know little of history, nothing of philosophy, and adopt their political ideas from the daily lectures of a paper established solely to gain their favour to one party, the party possessed of present power; zealous for its extension and prolongation, and naturally desirous of preventing all scrupulous enquiry into its abuse. Such means, so used, certainly serve the cause of persons in office, and gratify avarice and pride; but it is a service which, while it promotes the sordid views of a few individuals, militates against the spirit of constitutional freedom. It is a vile cause, which cannot be maintained to the security and satisfaction of those who wish to maintain it, without recourse to daily falsehood, and the cowardly concealment of conscious malversation. Honest purposes love the light of truth, and court scrutiny; because the more they are known, the more they must be honoured. The friends of liberty and man are justly alarmed, whenever they see the press pre-occupied by power, and every artifice used to poison the sources of public intelligence.

In every free country the people, who pay all expences, claim a right to know tbe true state of public affairs.. The only means of acquiring that knowledge, within.reach of the multitude, is the press: and it ought to-supply them with all important information, which.may be divulged without betraying.intended measures, the accomplishment of which would be frustrated by communication to a public enemy. The very papers themselves, which communicate intelligence, pay a tax above the intrinsic value of the work and materials, to the support of the government: and the stamp, which vouches for thepayment, ought, at the same time, if any regard were paid to justice and honour, to be an authentic testimony that government uses no arts of deception in the intelligence afforded.

But let any one review, if it be not too nauseous an employment, the prints which of late years have been notoriously in the pay of ministerial agency. There he will see the grossest attempts to impose on the public credulity. He. will see the existence of known facts, when they militate against the credit of a ministry, doubted or denied; doubtful victories extolled beyond all resemblance to truth; and defeats, in the highest degree disgraceful and injurious, artfully extenuated. All who have, had opportunities of receiving true intelligence, after some great and unfortunate action, have been astonished at the eft frontery which has diminished the number of lives lost' to a sum so small, as contradicts the evident conclusions of common sense, and betrays the features of fajsehood at the first appearance. All who have been able to judge of the privileges of Englishmen, and the rights of human nature, have seen with abhorrence, doctrines'boldly broached and sophtetically defended, which strike at once at the English constitution, and the happiness of man in society. They bhVe seen this done by those who pretended an almost exclusive regard to law, order, and religion; themselves grossly violating all of them, while they are reviling others for the supposed violation; in the bitterest language which rancour, stimulated by pride and avarice, can utter.

■ When great ministers, possessed of a. thousand means of patronizing and rewarding obsequious instruments of their ambition, are willing to corrupt, there will never be wanting needy, unprincipled, and aspiring persons to receive the infection. But can men be really great, really honourable—Ksan 'they.be patriots and philanthropists—-can they be zealous and sincere friends to law, order, and religion, who thus hesitate not to break down all the fences of honour, truth, and integrity 4 and render their administration of affairs more similar to the juggling tricks of confederate sharpers, than to tjbe grave,,- in-' genuous conduct of statesmen, renowned for their wisdom and revered for their virtue ? Do men.thus exalted, whose conduct is a model, and whose opinion is oracular, mean to teach a great nation that conscience is but.a name, and honour a phantom? No books, of those innovators, whom they, persecute, contribute to discredit the system, which: these men support, so.much as their own sinister measures of self-defence..:   ;   : •   :>

There is little hope of preventing the corruption of the diurnal papersby any remonstrance addressed to men, who, entrenched behind wealth and power, scorn to yield at the. summons of reason. There may be more hope in appealing to the readers and encouragers of such papers. Do they wish to be deceived?/ Is it pleasant.to be misled by partial; mutilated, and distorted narratives ? Is it manly to:

become voluntary dupes? Or is it honourable, is it honest, to co-operate with any men, for any purposes, in duping others? No; let the press, however it may be perverted by private persons, to the injury of society, be preserved by the public, by men high iu office* the guardians of every valuable institution, as an instrument of good to the community, as the support of truth, as the lamp of knowledge.

Though the liberty of the press should be pre* served, yet let it be remembered, that the corruption of the press* by high and overbearing influence, will be almost as pernicious to a free country as its destruction. ■ An *imprimatur* on the press would spread an alarm which would immediately remove the re* straint; but the corruption of the press may insinuate itself unperceived, till the spirit of despotism, pro* moted by it, shall at last connive at, Or even consent to, its total abolition..

SECTION VII.

*The fashionable Invectives against Philosophy and
' Reason, a Proof of the Spirit of Despotism.*

PERSONS who owe all their pre-eminence to the merit of their forefathers, or to casual events, which constitute good fortune, are usually desirous of fixing a standard of dignity, very different from. real worth, and spare no pains to depreciate personal excellence; all such excellence as is, in fact, the most honourable, because it cannot exist without talents or virtues. Birth and riches, fashion and rank, are in their estimation infinitely more honoufr able and valuable than all the penetrating sagacity and wonderful science of a Newton. Such person; value Newton more as a knight than as a philosopher; more for the title bestowed upon him by Queen Anne, than the endowment given him by God, and improved by bis own meritorious exertion.

Upon this principle, many men in our times, who wish to extend and aggrandize that POWER, from whose arbitrary bounty they derive all the honour they are capable of acquiring, endeavour to throw contempt on PHILOSOPHY. It may indeed be doubted, whether they all know the meaning of the word; but they know it implies a merit not derived from princes, and therefore they wish to degrade it. Their fountain of honour, they conceive, has no resemblance, in its nature or efficacy, to the famed fountains of Parnassus.: it conveys no inspiration, except that which displays itself in the tumour of pride.

The present age has heard upstart noblemen give to philosophers (whose genius and discoveries entitle them to rank, in Reason's table of precedency, above every nobleman in the red book) the opprobrious appellation of wretches and miscreants. Philosophy and philosophers have been mentioned by men, whose attainments would only qualify them for distinction in a ball-room, with expressions of hatred and contempt due only to thieves, murderers, the very outcasts and refuse of human nature.

The mind is naturally led to investigate the cause of such virulence, and to ask how has Philosophy merited this usage from the tongue of factitious grandeur. The resentment expressed against Philosophy is expressed with a peevishness and acrimony that proves it to proceed from the sense of a sore place. How has pride been so severely hurt by Philosophy? It has been exposed, laid open to the eye of: mankind in all its nakedness. Philosophy has held the scales, and rejected the coin that -wanted weight. Philosophy has applied the touchstone, and thrown away the counterfeit. Hence the spirit of despotism is incensed against Philosophy; and if proclamations or cannon-balls could destroy her, her perdition would be inevitable and eternal. Polly exclaims aloud, "Let there be no light to de- "tect my.paint and tinsel." But happily, the command of Folly, however imperial her tone, is not the fiat of Omnipotence. Philosophy therefore will survive the anathema; and, standing on the rock of truth* laugh at the artillery of confederated despots.

When she deserts truth, she no longer deserves to be called Philosophy: and it must be owned, that when she has attacked religion, she has justly lost her reputation. But here it is well worthy of remark, that those who now most bitterly revile her, gave themselves little concern about her, till she descended to *politics.* She might have continued to argue against *religion;* and many of her present opposers would have joined in her cry with alacrity: but the moment she entered on the holy ground of politics, the ignorant grandees shuddered at the profanation, and "₁ A vaunt, Philosophy," was the word, of alarm.

Philosophy, so far from deserving contempt, is the glory of human nature. Man approaches by contemplation to what we conceive of celestial purity and excellence. Without the aid of Philosophy, the mass of mankind, all over the terraqueous globe, would have sunk in slavery and superstition, the natural consequences of gross ignorance. Men at the very bottom of society, have been enabled by the natural talents they possessed* seconded by favourable opportunities, to reach the highest improvements in Philosophy; and have thus lifted up a torch in the valley, which has exposed the weakness and deformity of the castle on the mountain, from which the oppressors sallied, in the night of darkness, and spread desolation with impunity. Despots, the meanest, the basest, the most brutal and ignorant of the human race, would have trampled on the rights and the* happiness of men unresisted, if Philo* sophy'.'had not opened the- eyes of the sufferers, shewn them their own power and dignity, and taught them to despise those giants of power, as they appeared through the mists of ignorance, who ruled a vassal world with a mace of iron. Liberty is the daughter- of Philosophy; and they who detest the offspring, do all that they can to vilify and discountenance the mother^

> But let us calmly consider what is the object of this Philosophy, so formidable in the eyes of those who are'bigotted to antient abuses, who hate every improvement* and who wish to subject the many to the controul of an arbitrary few. Philosophy is ever employed in finding out whatever is GOOD, and whatever TRUE. She darts her eagle eye over all the busy world, detects error, and mischief, and points out modes of improvement. In the multiform state of human affairs, ever obnoxious to decay and abuse, it is her's to meditate on the means of melioration. She wishes to demolish nothing but what is a nuisance. To build, to repair, to strengthen, and to polish, these are the works which she delights to plan; and,, in concerting the best methods of directing their accomplishment, she consumes the midnight oil. How can she disturb human affairs, since she dwells in contemplation, and descends not to action? neither does she impel others to action by the arts of delusive eloquence She applies to reason alone; and if reason is not convinced, all that she - has done, is swept away, like the. web- of Aracbne..

But it is modern Philosophy, and *French* Philosophy, which gives such umbrage to the lovers of old errors, and the favourers of absolute powers just as if Philosophy were mutable by time or place. Philosophy, by which I mean the investigation of the good and true, on all subjects, is the same, like the sun, whether it shines in China or Peru. Truth and good are eternal and immutable; and therefore Philosophy, which is solely attached to these, is still one and the same, whether antient or modern, in England or in France, , ,, ·

It is *sophistry,* and not Philosophy,.which is justly reprobated; and there has at air times been more sophistry displayed by the sycophant defenders of despotism, than by the friends to liberty. England has ever abounded. with sophists, when the high prerogative notions, Toryism, andJacobitism, and the servile principles which, flow, from them, have required the support of eloquence, either written or oral. Besides our modern *Filmrs,* we have had an army of ten thousand mercenary speakers-and wri* ters, whose names are as little rememberedas their venal productions. Such men*. contending against the light of nature, and common sehs,e*;.haye been obliged to seek succour of sophistry. Theirs, is the Philosophy, falsely so called, which deserves reprot batfon. They have had recourse to VERBOSITY, to puzzle and perplex the plainest points; they: have seduced the reader from the direct road of common sense, to delude his. imagination in the fairy land of metaphorthey have fine-spun their arguments to a degree of tenuity neither tangible nor visible, that they might excite the awe which is always felt for the *incomprehensible* by the ignorant; and, at the same time, elnde the refutation of the learned and the wise: they have acquired a lubricity, which, like the eel, enables..them to slip from the grasp of the captor, whom they coaid not have escaped, by. the fair exertion of muscular vigour. Animated with the hope of reward from that POWER which they labour to extend, they have, like good servants to their masters, bestowed art and labour in proportion to the weakness of their cause: they have assumed an air of wisdom to impose on the multitude, and uttered the language of knavery and folly with the grave confidence of an oracle. It is not necessary to cross the Channel in order to find Sophistry, decking herself, like the ass in the skin of the lion, with the venerable name of Philosophy.

As we value a free press, or wish to preserve a due esteem for genius and science, let us ever be on our guard, when we hear GREAT MEN, possessing neither genius nor science, rail against Philosophy. Let us remember, that it was a Roman tyrant, in the'decline of all human excellence, (when Providence permitted such monsters to shew the world the deformity of despotism,) who wished to extinguish the light of learning by abolishing the finest productions of genius. There are men, in recent times, who display all the propensities of a Caligula; be it the PEOPLE'S care, that they never possess his power.

SECTION VIII.

Of Loyalty, and certain mistaken Ideas of it.

THE mass of the community, on whom the arts of delusion are chiefly practised by politicians, are seldom accurate in the use of words: and among others which they misunderstand, anct are led, by the satellites of despotism, to misapply, is the term, Loyalty.

Loyalty means, in its true sense, a firm and faithful adherence to the law and constitution of the community of which we are members, if monarchy be a part of that constitution, it certainly means a firm and faithful attachment to the person of the monarch, as well as to the monarchical form,' and all the other branches of the system. It is nearly synonymous with fidelity; but as fidelity may be actuated solely by principles of duty, loyalty seems, in its common acceptation, to include in it also a sentiment of affection. It is the obedience of love, and anticipates compulsion. It is a sentiment, which all good men will feel,, when they live under a good government honestly administered.

But mark the disingenuity of men impelled by high-church, high tory, or jacobitical principles. They would limit this liberal, comprehensive principle, which takes in the whole of the constitution, and therefore tends to the conservation of it all, in its full integrity; they would limit it to the *person of the monarch,* to that part of the whole, which favours, in their opinion, their own purposes, and the extension of jpower and prerogative, the largesses of which they hope to share in reward for their sycophantic zeal, their slavish, selfish, perfidious adulation.

They represent this confined loyalty as a religious duty, partaking the nature of divine worship. They set up an idol, and command all men, upon their duty, to adore it. The people are not entitled even to attention by the propagators of this inhuman, anti-christian idolatry.

Let us consider a moment the mischief this artifice has in former times occasioned to our country. It attached great numbers to the family of tbe Stuarts, after they had forfeited all right to the crown; to the *persons* of the Stuarts, and for a long period, harassed the lawful king and the people of this nation with wars, alarms, seditions, and treasons. Tory zealots shed their blood freely, on the impulse of this unreasonable loyalty, which disregarded the ruling powers of their country established by law; and, in promoting the interest of a dispossessed individual, considered a whole people, either as a non-entity, or as worthy to be sacrificed for ONE MAN. Sncb men, acting in consistency with their principles of false loyalty, would have drenched their country in blood to restore an exiled Nero, of the *true-bred,* royal family.

Narrow loyalty, like this, which is but another name for bigotry, must ever be inimical to a mo* natch limited by laws, wishing to govern by them, and owing his seat on his throne to a revolution,- to the expulsion of a pre-occupant, apd the refusal of a pretender's claim. It must ever keep alive a doubt of his title. If it assumes the appearaneeofaffection for him, it may be suspected as the kiss of Judas. If it should seduce him to extend his power beyond the constitutional.limjts, it would lead., him to destruction; and involve, a people in all the mi?sery of revolutionary disorder. Is then such loyalty a public virtue ? In cunning men it is but mean servility endeavouring to ingratiate itself with the prince, for honours and emoluments.. In the simple ones, it is silly superstition. In both, it is injurious to the king of a free country and to the constitution. It confines that attention to one branch, which ought duly to be distributed among ALL, and to comprehend, in its attachment, that *main root and stock*, from which all the branches grow, the PEOPLE AT LARGE.

Nevertheless, such is the subtle policy of those who are actuated by the principles of Tories, Jacobites, royalists, despots, (call them by which name you please,) that they continue to represent every spirited effort in favour of the people's rights, as originating in disloyalty. The best friends to the constitution in its purity, and therefore thp.best friends to the limited monarch, are held out, both to public and to royal detestation, as disaffected to the person of the prince. Every stratagem is used to delude the common and unthinking part of the people-into a belief, that their only/way of displaying loyalty is, to display a most servile obsequiousness to the throne, and to oppose every popular measure.

OF DESPOTISM.

The procurers of addresses couch them in the most unmanly language of submission, and approach with a degree of prostration of sentiment, worthier to be received by the great mogul or the Chinese emperor, than the chief magistrate of a free people. The composers and presenters of such testimonies of loyalty, hoping-for knighthood at least, if not some more splendid or substantial effect of royal gratitude, exhaust the language of all its synonymous terms, to express their abject servility. Yet after all, of such a nature is their loyalty, that, if a Stuart or a Robespierre were the possessor of power, their mean and hollow professions of attachment would be equally ardent and importunate. *The powers that be ^re* the powers which they worship. The proffer of their lives and fortunes is the common sacrifice. Bat to distinguish their loyalty, they would go. farther than the addressers of the foolish and unfortunate James, and present their very souls to>be disposed of by their earthly Deity; knowing it to be! a *safe* oblation.

As. great respect is due to the office of the supreme magistrate, so also is great affection due to his 'person,; while be conducts himself with propriety* and consults the happiness of the people. Tfaie most decorous language should be used to him, the most respectful behaviour preserved towards him; every mode adopted of shewing him proofs of love and honour, *on this side idolatry.* Arduous is his task, though honourable. It should be sweetenedby every mode which true and sincere loyalty can devise. 1 would rather exceed than foil short of the deference due to the office and the man. But I will not pay a limited monarch, at the head of a free people, so ill a compliment, as to treat him as if he were a despot, ruling over a land of slaves. I cannot adopt the spirit of despotism in a land of liberty; and I must reprobate that false, selfish, adulatory loyalty, which, seeking nothing but its own base ends of avarice or ambition, and feeling no real attachment either to the person or the office ■ of the king, contributes nevertheless to diffuse by its example, a servile, abject temper, highly promotive of the despotic spirit. :•

. But the *ministers* of state have sometimes presumeed so far on present possession of power, as to attempt to make the people believe, that a *loyalty* is due to *them;* that an opposition to tAeirwill is a proof of defective loyalty; a remonstrance against *their* measures, a mark of disaffection. They have not been unsuccessful. The servile herds who come forward into public life, solely *to be bought up,* when marketable, are, for the most part, more inclined, to worship the minister than the monarch.. While it is *the priest* who divides among the sacrificers the flesh of the victim, many attend with devotion at the sacrifice; who are more desirous of propitiating the priest than the Deity. There are many who, if they had it in their power, would make it constructive treason to censure any minister, whose continuance in place is necessary to realize their prospects of riches and titular distinction. Such men,.wander up and down society as spies,, and mark.those.who blame the *minister,* as persons.to.be suspected of disloyalty. They usually fix on them some nickname, in order to depreciate their characters m the eyes of the people, and prevent them from ever rising to such a degree of public esteem, as might render them competitors for ministerial douceurs. Associations are formed by such men, under pretence of patriotism and loyalty, but with no other real design, than that of keeping the minister in place, whom they hope to find a bountiful paymaster of their services, a't the public expence.

True loyalty has no connexion with all this meanness and selfishness. True loyalty is'manly, while obedient, and respects itself, while it pays a voluntary and cheerful deference to authority and the persons invested with it. It throws sordid considerations aside, and haying nothing in view but the general good, bears an affection, and shews that affection, to the whole of a system established for the preservation of order and liberty. It is not misguided by pompous names, nor blinded by the glitter of external parade; but values offices and officers in the state, for the good they actually promote, for the important functions they perform, for the efficient place they fill, in the finely constituted machine ₍of a well-regulated community.

Such loyalty, I believe, does abound in England, notwithstanding the calumnies of interested men, who would misrepresent and cry down all real patriotism, that their own counterfeit may obtain currency. Men who possess such loyalty will be found the best friends to kings; if ever those times should return, which are said to afford the truest test Of friendship, the times of adversity.

May those times never come! but yet let us die*rish the true loyalty and explode the false; because the true is the best security to limited monarchy and constitutional liberty: while the false, by diffusing a: spirit of despotism, equally inimical to the constitution and to human happiness, is destroying the legal limitations, undermining the established systems, and introducing manners and principles at once degrading to human nature^ and pregnant with misery to nations.

SECTION IX.

On taking 'Advantage of popular Commotions, accidental Excesses, and foreign Revolutions, to extend Prerogative and Power, and encroach on the Li-' berties of the People.'

The riots in London, which, to the disgrace of magistracy, and the boasted vigilance of ministers, (richly paid as they are, to guard the public safety,) arrived from contemptible beginnings to a formidable magnitude in the year 1780, have been considered by courtiers, and those who are continually labouring to exalt prerogative at the expence of liberty, as extremely favourable to their purpose. They caused an universal panic. The cowardice, folly, and perhaps wickedness of certain public functionaries, were the true cause of the extensive mischief; but the excesses of a few most wretched rioters, who scarcely knew what they were doing; children, women, and drunken persons, were attributed to the PEOPLE. Arguments were drawn from the event against popular characters, popular books, popular assemblies, and in favour of military coercion. Military associations, in the capital were encouraged, and tbe bank of England became a barrack. Liberty has few votaries in comparison with Property. The alarm was artfully increased, and the spirit of despotism grew under its operation. The Tory mid Jacobite party exulted over the ruins, and would have rejoiced in building a Bastille with the dilapidations. "See," said they, as they triumphed over the scene, "the effects of *power* in the hands of the PEOPLE!"

But the truth is, the *people*, the grand mass of the community, were not at all concerned in effecting the mischief; for I cannot call a fortuitous assemblage of boys, beggars, women, and drunkards, the people. The first irregularities might have been suppressed by the slightest exertions of manly spirit. But those who were possessed of efficient places and their emoluments, enjoying the sweets of office without suffering a sense of its duties to embitter them, displayed no spirit, and left it to be fairly inferred that they had it not. The people at large were not to be blamed for these unfortunate events; the whole t>f the culpability belonged to the appointed ministers of the law, in whom the people trusted and were deceived. The blame, however, was laid on the people; and those who, from their arbitrary principles, wished to discredit all popular interference in government, rejoiced at the calamity, as an auspicious event, confirming all their theories and justifying their practice. *

The artful encroachers on liberty were not deceived in calculating the effects resulting from this total dereliction of duty oh the part of the civil magistrate. Almost immediately a damp was cast on the generous ardourj which, under a Wyvill, a Richmond, a Portland, and a Pitt, was seeking the salvation of the eountry, in a well-timed and deliberate reform of the house of commons. A few, indeed, remained equally zealous in the virtuous cause; but tbe minds of the many were palsied by the panic* and seemed ready to acquiesce under every corruption attended with tranquillity, rather than risk a reform, which, they were taught to believe, could not be effected without popular commotion. Toryism saw the change with delight, and employed all its influence in augmenting aud continuing the political torpor.

Jn a few years the public mind seemed to have relinquished its intentions of effecting a speedy reform. It seemed to adopt the physician's maxim, *Malum bene* positum ne moveto;* and hesitated to undertake the removal of a local pain, lest it should throw the morbid matter over the whole habit. The fear of exciting a general inflammation prevented men from probing and cleaning the inveterate ulcer. In the mean time, the sore is growing worse, and if not stopped in its progress, must terminate in a mortification.

Thus important and extensive were the consequences of a popular tumult, dangerous indeed and terrible in itself, but artfully exaggerated and abused by interested courtiers, for the prevention of parliamentary reform, and the discredit of all popular proceedings. When any appeal to the people was in agitation, on any business whatever, it was sufficient to say, "Remember the riots," and the intended measure was immediately relinquished. A glorious opportunity for the growth of despotic opinions! The high-church and high-government bigots re-

---

* Though this evil is *malum* mate *positum.*

joiced as if they had gained a complete victory. They already sang Te Deum.

But in the midst of their triumphs, as human affairs are seldom long stationary, the French revolution commenced. Every honest and enlightened mind exulted at it; but the news was like a death-bell to the ears of the sycophants. So' large, so powerful a part of Europe emancipated from the fangs of despotism, blasted all the budding hopes of those who were rather meditating the establishment than the demolition of absolute rule. Aristocratrcal pride was inprtified. Every sullen sentiment,' ettery angry passion, rose in the disappbinted bosom 'Of that ambition, which seeks its own elevation'oh the depression bf the people. But liberty and'ttumanity sympathized in the' joy of millions, restored 'to the rights which God and Natifre gave them; and which had been gradually stolen from them by the spirit of despotism, acting, for mutual aid, in alliance with superstition.   ' ' :   • *' . •!'>

But the morning which rose so beautifully in the political horizon of France was soon overclouded/ The passions of leaders, jealous of each other, menaced from within and from without, hunted by surrounding enemies till they were driven to phreuzy,' burst forth in tremendous fury. Cruelties, which even despots might shudder to perpetrate, were the effects of a situation rendered dangerous in the extreme, and almost desperate, by'the general attack of all neighbouring nations. The friends of liberty and humanity wept; but the factors of despotism triumphed once more. "Here," said they, ** we

OF DESPOTISM. 63

have another instance of the unfitness of the people foE the possession of power, and the mischievous effects of excessive liberty." Every art which ingenuity. eanpractise, and influence assist in its operation^ was exerted to abuse and vilify the French revolution. -Associations were formed to disseminate ehiidish books, favouring the spirit of despotism, addressed to the meanest of the people, who yet had too much sense to be seduced by sentiments, doctrines, and laqguage calculated only for the meridian of the nursery. Prosecutions and persecutions abounded p and it became *sedition* to hint the propriety of parliamentary r/Wmation. The alarmists, - as they were called, were so successful in propagating tbe old tory tenets, under the favourable influence' of the papic of real dangers and the detestation which French executions had justly occasioned, tbat sotoe of the staunchest friends of the people, men brought into the country at the revolution* owing all their honours and emoluments to it,aud hitherto professed and zealous whigs, deserted the 'Standard of liberty,^ and took distinguished posts under the banners of the enemy:

i The spirit of despotism now went forth with greater confidence than it had ever assumed since the expulsion of the Stuarts. Its advocates no longer sculked; no longer walked in masquerade. They boasted of their principles, and pretended that' they' alone were, friends to law, order, and religion. They talked of the laws of England not being severe enough for the punishment of sedition, and boldly, expressed a wish that the laws of Scotland might be' adopted in their place. Active promoters of parliamentary reform were now accused of treasonable intentions by tbe very persons who were once loudest in their invectives agaiust the corruption of the house of commons. Newspapers were hired to calumniate the best friends of freedom. Writers ap* peared in various modes, commending the old government of France; and pouring the most viruleht abuse on all who promoted or defended its abolition. Priests who panted for preferment preached despotism in their pulpits, and garretfoers. who hungered after places oτ pensions, racked tbeirinvention to propagate, its spiritby their pamphlets. Fear in the well-meaning, self-interest in the knavish,- and systematic subtilty in the great party of tones* caused a general uproar in favour of principles, and practices hostile to constitutional liberty.

It is, however, the nature of all violent paroxysms to be of transient duration. The friends of man may therefore hope that panic fears, servile sycophantism, and artful bigotry, will not long, prevail over cool reason and liberal philanthropy. The drunken delirium will pass off; and sober sense will soon see and acknowledge, that the accidental evils which have arisen in a neighbouring nation, during a singular struggle for liberty, can be no arguments in favour of despotism, which is a *constant evil* of the most destructive nature. The body in high and robust health is most subject to the heat of an inflammatory fever; but no man in his senses will therefore cease to wish for high and robust health.

' Sensible men, and true friends to the constitution, * and therefore to tbe king, who forms so considerable a part of it, will be on their guard against false alarms excited hy courtiers; lest in the fear of some future evil, from popular commotion, they lay aside that. ever-Waking vigilance which is necessary to guard the good in possession, their constitutional liberty, from the secret depredation of. the artful spoiler,: who is always on the watch to encroach on popular rights and privileges.

".Riots, tumults, and popular commotions, are indeed' truly dreadful, and to be avoided with the utmost • care by the lovers of liberty. Peace, good order, and security to all ranks, are the natural fruits of a free constitution. True patriots will he careful to discourage every thing which tends to destroy them; not only because whatever tends to destroy them tends to destroy all human happiness, but. also because even an accidental outrage in popular assemblies and proceedings; is used by the artful to discredit the cause of liberty. By. the utmost attention to preserving the public peace, true patriots will defeat the malicious designs of servile courtiers; but, whatever may happen, they will not desert the cause.of human nature. Through a dread ofilicentiousness,, they will not forsake the standard of liberty. It is the part of fools to fall upon Scy 11a in striving to avoid Charybdis. Who but a fool would wish to restore the perpetual despotism of the old French government, through a dread Of the transient outrages of a Parisian tumult? Both are despotic while they last. But the former is a tor-

• rent that flows for ever; tbe latter only a labd flood, that covers the meadows to-day, and disappears on the morrow.

Dr. Price has a passage so applicable to the pr&sent subject, that I shall beg leave to close this section by the citation of it: and on. the mention of his name, I must pay a trifling tribute to his memory, which is the more necessary, as his character has been scandalously aspersed by those who are ever busy in discrediting the people and their friends, and who, pretending a love of goodness and.religion, blacken with their foulest calumny those who are singularly remarkable for both, for no other reason than that, undo: the influence of goodness and religion, such persons espouse the cause of freedom, and prefer the happiness of millions to tbe pomp and pride of a few aspirants at unlimited dominion, Meek, gentle, and humane; acute, eloquent, and profoundly skilled in politics and philosophy; take him for all and all, the qualities of his heart, with the abilities of.his head, and you may rank **Price** among the first ornaments of his age. Let his enemies produce from all their boasted despots and despotical Satraps, any one of his contemporaries whom, iti the. manner of Plutarch, they may place by Ins side as a parallel. Posterity will do him: the justice of which the proud have robbed him, and snatch him from the calumniators, to place him in the temple of personal honour, high among thebe*nefactors to the human race.

But I return from the ^digression, into which I was led by an honest indignation against the vilest

OF DESPOTISM.

of calumnies against the best of men. These are the words of Dr. Price:

"Licentiousness and despotism are more nearly-"allied than is commonly imagined. They are both "alike inconsistent with liberty, and the true end of "government; nor is there any other difference be-. "tween them, than that one is the *licentiousness of* "GREAT MEN, and the other the licentiousness of "*little* men: or that by one, the persons and pro- "perty of a people are subject to outrage and inva- "sion from a king, or a lawless body of grandees; "and that by the other, they are subject to the like "outrage from a lawless mob. *In avoiding one of* "*these evils, mankind have often run into the other.* "But all well-constituted governments guard equally "against both. Indeed, of the two, the last is, on "several accounts, the least to be dreaded, and has "done the least mischief. It may truly be said, if "licentiousness has destroyed its thousands, despot- "ism has destroyed its millions. The former having "little power, AND NO SYSTEM TO SUPPORT IT, ne- "cessarily finds its own remedy; and a people soon "get out of the tumult and anarchy attending it. "But a despotism, wearing a form of government, " and being armed with its force, is an evil not to be "conquered without dreadful struggles. It goes on "from age to age, debasing the human faculties, "levelling all distinctions, and preying on the rights "and blessings of society. It deserves to be added, "that in a state disturbed by licentiousness, there is "an ANIMATION which is favourable to the human "mind, and puts it upon exerting its powers; but "in a state habituated to despotism, all is still and "torpid. A dark and savage tyranny stifles every "effort of genius, and the mind loses all its spirit "and dignity."

Heaven grant, that in guarding against a fever, we fall not into a palsy!

SECTION X.

When Human Life is held cheap, it is a Symptom of a prevailing Spirit of Despotism.

THERE is nothing which I can so reluctantly pardon in the GREAT ONES of this world, as the little value they entertain for the life of a man. Property, if seized or lost, may be restored; and without property, man may enjoy a thousand delightful pleasures of existence. The sun shines as warmly on the poor as on the rich; and the gale of health 'breathes its balsam into the cottage casement on the heath, no less sweetly and salubriously than into the portals of the palace. But can the lords of this world, who are so lavish of the lives of their inferiors, with all their boasted power, give the cold heart to beat again, or relume the light of the eye once dimmed by the shades of death? Accursed despots, shew me your authority for taking away that which ye never gave, and cannot give; for undoing the work of God, and extinguishing the lamp of life which was illuminated with a ray from heaven. Where is your charter to privilege murder? You do the work of Satan, who was a destroyer; and your right, if you possess any, must have originated from the father of mischief and misery.

There is nothing so precious as the life of a man. philosopher of antiquity, who possessed not the religion of philanthropy, who knew not that man came from heaven, and is to return thither; who never heard the doctrine authenticated, that man is favoured with a communication of the divine nature by the holy spirit of God; yet, tinder all these disadvantages, maintained that HOMO EST RES SACRA, that every HUMAN CREATURE is CONSECRATED to God, and therefore inviolable by his fellow man, without profanation. All the gold of Ophir, all die gems of Golconda, cannot buy a single life, hot'pay for its loss. It is above all price. '

Yet take a view of the world, and you will immediately be led to conclude, that scarcely any thing rs viler than human life. Grimes which have very little moral evil, if any, and which therefore cannot incur the vengeance of a just and merciful Deity, are punished with death at a human tribunal. I mean state crimes; such actions,conduct,' speeches, as are made crimes by despots, but are not recognized as such in the decalogue; such as may proceed from the purest and most virtuous principle, from the most enlarged benevolence,' from wisdom and unaffected patriotism; such as hiay proceed from mere warmth of temper, neither intending nor accomplishing any mischief; the mere effects of error, as innocent too in its consequences as its orb gin. But the despot is offended or frightened; for guilt trembles at the least alarm, and notfaihg brut the blood of the accused can expiate the offenCe.

Yet numerous as are the innocent victims-qf the tribunal, where to offend the state is the greatest abomination that man can: commit, they are lost and disappear when compared to the myriads sacrificed to the demon of war. Despotism delights in war. It is its element. As the bull knows, by instinct, that his strength is in his horns, and the eagle trusts in his talons; so the despot feels his puissance most, when surrounded by his soldiery arrayed for battle. With the sword in his hand, and his artillery around him, he rejoices in his might, and glories in his greatness. Blood must mark his path; and his triutnph is incomplete, till death and destruction stalk over the land, the harbingers of his triumphant cavalcade.

We hear much of necessary wars; but it is certainly* true, that a real, absolute, unavoidable necessity for war, such as alone can render it just, has seldom occurred in the history of man. The pride, the wanton cruelty of absolute princes, caring nothing for human life, have in all ages, without the least necessity, involved the world in war; and therefore it is the common cause of all mankind to abolish absolute power; and to discourage, by every lawful means, the spirit that leads to any degree of it. No individual, however good, is fit to be trusted with so dangerous a deposit. His goodness maybe corrupted by the magnitude of the trust; and* it is the nature of power, uncontrolled by fear or law, to Vitiate the best dispositions. lie who would have shuddered to spill a drop of blood, in a hostile contest, as a private man, shall deluge whole provinces, as an absolute prince, and laugh over the subjugated plains whicli he has fertilized with human goto.

What are the chief considerations with such men, previously-to 'going to war, and at its conclusion?

Evidently the expence of MONEY. Little is said or thought of the lives lost, or devoted to be lost, except as matters of *pecuniary* valne. Humanity, indeed, weeps in silence and solitude, in the sequestered shade of private life; but is a single tear shed in courts, and camps, and cabinets? When men high in command, men of fortune and family, fall, their deeds are blazoned, and they figure in history; but who, save the poor widow and the orphan, enquire after the very names of the rank 'and file? There they lie, a mass of human flesh, not so much regretted by the despots as the horses they rode, or the arms they bore. While ships often go down to the bottom, struck by the iron thunderbolts of war,- and not a life is saved; the national loss is estimated by the despot, according. to the weight of metal wasted, and, the magnitude and expence of the wooden castle. *

' ' Ploratur lachrymis amissa pecunia veris! Juv.

. God, we read, made man in his own image; and our Saviour taught us that he was the heir of immortality. God made no distinction of persons; but.behold a being, born to a sceptre, though a poor,, puny, shivering mortaL like the rest, presumes to: sell, and let out for hire, these images of God, to do, the work of butchers, in any cause, and for any paymaster, on any number of unoffending fellow-creatures, who are standing up in defence of their, hearths, their altars, their wives, their children, and their.liberty. Great numbers of pien, trained to the trade of. human butchery, are constantly ready to-be let to hire, to carry on the work of despotism^ and to support, by the money they earn in this hellish employment, the luxurious vices of the wretch who calls them his property. Can that state of human affairs be right and proper, which permits a miscreant, scarcely worthy the name of a man, sunk in effeminacy, the slave of vice, often the most abominable kind of vice, ignorant and illiterate, debilitated with disease, weak in body as in mind, to have SHch dominion of hundreds of thousands, his superiors by nature, as to let them out for pay, to murder the innocent stranger in cold blood?

Though, in free countries and limited monarchies, such atrocious villainy is never permitted, yet it becomes the friends of liberty and humanity to be on their guard against the prevalence of any opinions and practices which depreciate roan, as man, and vilify human life. None can tell to what enormous depravity small concessions may lead; when the horror of crimes is gradually softened by the wicked arts of proud intriguers, idolizing grandeur and trampling on poverty.

What shall we think of the practice of what is called CRIMPING? Is it to be allowed-in a free country ? Are not men bought, inveigled, or forced by it, as if they were cattle, beasts of tbe field or the forest, and capable of becoming the *property* of the purchaser or the captor? If a nation should behold with patience such a practice increasing and encouraged by the great, would there not be reason to suspect, that it had lost the spirit of freedom, and was preparing to submit its neck to the yoke of despotism? Is not an impressed sailor or a kidnapped soldier one of the images of God ? Is he not entitled to all the rights of nature, and the society of which he is a member? Does poverty disfranchize a man, rob him of his rights, and render \m hfe a commodity to be bought and sold, or thrown away, at the will of a rich man, who is enabled to take advantage of his want, and add to the misfortune of indigence the curse of slavery ? Are a few pieces of silver to be allowed, by connivance* if not by legal permission, as the price of blood, when poverty, but not the will, consents to the sale?

Even if BOXING were ever to become a spectacle patronized by princes, and encouraged by a people, there would be reason to.fear lest MAN, AS MAN, had lost his value; lest life Were estimated of little price; and lest the spirit of despotism were gradually insinuating itself into the community. - There would -be reason to fear lest times, like those of the latter Roman emperors, were returning, and that men might be kept like wild beasts, to be brought on the stage and fight for public diversion, and to be murdered for the evening's amusement of fashionable lords and ladies, at an opera-house.

The dignity of human nature, in despotical countries, is treated as a burlesque. A man is less dignified than a pampered horse, and his life infinitely less valued. But in a land of liberty, like ours* every man should learn to venerate himself and his neighbour, as a noble creature, dependent only on God, on reason, on law. Life, under such circumstances, is a pearl of great price. Every human being, under sucb circumstances, is of equal value in the sight of God. They, therefore, who, in consequence of civil elevation, hold any man's life cheap and vile, unless he has forfeited his rights by enormous crimes, are guilty of rebellion against God, and ought to be hunted out of society; as the wolf, once the native of.England's forests, was exterminated from the island.

SECTION XI.

Indifference of the middle and lower Classes of the People to public Affairs, highly favourable to the Encroachments of the Tory Principle, and therefore to the Spirit of Despotism.

THE opinion, that the majority of the PEOPLE have no concern in political disquisitions, is at once insulting and injurious. They who maintain it, evidently mean to make a separation in the minds of men, between the government and the nation. It is insulting to the nation, as it insinuates that they are either incapable or unworthy of interfering; and it is injurious to the government and the whole community, as it renders that power, which ought to be an object of love, an object of terror and jealousy.

Such an opinion is fit only for a country subject to absolute power, and in which the people, considered only as conquered slaves, hold their lives and all their enjoyments at the will of the conqueror. As it originates in despotic principles, so it tends to produce and diffuse them.

As to the intellectual abilities of the people, it is certain that some of the ablest statesmen, lawgivers, and men of business, have originated from that order which is called plebeian. There is a singular vigour of mind, as well as of body, in men who have been placed out of the reach of luxury and corruption by their poor or obscure condition; and when this vigour of mind has been improved by a competent education, and subsequent opportunities of experience and observation, it has led to very high degrees of menital excellence. Plebeians have arrived at the very first rank in all arts and sciences; and there is nothing in politics so peculiarly abstruse or recondite, as to be incomprehensible by Intellects that have penetrated into the profoundest depths of philosophy.

As to the right of the people to think, let him who denies it; deny, at the same time, their right to breathe. They can no more avoid thinking than breathing. God formed them to do both; and though statesmen often act as if they wished to oppose the will of the "Deity, yet happily they want the power. And since men must think, is it possible to prevent them from thinking of the *government* ? Upon the right conduct of which depend their liberty, their property, and their lives. It is their duty to watch over the possessors of power, lest they should be prevented, by the encroaching nature of power, from leaving to their posterity that freedom which they inherited; a natural right, preserved from the oppressor's infringement by the blood of their virtuous ancestors.

. But such is the effect of political artifice, under the management of court sycophants, that the middle ranks of people are taught to believe, that they ought not to trouble themselves with affairs of state. They are taught to think that a certain set of ! men come into the world like demigods, possessed of right, power, and intellectual. abilities, to rule the earth, as God rules the universe, without controls They are taught to believe, that free inquiry and manly, remonstrance are the sin of sedition. They are taught to believe, that they, are: to labour by. the sweat of their brow to get money for the!taxes;' and when they have paid them, to.go to work again for more, to pay the next demand without a murmur. Their children may starve: they may be. obliged to shut out the light of heaven, and the common air which, the beasts on the waste enjoy; they may he prevented from' purchasing the means of artificial light ini the;absehce of natural; they may he disabled: from procuring a draught of wholesome add refreshing: beverage after the day's labour which has raised the money to pay the tax; they may not be able to buy the materials for cleanliness of their persons, when defiled by the day's labour; yet they must acquiesce in total silence. They must read no obnoxious papers or pamphlets, and they must not utter a complaint, at the house where they are compelled to go for refreshment, which the tax prevents them from enjoying at home with their little ones!. Yet they have nothing to do with public affairs; and if they shew the least tendency to inquiry or opposition, they suffer a double punishment; first, **from** their lordly landlord and employer,.and secondly, from prosecution for turbulence and sedition.

The legal punishments attending the expression of discontent, by any overt-act, are so severe, and

OF DESPOTISM. 79

the ill-grounded terrors of them so artfully disseminated, that rather than incur the least dahger, they submit in silence to the hardest oppression.

Even the middle ranks are terrified into a tame and silent acquiescence. They learn to consider politics as a dangerous subject,, not.to be touched without hazard of liberty or life. They shrink there? five from the subject They will'neither read'nor converse upon it They, pay their contribution to a war, and take a minister's word that it is just and necessary. Better part with a little inoney patient*ly, since part with it we must, say they, than by daring to investigate tbe causes or conduct of public measures, risk a prison or a: gibbet.

Great and opulent landholders often exercise a despotism;intheir petty dominions, which stifles the voice of truth, and blinds the eye of inquiry. If tenants utter a sentiment[1] in public, adverse to the courtly opinions of the great mAn, who is looking up to a minister for a douceur fol* himdelf, his sons, his natural sons, or his nephews, olr cbusins, the beneficial lease will not be renewed at its expirationt What has such a fellow to do trith politics?' Fine times, indeed, when rustics dare to have an, bpinioh on the possibility of avoiding a wUr, which a minister has declared unavoidable f A thousand modes of harassing and embarrassing the subordinate neigh>bour, who dares think for himself, are practised by the slavish rich man, who,possessingenough to maintain a thousand 'poor families, is yet greedily grasping at a place or a pension; or, if he be too opulent to think of snch addition, which is seldom the case, still views with eager eye and panting heart,, at least a baronetage, and perhaps a coronet, glittering on high with irresistible brilliancy.

Gross ignorance, unmanly fear of punishment, and obsequiousness to overgrown aristocrats, at once servile and tyrannic, operate in conjunction to prevent the middle and lower ranks from attending to the concerns of the community, of which they are very important members; contributing to its support by their personal exertions, their consumption of taxed commodities, and the payment of imposts.

There is also an habitual indolence which prevents many from concerning themselves with any thing but that which immediately affects their pecuniary interest. Such persons would be content to live under the Grand Seignor, so long as they might eat, drink, and sleep in peace. But such must never be the prevailing sentiment of a people, whose ancestors have left them the inheritance of liberty* as an estate unalienable, and of more value than the mines of Peru. Such indolence is treachery to posterity; it is a base and cowardly dereliction of a trust, which they who confided it are prevented by death from guarding or withdrawing..

The middle and lower ranks, too numerous to be bribed by a minister, and almost out of the reach of court corruption, constitute the best bulwarks of liberty. They are a natural and most efficacious check on the strides of power. They ought therefore to know their consequence, and to preserve it with uuwinking vigilance. They have a stake, as it is called, a most important stake, in the country.

Let not tbe overgrown rich only pretend to have a stake in the country, and claim from it an exclusive privilege to regard its concerns. The middle ranks have their native *freedom* to preserve; their birthright to protect from the dangerous attacks of enormous and overbearing affluence. Inasmuch as liberty and security are more conducive to happiness than excessive riches, it must be allowed, that the poor man's stake in the country is as great as the rich man's. If he should lose this stake, his poverty, which was consoled by the consciousness of his liberty and security, becomes an evil infinitely aggravated. He has nothing left to defend him from the oppressor's wrong aud the' proud man's contumely. He may soon degenerate to a beast of burden; for the mind sinks with the slavery of the condition. But while a man feels that he is free, and fills a respectable rank, as a freeman, in the community, he walks with upright port, conscious, even in rags, of comparative dignity.

While the middle and lower ranks acquaint themselves with their rights, they should also impress on their.minds a sense of their duties, and return obedience and allegiance for protection.

To perform the part of good members of the community, their understandings must be duly enlightened, and they must be encouraged, rather than forbidden, to give a close attention to all public transactions. Disagreements in private life are often justly called, misunderstandings. It is through want of clear conceptions that feuds and animosities frequently happen in public. The *many* are not so mad as lliey are represented. They act honestly and zealously according to their knowledge. Give them fair and full information, and they will do the thing that is right, in consequence of it. But nothing more generally and justly offends them, than an attempt to conceal or distort facts which concern them; an attempt to render them the dupes of interested ambition, planning its own elevation on the ruins of their independence.

I wish, as a friend to peace, and an enemy to all tumultuary and riotous proceedings, that the mass of the people should understand the constitution, and know, that redress of grievances is to be sought and obtained by appeals to the law; by appeals to reason; without appealing, except in cases of the very last necessity, which seldom occur, to the arm of violence. I advise them patiently to bear, while there is but a hope of melioration, even flagrant abuses, if no other mode of redress appears, for the present, but convulsion. I would exhort them, not to fly from the despotism of an administration, to the despotism of an enraged populace. I would have them value the life, the tranquillity, the property, of the rich and great, as well as those of the poor and obscure. I would wish them to labour at promoting human happiness in all ranks, and be assured, that happiness, like health, is not to be enjoyed in a fever.

To accomplish these ends, 1 think too much pains cannot be bestowed in teaching them to understand, the true nature of civil liberty; and in demonstratng to them, that it is injured by all excesses, whether the excesses originate in courts or cottages.

And surely those men are neither friends to their country nor to human nature, who, for the sake of keeping down the lower orders, would object to teaching the people the value of a pure representation, free suffrage, a free press, and trial by jury. These are the things that are most likely to endear the constitution to them, to render them truly loyal, chearfully obedient, and zealously peaceable.

It is not the delusive publications of interested and sycophantic associators which can produce this valuable purpose. Writings so evidently partial persuade none but those that are already persuaded; and deceive none but those that are willing to be deceived. Truth only will have weight with the great body of the people, who have nothing to hope from ministerial favour, or to fear, while the constitution is unimpaired, from ministerial displeasure.

Let the people then be at liberty, uninterrupted by persons actuated by tory and high prerogative principles, to study politics, to read pamphlets, and to debate, if they choose it, in societies. The more they know of a good constitution and a good administration, the better they will behave. Ministry need not hire newspapers, or employ spies. Let them build their confidence in truth and justice, and the enlightened people will constitute its firmest buttress. Let it never be said, that the people have nothing to do with politics, lest it should be inferred, that such politics have no regard to the people.

SECTION Nil.

The despotic. Spirit is inclined to discourage Cony merce, as unfavourable to its Purposes.

Jg man a reasonable creature? Is he then most perfect and happy, when his conduct is regulated by reason? If so, then the boasted age of CHIVALRY was an age of folly, madness, and misery. It was an age in which a romantic imagination triumphed by force over the plainest and strongest decisions of common sense. It was an age in which pride and wanton insolence trampled on the rights and happiness of human nature. To express my idea of it in a word, it was an age of QUIXOTISM, in which Europe appeared as one vast country of bedlamites. Yet, wonderful to relate, men have lately arisen, pretending to extraordinary degrees of the distinctive faculty of mail, professing the most unbounded philanthropy, but at the same time regretting that the age of chivalry is no more.

The truth is, the spirit of chivalry was highly favourable to' the spirit of despotism. Every feudal baron was a petty tyrant, little differing from the chieftain of banditti. They were absolute sovereigns over their vassals. Tbeir castles were fortified palaces, from which they issued, regardless of government or law, like lions or tigers from their dens, to deform the land with blood and devastation. What was the situation of the PEOPLE, the million, in those days of mischievous folly? It was scarcely better than that of the negroes in the islands of America. And are these times to be regretted in the present day? Yes, certainly, by those who pine at seeing the condition of the multitude meliorated, and who consider the unfortunate part of their fellow-creatures as a herd of swine.

At this period of English history, slaves, natives of England, were bought and sold on English ground, just in the same manner as the negroes in Africa. One of the chief articles of export from England, in the time of the Anglo-Saxons, was the SLAVE. Slaves were always appendant to manorsj like the stock of cattle on a farm. They were attached to the soil, and were conveyed or descended with the estate, under the name of *villains regardant, glebce adscriptitii.* They were never considered as *citizens;* they had no vote, no rights; and were in every respect, in the eye of the great men who possessed them, like goods, chattels, and beasts of burden.

[1] As honest labour was considered as SLAVISH, so also was every kind of TRADE. The only class esteemed, was that which we should now call GENTLEMEN or ESQUIRES. And what was their employment? *Destruction of their fellow-creatures.* They neither *toiled nor spun;* but they wielded the sword, and shed blood under the banners of their chief, whenever he thought proper to wage war with an unoffending neighbour. They were, however, honourable men; *all, all honourable* men. But honour will hot fill the belly, nor clothe the back;

and pride was obliged to stoop for food, raiment dwellings, and all the comforts and accommodations of life, to the villain and vassal; who were exactly in the rank occupied by modem tradesmen, mechanics, and artisans. The GENTLEMAN of those days availed himself of their labour and ingenuity, and then despised them. The GENTLEMEN of modern days, who admire the age of chivalry, and who adopt tory and arbitrary principles, would be glad to consider this useful and ingenious class of citizens in the same light. "*Perish our commerce, live our constitution.* Perish the loom, the plough, "tbe hammer, the axe; but flourish the sword. "Sink the merchant ship, but let the man of war "ride on the waves in all her glory."

Such sentiments resemble those of the feudal barons, tbe most despotic GENTLEMEN that ever disgraced human nature. Tbe old feudal barons, however, could not always find employment for the Sword at home; and Peter the monk told them they would be rewarded in heaven by waging war on Palestine. They embarked with the blessings of the pope on their banners. It was a fortunate event for the despised vassals who were left at home. Both commerce and liberty are greatly indebted to the crusades for their subsequent flonrishing state. In the absence of the tyrants, the tradesmen and artisans exercised their art and industry on their own account, and gradually acquired a degree of independence. Many of the barons never returned to oppress them. Many returned, greatly injured in strength, spirit, and property. Consequently they lost their power. Charters were now sold or granted, and Commerce lifted up her front in defiance of Pride, that, looking down from her castle on the ship and manufacturer, despised her lowly occupation, while she envied her opulence. The country was enriched by arts which the nobles deemed vile. The mass of the people acquired property, and with it, power and independence. The tyranny of the feudal Bystem, and the nonsense of chivalry, which endeavoured to create a fantastic merit, independent of virtue and utility, soon vanished when tbe human mind was at liberty to think for itself; and men were emboldened to act freely by a consciousness of possessing skill and property..

But while the human heart is subject to pride, aud fond of power, the spirit of tyranny, which actuated the old barons in feudal times, will manifest itself, in some mode or degree^ whenever opportunities occur. Commerce was despised under the late monarchy in. Prance; and commerce, we have reason to. think, is looked upon with a jealous eye in England, by those who are violently attached to senseless grandeur.

. Men of this description are averse to commerce* not only from pride, but from policy. They see commerce enriching and exalting plebeians to a rank m society equal to their own; and often furnishing the means of luxurious enjoyment and splendour, >ybieh they them salves, with all the pride pf birth and the presumption of office, cannot support. Though a war may injure trade, and ruin manufacturing towns, yet it is eagerly engaged in, if it gratifies the revenge of courts, and the pride of noblest Its ill effects on commerce may be a recommendation of it to those who exclaim, *"Perish commerce, live our constitution."* It reduces that aspiring greatness of the merchant, which treads on the heels of the grandee, and overtops him. It bleeds the body which appears in the eyes of the great to shew symptoms of plethora. It clips the wings which seem ready to emulate the flight of the eagle. It lops the tree which gives umbrage by its shadow, The favourers of absolute power would have a nation of gentlemen soldiers, of courtiers, and of titled noblemen; and they view with pain, a nation of gentlemen merchants, of men independent' both in spirit and fortune, enlightened by education, improved by expedience, enriched by virtues and useful exertion, possessing principles of honour founded on honesty; and therefore quite as scrupulous and nice as if they had been bred in idleness, bloated with the pride of ancestry, tyrannically imperious over the active classes, and at the same time abject slaves to courtly fashion..

But, as in a commercial nation, it is impossible to prevent men of this description from sometimes acquiring princely fortunes, it becomes a very desirable object, among the politicians attached to arbitrary power, to corrupt the principal commercial houses, by raising in them the spirit of vanity and ambition. They have already acquired money more than sufficient for all the purposes.of aggrandizement. The next object is honour; that is, a title. A baronetage is a charming lure to the whole family. Any favour indeed from the court is' a feather. A title is now and then judiciously bestowed. This operates on the rising race, and teaches them to undervalue their independence in competition with the smile of a minister. The minister, indeed, has means of gratifying the avarice as well as the vanity of the commercial order. Contracts are delicious douceurs to the aspiring trader: they not only enrich, but lead to a connection with the powers'that be, and pave with gold the road of ambition.

But'the sun of tory favour which irradiates the tops of the mountain, seldom reaches the vale. The millions of humbler adventurers in commerce and manufacture, who are enriching their country,- and accommodating human life, in ten thousand modes that require both virtue and skill, are viewed by the promoters of arbitrary power with sovereign contempt. The truth is, that most of these, notwithstanding the disdain with which they are treated, are some of the most independent members of the community. They constitute a very large portion of the middle rank. They are a firm phalanx, and commonly enlisted on the side of liberty. They can scarcely be otherwise; for they have little to hope or fear from those who call themselves their superiors. They perform a work, or vend a commodity, equivalent to the compensation they receive; and owe no obligation beyond that which civility or benevolence, towards those with whom they negociate, imposes. The customer applies tothem for his ownconvenience. If they be fair traders,-they vend their wares at the market price; and if, one wilt not accede to it, they wait patiently for another ofier. They do not think themselves hound to make any unmanly submissions to those who deal with them for their own advantage.

A numerous body of men like these, possessing, in the aggregate, a vast property, and consequently, if.they could act in concert, a vast power also, cam not but be an object of uneasiness to the copartners in a proud aristocracy, wishing to engross to themselves the whole world, with all its pleasures, honours, emoluments, and rights^ As they cannot destroy this body, their next endeavour is to vilify it, to render it insignificant, to discourage its attention to public affairs, to lessen its profits, and to embarrass its operations, by taxes on its most vendible productions. They would gladly render a tradesman as contemptible in England as it was in France before the revolution. In France, we all know, under its despotic kings, no virtue, no merit, no services to the public or mankind, could wipe off the filthy stain fixed on tbe character by merchandize. The poorest, most villainous and vicious idiot, who partook of noblesse, would have been esteemed, in that unhappy period, infinitely superior to a Gresham, a Barnard, or a Skinner.

My purpose in these remarks is to exhort the mercantile order to preserve their independence, by preserving a just sense of their own dignity. I see with pain and alarm the first men in a great city, the metropolis of the world, whose *merc/umts are princes*, crouding with slavish submission to the minister of the day, seconding all his artful purposes in a corporation, calling out the military on the slightest occasion, at once to overawe the multitude, and at the same time to annihilate their own civil and constitutional authority. If they would but preserve their independence, and retain a due attachment to the people, and the rights of their fellow-citizens, their power and consequence would be infinitely augmented, and the very minister who buys or cajoles diem would hold them in high estimation. Ultimately, perhaps, their present sordid views might be accomplished with greater success; as they certainly would be, if accomplished at all, with more honour and satisfaction.

Instead of separating their interests, I would say, let bur commerce and our constitution ever flourish together. Certain I am, that a flourishing commerce, by giving power and consequence to the middle and lower ranks of the people, tends more than all the military associations to preserve the genuine [spirit of the constitution.

'SECTION XIII.

The Spirit of Despotism displaying itself in private Life, and proceeding thence to avail itself of the. Church and the

■MANY who enjoy the great advantages of distinguished rank and enormous wealth, either hereditary or acquired, not contented with those advantages, seem, by their behaviour, to envy the less fortunate of their species the little happiness they retain in their humble sphere. Unsatisfied with the elevation which their birth or fortune has given them, they wish to trample on their inferiors, and to force them still lower in society. Base pride! sordid greediness, of wretches, who, notwithstanding they are gratified with all external splendour, and pampered even to loathing with plenty of all good things, yet insult those who minister to their luxuries, and who (however deserving by virtue all that the others possess by chance) sit down with a bare competence, and often in want of veal necessaries, food, raiment, and habitation.

The insolence of many among the great, who possess neither knowledge nor virtue, nor any quality useful to mankind, and the contempt with which they Ipok down upon men, whom, though both virtuous and useful, they call their inferiors, excites the honest indignation of all who can think and feel, ^nd who are remote from the sphere of corrupting influence. The natural sensations of an honest heart revolt agaiust it. It is not only most highly culpable in a moral view, but extremely dangerous in a political. It arises from the genuine spirit of despotism, and if not checked by the people, must lead to its universal prevalence. Such a spirit would allow no rights to the poor, but those which cannot be taken away, such as the swine possess; the rights of mere animal nature. Such a spirit hates the people, and would gladly annihilate all of them, but those who administer to pride and luxury, either as menial servants, dependent tradesmen or mechanics, or common soldiers, ready to shed their own and others' blood for a morsel of bread. -

Even the beasts are held in higher, honour by the *aristocrats* than the poor people in their vicinage. Dogs and horses are fed, lodged, nay^ the horses sometimes clothed sumptuously; while:the poor labourers in the cot on the side of the common, are starved, scarcely sheltered by their roofs, and almost naked. As you ride by the splendid palace and extensive park of some inheritor of overgrotvn opulence, some fortunate adventurer, some favoured contractor, pensioner, or placeman, you behold sta^ bles and dog-kennels erected in a style of magnificence; externally grand and internally commodious. The dogs and horses are waited on by MEN appointed for the purpose, and more amply paid than the labourer, who rises early and late takes rest in the work of agriculture or manufacture. After viewing the magnificent stables, proceed a little, farther, and you see, on the road-side, and in the village, wretched houses, without glass-in the windows; tbe poor labourer, his wife, and children in rags; scarcely able to procure the smallest fire in the coldest weather, threatened with prosecution if they pick up sticks in the park; and, if they refuse to *endure* extreme cold and hunger, in danger of being hanged, and certain of imprisonment. The great man, who spends much of his time in the stable and kennel, and who caresses the horses and dogs, condescends not to enter the cottages. He receives the lowly obeisance of the inhabitants without returning it. Look at yonder corner of his park, and you see a board with an inscription, threatening all who enter with MAH traps and spring guns. If, tempted by hunger, the poor man should venture to catch a bare or partridge, the horsewhip is threatened, and perhaps indicted, in the first instance: and on a repetition of the atrocious crime, he and his whole family are turned out of their cottage; happy if himself be not imprisoned, though the bread of the helpless depends on his liberty and labour.

This petty tyrant of a village domain shall nevertheless think himself entitled to represent the next borough in parliament. What can be expected from such'a wretch, but that he should beas servilely mean and obsequious to a minister, as he is cruel and unfeeling in his behaviour to the poor of bis vicinity ? He has shewn already the dispositions of a Nero and Domitian in miniature; and if he could obtain a throne, his sceptre would be a rod of iron. He Would be inclined- to consider all the *people* as a tribe of POACHERS.

If no considerable district of a country be withont such overbearing despots; if they are viewed without abhorrence, and considered as assuming only the common privileges of country gentlemen; if such men, availing themselves of a corrupt state of representation; often procure a share in the legislature; is not that country, if there be such an one, in danger of being over-run with the spirit of despotism ? Are not the YEOMANRY, who are usually tenants of these lordly Nimrods, likely to be influenced by them, through fear of losing their farms, in their votes, and in all their sentiments and conduct? And will not Liberty lose some of her ablest* as they were probably among her sincerest and manliest; defenders, when the yeomanry desert her banners ?

Among all that description of persons who have been lately called ARISTOCRATS, proud and selfish in their nature, Tories and Jacobites in their political principles, it is obvious to remark the most haughty, overbearing manners in the transactions of common life, in their domestic arrangements, in their pleasurable excursions, their visits, their conversation, and general intercourse. In all these, their grand object is to keep the *vulgar,* urider which appellation they comprehend many truly, though not nominally, NOBLE, at a distance. They form a little world of their own, and entitle it, the *eircies of fashion.* Folly and vanity govern this little world With despotic rule; and virtue, learning, usefulness, have rio daim to admassioa into it. Pride, servility to courts, and a mutual though tacit agree*-

meat to treat the people with contempt, are among the principal recommendations to it. The grand secret of its constitution, is to claim dignity, distinction, power, and place, exclusively, without the painful labour of deserving either by personal merit or by services to the commonwealth.

. These people push themselves forward to notice at all public places. Though they contribute no more than others to the support of such, places, (fortheyare *sordidly parsimonious,*) yet they claim a right to dictate every regulation. Countenanced by each other, they assume at theatres a bold behaviour, such as argues a'sovereign contempt of the *canaille.* They talk loud, they laugh loud, they applaud each other's wit, they strut with airs of perfect self-complacency; but would not be.supposed to cast an eye at the inferior crowd, whose admiration thiey are at the same.time, courting, by every silly effort of pragmatical vanity. They cannot live long at home. No; they must have the eyes,of the very people whom they affect to despise, constantly upon their persons, their coaches, their livery servants; or else wealth loses its power to gratify,- hod grandeur is no better than insignificance.

Nothing flatters such persons more, than to have a number of their fellow-creatures engaged as/ 'servants about their *persons,* with nothing to do, or with such employments as a man, properly so called, could not endure to have done by.another, it adds greatly to.their happiness, if they can clothe these superfluous menials in very fine and costly dress, far exceeding any thing which the middle yet indepen-

Kj

dent ranks of the people can either afford or would choose to display. They also choose that their footmen should be handsome in their persons, as well as sumptuously clad; the intention being to lead the spectator to exclaim, when even the servants ate such' respectable personages, "how stupendously "great must be the lordly master!"

A court, with all its forms and finery, is the very element of such persons. They flutter about it like butterflies in the sunshine; and happy he, who, in his way: to it, excites the most admiration of his gaudy coach and coat in the crowd of St. James's-street; that crowd, which nevertheless they *scorn*, through fear of pollution, to look at, with eyes destined,in a few minutes to enjoy the beatific vision of royalty. But as a court is their delight, no wonder that their sentiments on political matters are perfectly courtier-like. They are for extending the powers and prerogatives of royalty, from a selfish idea that they can recommend themselves to the notice: and patronage of courts by servile compliance, ' by riches and pomp; whereas the *people* would require *personal merit* as the passport to their favour. They think the people have little to bestow but. bare esteem, or such offices as are honourable onlyin proportion as they are well or ill discharged; such; as require virtues and. abilities: whereas a court can bestow on its favourites, without requiring painful virtues, ribands, garters, stars, and titles, all which gratify superficial minds by their external finery and distinction, independently of any idea that they are, or should be, the public rewards of long and faithful services, in promoting die welfare of the community, and the happiness of the human race. ....

To form an adequate idea of the proud and frivolous minds of those who are intent on nothing but aggrandizing themselves by augmenting the power of courts and ministers, whose favour they seek with the most despicable meanness, it will be necessary to entertain right notions of the court of France, and the manners of the noblesse, previously to the revolution. "The two great aims" (says an observing French writer) "of the modern courtiers of "France, like some of another nation, were *cUssipa* "tiotiy* and the *means of repairing* the ruinous "consequences of that dissipation to their private "fortunes. To obtain the former end, they pursued "her through all the fantastical labyrinth of versa- "tile folly; and to accomplish the latter, they "startled at no depravity or corruption which pre- "sented itself." Thus the greatest personages in the nation were most distinguishable for vice and meanness; the sole object was to indulge in every vaid and every sensual gratification, and then to procure places and appointments, the profits of which were to pay the expences of pride and debauchery. The financier robbed the people. The great (as they are abusively called) received tbe stolen goods; and the people, in return for their property thus extorted from them, were at once oppressed, plundered, and despised. If a nobleman, impoverished by his normous vices and silly vanity, married into a. riob but plebeian family, they called this degrading- con-

OF DESPOTISM.

duct, the taking **dung** to fertilize their estates. At the same time, *pollution* as it was to *marry* the honest daughter of an honest merchant, they prided themselves in choosing for *mistresses* not only the lowest, but the most vicious persons, opera-dancers, and actresses, notorious for prostitution. Such were many of the courtiers, the noblesse, and sticklers for arbitrary power, in France; and have there not appeared in other nations, instances of similar conduct in persons of similar rank, and similar political principles?

In France, bishoprics were usually considered as genteel provisions for the sons of noble families. Religious considerations had little influence in the appointment of them. Learning was not a sufficient recommendation. **Blood** was the prime requisite; If by chance a man, with every kind of merit prosper for that station, rose to a bishopric, without; the recommendation of blood, he was despised by the fraternity, and called a **bishop of fortune**. I have heard in England such men as Dr. "Watson, and Dr. Porfeus, and Dr. Seeker, with all their learning, spoken of as men that must not think themselves of any political consequence; as men who should be satisfied with their *good fortune,* and not pretend to vie with the **Norths,** and Comwallises, and Keppels. How would such men have despised **Jesus Christ** and the poor fishermen 1 yet they love bishoprics, so far as they contribute to secular pomp End parade.

A similar spirit must produce similar conduct. Therefore those who would not wish the manners of 'the French, as they, existed before the revolution; to prevail'in their own country, will check the spirit that gives rise to such manners, by every rational: means of opposition to it.; That spirit and those manners at once supported the French monarchy, and caused its abolition.

- Indeed, the overbearing manners of the Tories, or friends of arbitrary power, are so disgusting in private life to every man of sense and independence, that they must be exploded, wherever sense and independence can prevail over the arts of sycophantism. They are no less offensive to humanity, and injurious to all the sweet equality of social. intercourse, than they are to public liberty. Observe one of. these persons, who swells to an unnatural size of self-consequence, from the emptiness of his head mid the pride of his heart, entering a coffee-house or public room at a watering place. To shew his contempt of all. around him, he begins *whistling,* or beating a tune with his. fingers or with a stick on the table. He stands;with his back to the fire, holding up the skirts of his coat, protruding his lips, picking his teeth, • adjusting his cravat, surveying his buckles, and turning out his knees or toes; shewing, by every sign he can think of, his own opinion of his own importance, and his sovereign contempt for the com* pany. Presently he calls the waiter with a loud voice and imperious tone. "Damn you, Sir, why don't you bring me a paper?" Then after strutting up and down two or three times, viewing himself in the glass, bowing through the window to a coach' with coronets on the sides, he hastily rushes out, shutting the door with a sound that disturbs the whole room. He steps back a moment, and having hallooed to the waiter—"Has Sir John been here?" shuts the door still louder, and departs to the other rooms, to display the same airs of self-importance.

Listen to him while he gives orders to his servants or workmen. His tone is so imperious, you might imagine them negroes, and himself a negro-driver. And happy, he thinks, would he be, if the laws of this country would allow him to use the whip at once, instead of wearing out his precious lungs on such low-born wretches. But as he *dares not* use the whip, (and, indeed, he is generally a coward as well as bully,) he makes up for it as well as he can, by *threatening* to use it on all occasions, whenever his will is not minutely and instantaneously-executed. He urges the propriety of keeping -these people at a distance, making them know their station, and preserving his own dignity. Porters, hackney-coachmen, chairmen, whoever is so unfortunate as to be obliged, through poverty and a low station, to minister to his luxury, are sure, at the same time, to be insulted by his insolence. *He pays no more than others;* often less; but* he swears and calls names. In truth, he considers this order of useful people, certainly respectable when honest, sober, and industrious, as not of the same flesh and blood with himself, but to be ranked with the ass and the swine..

Aminos servorum et corpora no§tr&
' Materia constare putat, paribusque elementis ?
"O Demens! ita *serous* ʜᴏᴍᴏ est ?"*—Juv.

This proud pretender to superiority, this sneaking slave of courts, and tyrant of his household, would monopolize not only all the luxuries of habitation, food, raiment, vehicles, attendants, but all notice, all respect, all consideration. The world was made for him, and such as he, to take their pastime in it. His family, his children, his house, must all be kept from plebeian contamination. It is worth While to observe the fences of his premises, his high rails, gates, the walls before his house, the grim porter at his door, and the surly mastiff, taught to hunt down the poor man and the stranger that sojourns near the magnificent palace of selfish grandeur. The well-barred portals, however, fly open at the approach of lords and dukes; and he himself would lick the shoes of a king or prime minister, if such should, for the sake of securing the influence of his wealth in parliament, condescend to enter his mansion.

The aristocratical insolence is visible where one would least expect it;'where all the partakers of this frail and mortal state should appear in a state of equality; Oven at chturcb, in the immediate presence of Him who made' high and low, rich and

* Have servants souls ?—and are their bodies then
  Of the same flesh and blood as gentlemen ?
  Have servants *rights of men* to plead ? O sure
  *Tis madness thus to patronize the poor.

poor; and where the gilded and painted ornaments on die walls seem to mock the folly of all human pride. The pew of the great man is raised above the others, though its elevation is an obstacle both to the eyes and ears of those who are placed in its vicinity. It is furnished with curtains, adorned with linings, and accommodated with cushions. Servants walk in his train, open the door of his luxurious seat, and carry the burden of the prayer-book. The first reverence is paid to persons of condition around. Those who do not bow at the name of Jesus Christ, bend with all lowliness to the lord in the gallery. The whole behaviour leads a thinking man to conclude, that the self-important being would scarcely deign to enter Heaven, any more than he does the church, if he must be reduced to an equality with the rustic vulgar.

Such persons, consistently with their arbitrary principles* are always high-churehmen. Though they may be indifferent to religion, they are zealous &r the church. They consider the church as useful* not only in providing genteelly for relations and dependents, but as an engine to keep down the people. Upon the head of their despot, they would put a triple covering; the crown, the mitre, and the helmet. The Devil offered our Saviour all the king doins p£ this world, and their glory, if he would fall down and worship him; and there is reason to fear, that such idolaters of the kingdoms of this world and their glory would apostatize from him who said *his tengdom was not of this world,* if the same evil b)eing were to make.them the same offer.: The temporalities and splendours of the church triumphant endear it to them; but, if it continued in its primitive state, or in the condition in which it was when poor: fishermen were its bishops, they would soon side, in religious matters, with the *miscreant philosophers* of France. But while mitres and stalls may be made highly subservient to the views of a minister, and the promoters of arbitrary power and principles, they, honour the church, though they know nothing of Christ; they stickle for the bench, though they abandon the creed. An ally, like the *church*, possessed of great power, must be cherished; though the very persons who wish to avail themselves of that power, would be the first, if that power were in real danger, to question its rights, and to accelerate its subversion.

There is one circumstance in the conduct of the *Tory* friends to *absolute sway* truly alarming i to the champions of liberty. They are always inclined, on the smallest tumult, to call in the military. They would depreciate the civil powers, and break the ' constable's staff to introduce the bayonet. In their opinion, the best executive powers of government are a party of dragoons. They are therefore constantly sounding alarms, and aggravating every petty disturbance into a riot or rebellion. They are not for parleying with the many-headed monster; they scorn lenient measures; and while their own persons are in perfect safety, boldly command the military to fire. What is the life or the limb of a poor man, in their opinion? Not so much as the life:or limb of a favourite pointer or racehorse. They' are always eager to augment the army. They would build barracks in every part of the country, and be glad to see a free country overrun, like some of the enslaved nations of the continent, from east to west, from north to south,- with men armed to overawe the saucy advocates of charters, privileges, rights, and reformations.

Against principles so dangerous in public life, and odious in private, every friend to his king and country, every lover of his fellow-creatures, every competent judge of those *manners,* which sweeten the intercourse of man With man, will shew a determined opposition. But how shall he shew it with effect? By **ridicule.** Nothing lowiers the pride from: which such principles proceed, so much! as general contempt and' derision. The insolence of petty despots in private life should be laughed at by an Aristophanes, while it is rebuked by a Cato. ■

SECTION XIV.

The despotic Spirit inclined to avail itself of Spies, Informers, false Witnesses, pretended Conspiracies, and self-interested Associations affecting Patriotism *

IT is not unfair to infer the existence of similar principles from similarity of conduct. In that black page of history which disgraces human nature; I mean the records of the Roman emperors in the decline of Roman virtue; we read, that: spies and informers were considered as necessary functionaries of government; that.they became favourites at court, and were encouraged by rewards due only to exemplary patriotism and public, service. There have been periods also in the history of England, when spies, informers, false witnesses, and pretended plots, were deemed lawful and useful expedients by the rulers of the state. In testimony of this assertion, we need only call to mind the pretended Popish plot, with all its villainous circumstances, in the reign of Charles the Second; a reign in many parts

---

* "*Sub Tibcrio Casare fuit accusandi frequens et pome pubUca* ra-"*bies, qua omni cwili hello gravius togatam civitatem corfecit. Exci-*"*piebatur* EBRIORUM *sermo, simplicitas* JOCANTIUM*.*"—SENECA de Benef.

"*Under Tiberius Casar the rage qf* accusing or informing *was so* "*common as to harass the peaceful citizens more titan a civil war. The* " *words* qf drunken men, *and the unguarded joke of the thoughtless**"*were taken down, and handed to the Emperor*"

OF DESPOTISM. 107

of it resembling the times of the Homan Tiberius. But at whatever period spies, informers, false witnesses, and pretended plots are adopted by men in power, to strengthen themselves in office, and destroy virtuous opposition, there is reason to fear, in spite of all professions of the contrary, that the tyrannic spirit of the degenerate Caesars waits but for opportunities to display itself in acts of Neronian atrocity. Power is deficient; but inclination is equally hostile to the mass of mankind, denominated the People, whom some politicians scarcely condescend to acknowledge as possessed of any political existence.

The employment of spies and informers is a virtual declaration of hostilities against the people. It iirgues a want of confidence in them.. It argues a fear and jealousy of them. It argues a desire to destroy them by ambuscade. It is, in civil, government, what stratagems are. in, a state of, war. It tends also to excite retaliation.

A ministry must be sadly corrupt, and unworthy tie confidence either of king or people, which can 8Q far degrade itself as to require the assistance, of the vilest of the human, race. Such are the: whole race of spies, *sycophants** (I use tbe word: in its jwe-*per* sense,).informers,,and false witnesses.. So great is the unfortunate corruption of human nature, that men have been always found itd< execute the most infamous offices, when a government has thought proper to seek their co-operation..Extreme poverty, united with extreme profligacy of conduct,, and a total destitution of moral and religious principle,' prepare men for the most nefarious deeds which tyrants cap meditate. For tyrants only, the robbers and murderers of men, be such miscreants reserved. Tacitus has called them instrumenta reoni, *the implements of government*, when government falls into hands which are skilled in the use of no better; into the hands of Neros and Caligulas. May the minister of a free country, who has recourse to such tools, be himself the first to feel their destroying edge!

Seneca, in the quotation at the head of this section, has handed down a circumstance, in the reign of Tiberius, which must cause every man, who has a just regard for the comforts of free intercourse and conversation, to shudder at the prospect of being governed by a system, supported by spies and informers. He tells us, that the convivial merriment of friends assembled over a glass, the innocent raillery and banter of jocular conversation, were, through the encouragement given to informers, by the government, made the grounds of a serious charge of sedition and treason. *The words of the drunken,'* and *the unguarded openness, of the joker,* Were taken hold of, by persons who mixed with the guests, in order to recommend themselves to government, by reporting' the free language that might escape in the hour of unreserved confidence; when the; heart is opened by friendship, and the tongue loosened by wine.

He who dippeth with me in the dish, the same shall

betray me, said our Saviour. But be it remembered, that the same persons who hired and paid Judas Iscariot, crucified Jesus Christ.

' But what shall we say? Have there been no Judas Iscariots in modern days ? Have our coffee-houses, taverns, and places of public amusement, been quite free from hired wretches, who, while they *dipped in the same dish* with us, were seeking to betray us, if possible, to prisons and to death? Did they this wickedness of themselves, or were they hired and paid by persons influenced by tory principles or high in office ? Have not certain spies confessed, at a solemn trial, that they were hired and paid by men'in office? Have not the same spies led to those extravagant speeches, or those offensive measures, which they afterwards informed against for hire; hoping to deprive the persons they betrayed either of liberty or life ? If such things have been, is'it not time to be alarmed, to guard against spies, informers, and false witnesses ? And is it not right to express, and increase, if possible, the public indignation against both them and their employers ?

' When men high in office, of reputed abilities, and certainly possessing extensive knowledge, patronize such miscreants as spies and informers, they certainly corrupt the public morals, by leading the people, over whom their examples must always have great influence, to believe, that treachery, perjury, and murder, are crimes of a venial nature. They teach men to carry the profligacy of public characters and conduct into the sequestered walks of'private 'life. They teach one of the most corrupting maxims; for they teach, "That when ends eagerly desired by "knaves in power are to be accomplished, the "means must be pursued, however base and dis- "honest." They destroy at once the confidential comforts and the most valuable virtues of private life.

But state-necessity is urged in defence of that policy which employs spies and informers. I deny the existence of such necessity. There are excellent laws, and there are magistrates and officers dispersed all over the kingdom, who are bound to take cognizance of any illegal and injurious practices, and to prevent them by a timely interference.: if such magistrates and officers neglect their duty, it is in? cumbent on those who appointed them, and who are amply paid for their vigilance, to institute prose* 'cutions, to punish and to remove them. The law knows nothing of spies and informers. The only watchmen it recognizes are magistrates, regularly appointed. The whole body of a people, well governed, and consequently contented with their governors, are the natural and voluntary guardians against seditions, treasons, and conspiracies to subvert the state. When spies and informers are called in, it argues a distrust of the magistrates, and of the whole body of the people. It argues an endeavour to govern in a manner unauthorized by that constr tution which the employers of spies and informers pretend to protect, by instruments so dangerous and unjustifiable.

1 have a better opinion of men in power, in our times, corrupting as the possession of power is

OF DESPOTISM.

allowed to be, than to believe that any of them would hire a false witness. But let them be assured, that a hired spy and informer will, by an easy transition* become a false witness, even in trials where liberty and life are at stake. In trials of less consequence, there is no doubt but that his conscience will stretch with the occasion. His object is not truth or justice; but filthy lucre; and when he aspires at great rewards, great mnst be his venture. Having once broken down, as a treacherous spy, the fences of honour and conscience, nothing but fear will restrain him, as a witness, from overleaping the bounds of truth, justice, and mercy. He will rob and murder under the forms of law; and add to the atrocity of blood-guiltiness, the crime of perjury. No man is safe, where such men are countenanced by officers' of state. They themselves may perish by his false tongue; suffering the vengeance due to their base encouragement of a traitor to the public, by falling unpitied victims to his disappointed treachery. The pestilential breath of spies and informers is not to be endured in the pure healthy atmosphere of a free state, it brings with it the sickly despotism of oriental climes.

But how ominous to liberty, if large associations of rich men, either possessing or expecting places, pensions, and titles for themselves or their relations, should ever take upon themselves the office of spying and informing! by their *numbers* braving the shame, and evading the personal responsibility, that would fall on an individual or unconnected spy or informer! Such an association would.be a most dangerous conspiracy of sycophants against a free constitution. If the public should ever behold the venal tribe thus undermining the fair fabric of liberty, and behold them without indignation, would it not give reason to suspect, that the Tory and Jacobite, principles, or the spirit of despotism, had pervaded the body of the people.

. The honest, independent, and thinking part of the community will be justly alarmed when they see either individuals or bodies of men encouraged by ministerial favours, in calumniating the people, and' falsely accusing the advocates of constitutional freedom. They will think it time to stem the torrent of corruption, which, rolling down its foul but impe-. tuous tide, from the hills, threatens devastation to the cottages in the valley. But how shall they stop, an evil, promoted and encouraged, for private and selfish motives, by the whole influence of grandeur and opulence acting in combination? By bearing their testimony in favour of truth and justice; by. giving their suffrages to honest men; by rejecting the servile adulator of courts, and. the mean sycophant of ministers: and by shunning as pestilences *every description of spies and informers, whether poor or rich, mercenary or volunteer** If they fail, they

---

* I subjoin a curious passage from the 14th book of Ammianus Marcellinus, on the manner in which spies executed their office, under the imperial authority of Constantius Gallus.

*' *Bxcogitatum est super his, ut homines quidam ignoti,* VILITATP IPSA
parum cavendi, *ad colligendos rumores per Antiochia latera cuncta* "*destinarentur, relaturi qua au dirent. Hi peraqranter et dissimulanter* "*honoratorum circulis assistendo, peroadendoque divitum domtts egen»* "*tium habitu, quicquid noscere poterant vel audire, latenterjntrami&si*

OF DESPOTISM.

will feel the comfort of having discharged their duty.

"per posticas *in regiam, nuntiabant: id observantes conspiratione "concordi, ut fingerent quadam, et cognita duplicarent in pejus:* LAUDES
"VERO SUPPRIMERENT CIESARItf, *qUos* **INVITIS QOAMPLtJRTMIS,** *fotmido "malorum impendentium exprimebat."*

"Another expedient was to place at every corner of the city certain "obscure persons, not likely to excite suspicion or caution, because of "their apparent insignificancy, who were to repeat whatever they heard. "These persons, by standing near gentlemen, or getting entrance into " the houses of the rich, in the disguise of poverty, reported whatever they "saw or heard, at court, being privately admitted into the palace by the "BACK STATES: having concerted it between themselves to add a great "deal, from their own invention, to whatever they really saw or heard, "and to make the matter ten times worse. They agreed also to suppress " the mention of those (loyal songs or toasts, or) speeches, in favour "qf the Emperor, which the dread of impending evil squeezed out of "many against their will and better judgment."

The decline of the Roman empire was distinguished by spies' and informers: it is to be hoped that the use of spies and informers does not portend the decline of the British empire.

SECTION XV.

The Manners of Tory Courtiers, and of those whet ape them, as People of Fashion, inconsistent with Manliness, Truth, and Honesty; and their Prevalence injurious to a free Constitution, and the Happiness of Human Nature.

Among a thousand anecdotes of the frivolity of the governing part of a despotic country, I select the following, merely as a slight specimen of the trifling disposition of those who, as they pretend, claim their elevated situations for the good of mankind.

"In the summer.of the year 1775* the queen of "France, being dressed in a light brown silk, the "king good-naturedly observed, it was *couleur dd* "*puce,* the colour of fleas; and instantly every "lady in the land was uneasy till she had dressed "herself in a silk gown of a flea colour. The rage "was caught by the men; and the dyers worked "night and day, without being able to supply the "demand for flea colour. They nicely distinguished "between an old and a young flea, and subdivided "even the shades of its body. The belly, the back, "the thigh, the head, were all marked by varying tints. This prevailing colour promised to be the "fashion of the winter. The silk-mercers found it "would hurt their trade. They therefore presented "her majesty with patterns of new satins; who "having chosen one, Monsieur exclaimed, it was "the colour of her *majesty's* hair !

"Immediately the *fleas* ceased to be favourites at "court, and all were eager to be dressed in the "colour of her majesty's hair* Servants were sent "off at the moment from Fontainbleau to Paris, to "purchase velvets, ratteens, and cloths of this colour. "The current price of an ell in the morning had "been forty livres, and it rose in the evening to "eighty and ninety. The demand was so great, "and the anxiety so eager, that some of her majesty's "hair was actually obtained, by bribery,, and sent to "the Gobelins, to Lyons, and other manufactories, "that the exact shade might be caught and reli-"giously preserved.".

Such was the little, mean, adulatory spirit of the court of France, and of the people who at that time imitated the court with more than apish mimicry. To shew how little there is of truth and honesty in such servility, be it remembered, that the nation, so eager to catch the very colour of the queen's hair, soon afterwards cut off the head on which it grew. Nothing silly, nothing overstrained, can be lasting, because it wants a solid foundation. Let kings be careful how they confide in court compliments and the addresses of corruption. Mastiffs guard their master and his house better than spaniels.

While such a spirit prevails' among the great, it is impossible that the happiness of man can be duly regarded by those who claim a right to govern him. Where frivolity and meanness are general, it is impossible that the people can be wise or happy.

Gaiety founded on levity or affectation, is not happiness. It laughs and talks, while the heart is either unmoved or dejected. Happiness is serious. The noise of folly is intended to dissipate thought; but no man would wish his thoughts to be dissipated, who finds any thing within him to think of with complacency.

Princes have always something important to think of, which, it might be supposed, would preclude the necessity of trifling amusements to kill time. Yet courts have always been remarkable for frivolity. This frivolity is not only contemptible in itself um worthy of rational beings, especially when executing a most momentous tri)6t, but productive of mean* ness, weakness, and corruption. Long experience has associated with the idea of a courtier in despotic courts, duplicity, insincerity, violation of promises, adulation, all the base and mean qualities, rendered still baser and meaner, by assuming, on public occasions, the varnish of hypocrisy.

Erasmus gives directions to a young man, in the manner of Swift, how to conduct himself at court. I believe they have never been presented to the English reader, and therefore I shall take the liberty of translating them, not •only for the sake of affording amusement, but that it may be duly considered, whether or not persons who form their manners and principles after such models, are likely to be the friends of man, the assertors or the guardians of liberty: whether the slaves of *fqshim,* who seem to separate themselves from others, as if the; weto 3 chosen tribe among the sons of men; as if they were

OF DESPOTISM.

made of such clay as forms the porcelain, while others are merely earthen ware; whether, I Say, the slaves of *fashion,* which always apes a coart in all its extravagancies, are likely to consult the happiness of the majority of mankind, the middle, lowest, and most useful classes, whom they despise, as an inferior species of beings; as the whites in the West Indies formerly looked down upon the negroes with disdain.

"As you are bow going to live at court," (says Erasmus,) "I advise you, in the first place, never "to repose tbe smallest degree of confidence in any "man there who professes himself your friend, "though he may smile upon you, and embrace you, "and promise you; aye, and confirm his promise "with au oath. Believe no man there a sincere "friend to you; and do you- take care to be a * sincere friend to no man. Nevertheless, yon must "pretend to love all you see, and shew the utmost "suavity of manners and attentions to- every indivi-"dual. These attentions eost you not a farthing; "therefore you may be as lavish of them- as you "please. Fay your salutations with the softest "smiles in your countenance, shake hands with the "appearance of most ardent cordiality, bow and "give way to all, stand cap in hand, address every "body by their titles of honour, praise without bounds, and! promise most liberally.

"I would have yon every morning, before you "go to the levee, practise in making up your face "fop the day at your looking-glass at home; that it "may be ready to assume any part in the farce, and "that no' glimpse of your real thoughts and feelings "may appear. You must study your gestures. "carefully at home, that in the acting of the day "your countenance, person, and conversation may "all correspond, and assist each other in keeping "up your character at the court masquerade.

"These are the elements of the courtier's philoso-"pby, in learning which, no man can be.an apt "scholar, unless he first of all divests himself of all "sense of shame; and leaving his natural face at "home, puts on a vizor, and wears it constantly too. "In the next place, get scent of the various cabals "and parties of the court; but be not in a hurry to "attach yourself to any of them, till you have fluly "reconnoitred. When you have found out who is "the king's favourite, you have your cue; mind to "keep on the safe side of the vessel. If the king's "favourite be a downright fool, you must not scruple "to flatter him, so long as he is in favour with tho "god of your idolatry.

"The god himself, to be sure, will require the "main efforts of your skill. As often as you hap-"pen to be in the presence, you must exhibit a "face of apparently honest delight, as if you were "transported with the privilege of being so near the "*royal person.* When once you have observed what he likes and dislikes, your business is done."

He proceeds to advise his pupil to pursue his own interest, regardless of all honour and honesty, whenever they may be Violated without detection. He tells him, in consulting his interest, to pay more court to *enemies* than friends, that he may turn them hearts, and bring them over to his side. I cannot, in this place, give the whole of the letter; but the curious reader may find it under number fifty-seven, in the twenty-eighth book of the London edition.

Erasmus drew from the life. Though a most profound scholar, yet he was not merely a scholar. He read the book of tbe world with as much accuracy as the volumes of his library. I have brought forward this letter, because I find it exemplified in the Precepts of Lord Chesterfield, and tbe Diary of Lord Melcombe. It appears, under the testimony of their own hands, that these men actually were tbe characters which Erasmus, in a vein of irony and sarcasm, advises his court-pupil to become. It appears from them, that many of the persons, with whom they acted, were similar. It follows that, if such men were great, wise, and good men, truth, honour, sincerity, friendship, and patriotism are but empty names, devised by politicians to amuse and to delude a subject and an abject people.

But the people (I mean not a venal mob, employed by a minister or by a faction) are not so corrupted. They value truth, honour, sincerity, and patriotism; and in their conduct often display tbem in their utmost purity. Shall courtiers, then, be listened to, when they represent the people as a swinish multitude, or as venal wretches ? Shall courtiers, such as Lord Melcopibe, claim an exclusive right to direct human affairs, influencing senates to make and unmake laws at pleasure, and to cry havoc, when they please, and let slip the dogs of war on the *poor,* either at. home or abroad ? Shall a whole nation be proud to mimic a court, not only in dress, amusements, and all the vanity of fashion, hut in' sentiments, in morals, in polities, in religion, in no religion, in hypocrisy, in cruelty?

Lord Melcotnbe and Lord Chesterfield were leading men, able men, eloquent men, considered in their day as ornaments of the court and of the nation, But if even they exhibit hoth precepts and examples of extreme selfishness, of deceit, and of a total disregard to human happiness, what may we think of their numerous dependents, under-agents,.pers(ribands, titles, expecting favours for themselves, or their natural children, or their cousins? Can we suppose these men to retain any regard for the public? Would they make any sacrifice to the general happiness of human nature? Would they assert liberty, or undergo trouble, loss, persecution, in defence of a constitution? They themselves Would laugh at you, if you should suppose it possible. They can be considered in no other light than as vermin, sucking the blood of the people whom they despise,

Yet these, and such as these, are the men who are indefatigable in declaiming against the people, talking of the mischiefs of popular government, and the danger of admitting the rights of man. These, and such as these, are the strenuous opposers of ali re? form in the representation. These, and such as these, call all attempts at innovations, though evidently improvements, seditious. These are the alarmists, who cry out, the church or tbe state is in danger, in order to persecute honest men, or to introduce the military. The military is their delight and their fortress; and to compass their own base ends, they will not hesitate to bathe their arms in human blood, even up to their very shoulders. Their whole object is to aggrandize a power, of which they pant to participate, and from which alone, destitute as they are of merit and goodness, they can hope for lucre and the distinctions of vanity,

"Where the ruling mischief," says the author of the Estimate, "prevails among the great, then even "the palliative remedies- cannot easily be applied. "The reason is manifest: a coercive power is want-"iug. They who should cure the evil are tbe very "delinquents; and moral and political physic no "distempered mind will ever administer to itself.
- "Necessity therefore, and necessity alone, must "• *m* such a case be the parent of reformation. So "long as degenerate and unprincipled manners can "support themselves, they will be deaf to reason, "blind to consequences, and obstinate in tbe long-"established pursuit of oain and pleasure. IN **"SUCH MINDS, THE IDEA OF A PUBLIC HAS NO PLACE.** "Nor can such minds be ever awakened from their "fatal dream, till either the voice of an. abused "people rouse them into fear, or the state itself "totter, through the general incapacity, cowardice, "and disunion of those who support it.

"Whenever this compelling power, Necessity, "shall appear, then, and not till then, may we hope "that our deliverance is at hand. Effeminacy, ra-"pacity, and fectiqn will then be ready to *resign* the

"reins they would how usurp. One common dah-
"ger would create one common interest. Virtue
"may rise on the ruins of corruption.
"One kind of necessity, and which I call an in-
"teriial necessity, would arise, when the voice of
"an abused people should rouse the great into
"FEAR.
"I am not ignorant, that it hath been a point of
"debate, whether, in POLITICAL MATTERS, THE GE-
"NERAL VOICE OF A PEOPLE OUGHT to be held
"worth much regard ? Right sorry I am to ob-
"serve, that this doubt is the growth of *later times'*;
"of times, too, which boast their love of freedom;
"but Ought, surely, to blush, when they look back
"on the generous sentiments of ancient days, which
"days we stigmatize with the name of *slavish.'*

"Thus runs the writ of summons to the parlia-
"ment of the 23d of Edward the First:—*The King,
"to the venerable father in Christ R. Archbishop of
"Canterbury, greeting: As the most just law, estaA
"blished by the provident wisdom of princes, doth
"*OF *appoint, that what* concerns all, *should be* ap-
"proved *by* all; *so it evidently implies, that dangers
"common to all, should be obviated by remedies pro-
"vided by all.* Ut quod omnes *tangit,* ab omnibus'
"approbetur;■—sic et innuit evidenter, *ut* communi-
"bus *periculis per remedia proviso* communiter
"*obvietur.* A noble acknowledgment from an Eng-
"lish king, which ought never, sure, to be forgotten,
"or trodden under foot by English subjects.

"There are two manifest reasons why, in a *degenerate state,* and a *declining* period, the united' "voice of a people is, in general, the surest test of "truth in all essential matters on which their own "welfare depends, so far, as the ends of political "measures are concerned.

"*First*, Because in such a period, and such a "state, the body of a people are naturally the least "corrupt part of such a people: for all general cor-, "ruptions, of whatever kind, begin among the "leaders, and descend from these to the lower "ranks. Take such a state, therefore, in what period "of degeneracy you please, the *higher ranks* will, in "the natural course of things, be farther gone in the "ruling evils than the lower; and therefore the **"LESS TO BE RELIED ON.**

"*Secondly*, A still more cogent reason is, that the "geueral body of the people have not such a *bias* "hung upon their judgment by the prevalence of "*personal* and *particular* interest, as the **great**, in all things which relate to state matters. It is "of no *pdrticular* and *personal* consequence to the "*general body* of a people, what men are employed, "provided the general welfare be accomplished; "because nothing but the general welfare can be an "object of desire to the *general body*. But it is of "much particular and personal consequence to the "**great**, what *men* are *employed;* because, through "their connexions and alliances, they must generally "find either their *friends* or *enemies* in *power*. Their "own private interests, therefore, naturally throw a "bias on their judgments, and destroy that *impar-* "*tiality* which the general body of an uncorrupt "people doth naturally possess.

"Hence, then, it appear*, that the united voice of "an uncorrnpt people is, in general, the safest test "of POLITICAL GOOD AND EVIL."

Is it not then time to be alarmed for tbe pnblic good, when great pains are taken to depreciate the people; when the names of Jacobin, democrat, leveller, traitor, and mover of sedition, are artfully thrown, by courtiers and their adherents, on every man who has sense and virtue enough to maintain the cause of liberty; that cause, which established the revolution on tbe ruins of despotism, and placed the present family on the throne, as tbe guardians of a free constitution ? I cannot think such courtiers, however they may fawn, for their own interest, on the person of the monarch, friends, in their hearts, to a limited monarchy. If they could and dared, they would restore a Stuart. But as that is impracticable, they would transfuse the principles of the Stuarts into the bosom of a Brunswick. To expose their selfish meanness, and frustrate their base design, is equally the duty and interest of the king and the people.

SECTION XVI.'

The Spirit of Truth, Liberty, and Virtue, public as well as private, chiefly to be found in the middle ranks of the People.

> Nemo altero nobilior, nisi cui rectius ingenium et artibus bonis aptius. Qui imagines in atrio exponunt et nomina familiae suae.... Non magis quam *nobiles* sunt.... Dicenda haec fuerunt ad contundendam *insolentiam* hominum ex fortun& pendentium.*
> —Seneca *de Benef.*

THE people of this land are usually divided into nobility, gentry, and *commonalty.* The nobility and gentry seem to "be estimated as officers in an army; the commonalty, or the whole body of the people, as the rank and file.

There might be no original impropriety in these appellations; but that of *commonalty* has been often used, by aristocratical upstarts, with insolence. The commonalty comprize the grand mass of the nation; form the great fabric of the political building; while the GENTRY, after all, are but the carving and gilding, or the capitals of the pillars, that add to the

---

* "No man is nobler born than ANother, unless he is born with bet-"ter abilities and a more amiable disposition. They who make such a "parade with their family pictures and pedigrees, are, properly speak-"ing, rather to be called noted or notorious than noble persons. I "thought it right to say thus much, in order to repel the insolence of "men who defend entirely upon chance and accidental circumstances "for distinction, and not at all on public services and persoml merit."

support of the roof, but constitute neither the walls nor the foundation. The commonalty, therefore, being the main fabric, are worthy, in the eye of reason, of the highest esteem, and the first degree of a patriot's solicitude. There can be no rational end in our government but the happiness of the whole People, King, Lords, and Commons.

The commonalty are, beyond all comparison, the most numerous order: and as every individual of them is entitled to comfort and security in a well-regulated nation, the whole together must demand the greatest attention of the philosopher, the divine, the philanthropist, of every man of sense, goodness of heart, and liberality. The pomp and parade, the superfluous luxury, the vain distinctions of the few, sink to nothing, compared, in the mind of reasonable and humane men, with the happiness of the *million*.

It is certainly true, that the greatest instances of virtue and excellence of every kind have originated in the middle order. "Give me neither poverty nor "riches," was a prayer founded on a knowledge of human nature, and fully justified by experience. The middle station affords the best opportunities for improvement of mind, is the least exposed to temptation, and the most capable of happiness and virtue.

This opinion has long been received and acknowledged. I could cite, from the sermons of our best divines on *Ag&r's Prayer*, many passages in confirmation of it. I dwell upon it now, for no other reason, but because it has *lately* been the fashion, among those who are alarmed for their privileges by the French revolution, to run down the people, and to cry up that silly spirit of chivalry which established the systems of false honour, claiming rank and respect from society, without rendering it any service, without possessing any just claim to esteem, much less to public honour, exclusive privileges, and titular distinction. The terms *sans culottes, car naille, bourgeoise,* scum of the earth, *venal wretches,* and the never-to-be-forgotten *swinish multitude,* have been reserved for the people, especially those among them who have had sense and spirit enough personally, to oppose the progress of despotic principles and practices. Every thing that malice, urged by the fear of losing tbe ribands, the titles, and the solid pence which a corrupt and corrupting minister can bestow, has been thrown out, in newspapers hired by the people's money for the phrpose of vilifying the people.

It is time, therefore, that the people should vindicate their honour. What are these insolent courtieFS, what these placemen and pensioners, who live on the public bounty, that they should tbus insult those whose bread they eat? For the most part, they are persons who, if they were stripped of the false splendour of great mansions, numerous retinues, painted carriages, would appear among tbe meanest and most despicable members of society. They, indeed are to be pitied and borne with, while they abstain from insulting the people; but when their silly pride presumes to trample on the mass of the community, they become deserving of contempt as well as commiseration.

These are the persons whom a patriotic Lord describes "as giving themselves up to the pursuit of "honours and dignities^ as loving the splendour "of a court, and attaching'themselves to the cause "of monarchy, (uot from any conviction that mo-"narchy is the most favourable to human bapph "ness, not even from personal attachment to the "monarch,) but because they see in the *increased* "*power* of the monarch the source of additional "weight and splendour to those (that is them-"selves) who surround the throne, and an increase "of value to the favours which the sovereign can "confer; such as stars, garters, ribands, and "titles."

But is a passion, childish from its vanity, and diabolical in its unfeeling greediness, to be borne with any longer, when, not content with engrossing the profits of office and the pageantry of state, it dares to speak of the middle and tower elasses, as beings scarcely deserving notice, as mere *nuisances* when not employed in the servile office of administering to aristocratic pride ?

Virtue is nobility. Personal merit, useful, generous, benevolent exertion, the only honourable distinction. The trappings which every taylor can make to clothe a poor puny mortal, add no real dignity. In ages of ignorance, they might strike with awe. Those ages are no more. Nor will they ever return, notwithstanding the efforts of petty despots, (fearing the loss of those distinctions which they know they never earned,) to keep the people in the grossest ignorance.

God Almighty, who gives his sun to shine with as much warmth and radiance on the cottage as on the palace, has dispensed the glorious privilege of genius and virtue to the poor and middle classes, with a bounty perhaps seldom experienced in any of the proud pretenders to hereditary or official grandeur/ Let us call to mind a few among the worthies Who have adorned the ages that have elapsed: Socrates; was he *noble* in the sense of a king at arms? Would he have condescended to be bedizened with ribands, and stars, and garters? CrcerO; was-he not'a *novus homo?* a man unconnected with patricians, and deriving his glory from the-purest fountain of honour, his> own genius and virtue ? Demosthenes would have;scorded to owe his estimation 'to a pedigree.

Who were the great reformers, to whom we of England and all Europe are indebted for emancipation.' from the chains of superstition? [1] Erasmus and Luther; Erasmus, as- the mfonks of his day objected to him, laid tbo egg, and Luther batched it. But was it> Archbishop Erasmus?- Lord'Luther, Marquis Luther, Sir-Martin Luther? Did they, either of them, seek the favour of courts? Were they notamong the *swinish multitude ?* [s]

'• Thomas' Paine contributed much, by his *Common Sense,* to the happy'revolution in-America^; I'need' dot observe, that he had nothing of the lustre Of eourts or nobility to-recommend him.[8] The Virulent malice of courtiers and venal scribblers has blackened him as they once blackened Luther, when they assertad'of him,- that he was actually a *devil incar**

nate, disguised in the shape of a monk with a co%l< I do not advert to any of his subsequent publications. I only say, if they are so *contemptible* as they are said by.courtiers and aristocrats to be, why not undertake the *easy* task of refuting him ? Bloody wars and prosecutions are no refutation.

"Who is this *Luther* ?" (said Margaret,, governess of the Netherlands.) The courtiers around her replied, "He is an ILLITERATE MONK." "Is he so ?" (said she.) "I am glad to hear it. Then do you/ "gentlemen, who are not illiterate, who are both "learned and numerous, do you, I charge you, "write against this *illiterate monk.* That is all you "have to do. The business is easy; for tbe world "will surely pay more regard to a great many "*scholars,* and great men, as you are, than to. one "poor ILLITERATE MONK."

Many did write against him, and poured forth the virulence of a malice unchecked by truth, and encouraged by crowned heads. But *Luther* prevailed, and we Englishmen have reason.to celebrate the victory of truth and virtue over corrupt.influence and cruel persecution.

The greatest scholars, poets, orators, philosophers, warriors, statesmen, inventors and improvers of the arts, arose from the lowest of the people. If we had waited till courtiers had.invented the art of printing, clock-making, navigation, and, a. thousand others, we should probably haye continued in darkness to this hour. They had something else to do, than to add to the comforts and conveniences of ordinary life. They had to worship an idol,.with the incense of flattery, who was often much more stupid than themselves, and who sometimes had no more care or knowledge of the people under him, or their wants, than he had of arts or literature.

The education of the middle classes is infinitely better than the education of those who are called *great people*. Their time is less consumed by that vanity and dissipation which enfeebles the mind, while it precludes opportunity for reading and reflection. They usually have a regard to *character*, which contributes much to the preservation of virtue. Their honour and integrity are valued by them, as pearls of great price, These are their: stars, and these their coronets. They are for the most part attached to their religion. They are temperate, frugal, and industrious. In one particular, and that one adds a value above all that *Courts* can give, they greatly excel the GREAT, and that particular is SINCERITY. They are in earnest in their words and deeds. They have little occasion for simulation and dissimulation. Courtiers are too often varnished, factitious persons, whom God and nature never made; while the people preserve the image uneffaced, which the Supreme Being impressed when he created MAN,

SECTION XVII.

On debauching the Minds of the rising Generation and a whole People, by giving them Military Notions in a free and commercial Country:

In proportion as great men refuse to submit to reason, they ace inclined to govern, by violence. They who. hire the sword in their hands, are unwilling, to wait for. the. slow operation of argument. The sword cuts away, all opposition.i No; troublesome-contra* diction, no unwelcome truth, will. impede the progress of him who uses the *ratio ultima regum,* and mows down all obstacles, with the scythed car.. -

Hence the abettors of bighprerogative,of absolute monarchy, and aristocratical. pride, always delight in -war. Not.satisfied with attacking foreign nations, and keeping up a. standing army. even in time of peace, they wish, after they have once corrupted, the mass of the people by universal'influence, to render a whole nation military. The aggregate, of military force, however greats.being under their entire direcr tion, they feel their power infinitely augmented, and bid defiance to the unarmed philosopher and politician, who brings into the field truth without a spear, and argument unbacked with artillery.

But such a system tends to go.thicize a nation, to extinguish the light of learning and philosophy, and once more to raise thick fogs from the putrid pools of ignorance and superstition, the bane of all happiness, but the veryelement of despotism.

The diffusion of a military taste among all ranks, even the lowest of the people, tends to a general corruption of morals, by teaching habits of idleness, or trifling activity, and the vanity of gaudy dress and empty parade.

> The strict discipline, which is found necessary to render an ' army a machine in the hands of its direc-* tors,' requiring, under the severest penalties, the most implicit submission tb> absolute command, haS a direct tendency to familiarize, the mind to civil despotism. Men, rational, thinking animals, equal toi their commanders, by nature, and often superior* are bound to obey tbe impulse of a constituted authority, and to perform their functions as mechanically as the trigger which they pull to discharge their muskets.- They; cannot indeed help having a will of their own; but they must suppress it, or die. They; must consider their official superiors as superiors in wisdom; and in virtue, even though they know them to be weak and vicious. They must see,;if they: see at all, with the e^es of others: their duty is not; to have an Opinion of their own, but to follow: blindly the behest[1] of him who has had interest enough to obtain the appointment of a leader. They become liviiig automatons, aud self-acting tools of despotism;

While a few only are in this condition, the danger may not be great to constitutional liberty; but when a m&jdrity of the* people are made soldiers, it is evb dent that itbe same obsequiousness will become har bitual to the majority of the people. Their'minds will be broken down to the yoke, the energy of in-r dependence weakened, the manly spirit tamed'; like animals, that once ranged in the forest, delighting in their liberty, and fearless of man, caught in snares, confined in cages, and taught to stand upon their hind legs, and play tricks for the entertainment of the idle. They obey the word of command given by the keeper of the *menagerie*, because they have been taught obedience by hunger, by the lash of the whip, by every mode of discipline consistent with their lives, which are *saleable property*. But they are degenerate, contemptible animals. Compare a bird or a beast, thus broken down, with one of the same species flying in clear expanse of air, or roaming in the forest. Their very looks speak their degradation. The discipline of Mr. Astley causes the fiery steed to bend his knees in apparent supplication. But how are the mighty fallen! when the animal has broken from his obedience to nature, to. fall down prostrate before Mr. Astley!

Suppose a whole nation, thus *tamed,* and taught submission to the command of one of their own species. Be it remembered, the horse, in learning unnatural tricks, submits to one of another species, who is naturally his superior. But suppose a whole nation, or at least the mass of the *common people, thus broken in* by a skilful rider. Will they not lose all energy ? Will they dare, I do not say to speak, but to think of liberty? No; they will sink to the rank of *German mercenaries* let out for hire, claiming no rights, enjoying no privileges above the swine; a state of degradation at which the spirit of man, unspoiled by despotic government, revolts; and rather than fall into which, every true Englishman, from the palace to the hovel of the itinerant beggar, will be ready to exclaim, in the language of the scriptures, "Why died I not from the womb?"

Is it not time, then, for the virtuous guardians of Heaven's best gift, **Liberty**, to be alarmed, when they see a propensity in ministers, who have gained enormous power and corrupt influence, to render a whole people *military?* The gold chain of corruption is thus let down and ramified, in a million of directions, among those who never thought of courts or courtiers; but enjoying a noble independence, the independence of honest industry, chaunted their carols at the plough and the loom, glorying in the name of Englishmen, because England is free; and delighting in peace, because peace is the parent of plenty.

But, under the auspices of such a ministry, many an emulous esquire, hoping to be distinguished and rewarded, in some mode or other, by *court* favours, fond of the dress and name of a **captain**, and the privilege of *commanding* with absolute sway, bribes volunteers from behind the counter and the plough. He clothes them in the finest frippery that his own or his lady's imagination can invent. He himself parades at their head; a very pretty sight on a summer's day. And now **he** is distinguished as **a soldier**, who before only figured as a hunter of hares or foxes, and a prosecutor of poachers. Ambition, as well as vanity, begins to fire his soul.' The raising of so many men in his neighbourhood must please the minister; especially if the esquire uses, the influence he gains over the vicinity in a *proper* manner, at *a general election*. If the esquire wants not *money,* he may want *honour.* Then let;ths minister make him a baronet. If he has no sons of his own in the army, navy, law, or church, he may have nephews or cousins. If not these, he limit have *nominal* friends, to direct on whom the favours of ministers, though it proceed, not, from benevolence, must flatter pride, and add to rural consequence.

The whole of the military system is much indebted for its support to that prevailing.passion of human nature, Pride. Politicians know it, and flatter pride even in the lowest of the people. Hence recruiting-officers invite *gentlemen* only, who are above *servile* labour. "The vanity of, the poor men" (says a sagacious author) "is to be worked upon at "the cheapest, rate possible. Things we are ac- "customed to we do not mind, or else what mortal, "that never had seen a soldier, could look, without "laughing, upon. a man accoutred with so much "paltry gaudiness and affected finery ? The coarsest "manufacture that can be made of wool, dyed of a "hrick-dust colour, goes down with him, because "it is in imitation of scarlet or crimson cloth; and "to make him think himself as. like his officer as it "is possible, with little or no cost, instead of silver "or gold lace,, his hat is trimmed with- white or "yellow worsted, which in others would deserve "bedlam; yet these fine allurements, and the noise "made upon a calf-skin, have drawn in and been "the *destruction* of more men in reality, than all the "killing eyes and bewitching voices of women ever "slew in jest. To day the *swineherd* puts on his red coat, and believes every body in earnest that "calls him *gentleman;* and two days after, *Serjeant* "*Kite gives him a swinging rap with his cane,* for "holding his musket an inch higher than be shonld "do....When a man reflects on all this, and the "usage.they generally receive—their pay—and the "*care that is taken of them when they are not wanted,* "must he not wonder how wretches can be so silly "as to be proud of being called *gentlemen soldiers?* "Yet.if they were not so called, no art, discipline, "or money, would be capable of making them so "brave as thousands of them are."

When all the base arts which custom is said to have rendered *necessary* are practised only to raise and support a regular army, perhaps they might, however reluctantly, be connived at by the watchful friend of freedom. But when the major part of the labouring poor, and all tbe yeomanry, are made *gentlemen* soldiers, merely to support a minister, it is time for every virtuous and independent mind to express, as well as feel, alarm.

It appears from the above-cited passage of an authoPwho had anatomized human nature, to find out its most latent energies, that the *spirit of pride* is rendered, by artful statesmen, the chief means of supplying an army. But the spirit of pride is in fact the spirit of despotism; especially when it is that sort of pride which plumes itself on command, on external decoration, and the idle vanity of military parade.

When this pride takes place universally in a nation, there will remain little industry, and less independence. The grand object will be to rise above our neighbours in show and authority. All will bow to the man in power, in the hope of distinction. Men will no longer rely on their *own* laborious exertions; but the poor man will court, by the most obsequious submission, the favour of the esquire; the esquire cringe to the next baronet, lord, or'duke, especially if he be a lord-lieutenant of the county; and the baronet, lord, or duke, or lieutenant of the county, will fall prostrate before the first lord of the treasury; and the first lord of the treasury will idolize prerogative. Thus the military rage will trample on liberty; and despotism *triumphant* march through the land, with *drums beating and valours flying.*

SECTION XVIII.

Levity, Effeminacy, Ignorance, and Want of Principle in private Life, inimical to all public Virtue, and favourable to the Spirit of Despotism.

"The constitution of the British government" (says Bolingbroke) "supposes our kings may abuse their "power, and our representatives. betray their "trust, and provides against both these contingen-"cies. Here let us observe, that the same con-"stitution is very far from supposing the people "will ever betray *themselves;* and yet this case is "possible."

"A wise and brave people will neither be cozen-"ed nor bullied out of their liberty; but a wise and "brave people may cease to be such; they may de-"generate; they may sink into sloth and luxury; "they may resign themselves to a treacherous con-"duct; or abet the enemies of the constitu-*?tion, under a notion of supporting the friends "of government; they may want the sense to dis-"cern their danger in time, or *the courage to resist* "*when it stares them in the face.*

"The Tarquins were expelled, and Rome resumed "her liberty; Caesar was murdered, and all his race extinct; but Rome remained in bondage. Whence "this difference? In the days of Tarquin, the *pea-*"*pie* of Rome were not yet corrupted; in the days Qf Caesar, they were most corrupt,

"A free people may be sometimes betrayed; but "no people will betray themselves, and sacrifice "their liberty, unless they fall into a state of uni-"VERBAL CORRUPTION.

"As all government began, so all government "must end by the people; tyrannical government, "by their virtue and courage; and even free govern-"ments, by their vice and baseness. Our constitu-"tion indeed' makes if impossible to destroy liberty "by any sudden blast'of popular fury, or by the "TREACHERY OF 'THE FEW;' but"if"tbei:MANY wdH "ooncur with the few; if they will advisedly and "deliberately suffer their¹ liberty to *he taken away* "by those on whom they delegate power to pke-"serve it, this no constitution can prevent. God "would not support even his own theocraoy against "the concurrent desire of the children of Israel; "but *gave them# king in his anger,*

** How then should our human constitution of "government support itself against bo universal a "change; as we here suppose, in the temper and "character of the people. It cannot be. We "may give ourselves a tyrant, if we please. But "this can never happen, till the whole nation falls "into a state of political reprobation. Then, and "not till then, political damnation will be our lot."

So far a political writer* who strenuously supports the cause of liberty, and who has been, for that reason, lately depreciated. The words just now cited are worthy the serious consideration Of every man who wishes to leave the inheritance of liberty, which he received from his forefathers, unimpaired to his posterity. We are jealous of charters, privileges, and laws, but not sufficiently aware of the danger which liberty incurs from degeneracy of manners. Bqt what avail Jaws preventing *constructive* treason, and bills of rights ascertaining our liberties, without virtuous dispositions io the people?

.... Quid leges sine moribus
   Van as proficient?   Roe.

A charter, as an advocate at the English bar expressed it, is but a piece of parchment with a bit of wax dangling to it, if men have lost that energy of mind which is necessary to preserve the rights it. was intended to confer or secure. The trial by jury, the bulwark of liberty, as we have lately experieneed.it in very remarkable instances, will be but a tottering wall, when oaths have lost their sanctity, and When truth and, justice are considered only as phantoms. What will avail a constitution, when every one is immersed,in private concerns, private pleasures,,and private interest, acknowledging no public care,,uq *general* concern, nothing out of, the sphere of,do$_r$ mesticor personal affairs, worthy of lanxious. regard?

I:lately heard^a sensible man affirm, in a tope of apparent despondency, that in.England there was, at the time he spoke, mo public^....I thought[1] the expression strong, and paused to: consider it. I hope it-was the ebullition of sudden vexation at circumr stances, which, when it was spoken, seemed to argue a? general insensibility in, the peqple to the blessings efo. free country. It waR. uttered at;a time wheu a zeal, red or pretended* for the *minister?*.of goyern$_T$

ment, seemed totally to overlook, in its mistakerf ardour, the public welfare.

"There is no public," said the sagacious observer. I understood him to mean, that from an ambitious attachment to party, in some of the higher ranks; to self-interest, in some of the lower; to general dissipation, in all, the number of independent, liberally minded, and well-informed men, who zealously wished and sought the *public good* and tbe *happiness of man,* was too inconsiderable to effect any great and important purpose. Public virtue must arise from private. Great pretensions to it may be made by the profligate, but they will be found to originate in selfishness, in rancour,, in envy, or some corrupt principle inconsistent with a virtuous character and benevolent conduct.

If there be such a defection from private and public virtue, what is to preserve a regard for the constitution, whenever ministerial influence shall so far prevail as to render it the personal interest of great majorities of powerful, because rich, men, to neglect it, or even to connive at infringements upon it? If the people fall into universal corruption, the words *liberty* and *constitution* will be considered by them as fit only to adorn a school-boy's declamation. In such a state there will be no more security for. the tenant of a throne than of a cottage. A junto/.that has no regard for either, and is solely actuated by the love of power, its distinctions and emoluments, may, by distributing distinctions and emoluments on *many,* and by raising the hopes and expectations of *more,* make the mass of the people themselves.

(tbus corrupted at,the very fountain-head) become the instruments of annihilating the best part of the constitution. A limited monarch, whose throne is founded on the basis of a people's affection* and a judicious preference both of his person and form of government, will be as reasonably anxious as any among the people can be, to guard against the prevalence of such corruption, and the success of such eorruptors. It is the cause of *courts*, if they mean to consult their stability* as much as it is of popular conventions, to preserve public virtue, and prevent the people from losing all *sensibility* to the value of a free constitution, the liberty of the present age, and of ages to come*

I firmly maintain, that the prevention of this popular degeneracy is to be effected, not by political artifices, not by prosecutions, not by sycophantic associations of placemen, pensioners, and expectants of titles and emoluments, but by reforming the manners of the people. Principles of religion, honour, and public spirit must be cherished. The *clergy* must be *independent,* and the **pulpit free.** Books written without party views, intending to promote no interests but those of truth and philanthropy, must not only not be checked by *crown* lawyers, but industriously disseminated among the people. Religion must be considered by the **great**, not merely as a state engine, but as what it is, the source of comfort and the guide of conscience. Its professional teachers must be advanced from considerations of real merit and services, and not from borough interest, and the prostitution of the pulpit to the unchristian purposes of ministerial despotism.

No writings of sceptical or infidel philosophers do so much harm to Christian faith and practice, to religion and morality, as tbe using of church *revenues* and church *instruction as* instruments of court corruption. The very means appointed by Godi and the laws, for checking the depravity of the people, contribute to it, When they appear to be-considered by the great as' little more 'than artificeh of politicians, designed to keep the vulgar (as tbey are often unjustly called): in subjection to wicked!' upstarts, possessed of temporary and official powers by 'intrigue and unconstitutional influence.

It is certainly in the power of a well regulated government, by rendering the church effective, and by good examples and sincere attachment do virtuous men and virtuous principle^ to correct the levity effeminacy, and want of principle in private life, which leads to the'loss of liberty. The church wiH be effective, as soon; as the people: are convinced, that all preferments in it are bestowed*on those who have preached the gospel faithfully; and not on time-servers,; and[1] the friends and[1] relations- of parasites, who have no other view in seeking seats in the senate, but to-serve a minister-for their own advantage. - Till the people>are convinced that an *administration is sincere in religion,* they -will be too -apt to Consider not only *religion,* but common *honesty,* as an empty name.

The religions principle being thus destroyed by

the greedy aspirants at worldly grandeur, no wonder the people lapse into that dissolute conduct, which seeks nothing seriously but selfish pleasure and private profit. Levity of manners both proceeds from, and produces, *defect of moral principle.* JEfifeminacy, the natural consequence of vice and luxury caused by *defect of moral principle*, precludes, courage, spirit, and all-manly, virtuous exertion. Ignorance must follow; for to obtain knowledge requires a degree of labour and laudable application, which those who are sunk in indolence and sensuality will never bestow. When ignorance is become gerieral, and vice reigns triumphant, what remains to oppose the giant Despotism, who, like a Colossus, strides over the pigmy and insignificant slaves of oriental climes, from trampling on men in countries once free?

Farewell, then, all that truly ennobles human nature. Pride, pomp, and cruelty domineer without controul. The very name of liberty becomes odious; and man, degenerated, contents himself with the licence to eat, drink, sleep, and die at the will of an ignorant, base, libidinous superior. The sword rules absolutely^ Reason, law, philosophy, learning, repose in the tomb with departed liberty. The sun of the moral world is extinguished; and the earth is overshadowed with darkness and with death* Better had it been for a man not to have been born,- than born in a country rendered by the wickedness of government, corrupting and enslaving a *whole people*, a hell anticipated.

SECTION XIX.

Certain Passages in Dr. Brown's "Estimate" which deserve the serious Consideration of all who would oppose the Subversion of a free Constitution by Corruption of Manners and Principles, and by undue Influence.

FEW books have been more popular than Brown's *Estimate of the Manners and Principles of the Times.* He wrote with sincerity and ability; but his unfortunate end, occasioned by mental disease, had a very unfavourable influence on the circulation of his book, and his posthumous fame. Nothing can, however, be more unreasonable, than to depreciate a book, allowed by all, at its first appearance, to contain indisputable and important truth, because of the misfortune, or even misconduct, of its author subsequent to its publication. I confidently recommend the following passages to the consideration of every true lover of that free constitution which renders our country conspicuously happy and honourable among the nations which surround it.

"The restraints laid on the royal prerogative at "the revolution, and the accession of liberty thus "gained by the people, produced two effects, with "respect to parliaments. One was, that instead of "being *occasionally,* they were thenceforward *animat-* "*ly* assembled; the other was, that whereas on any "trifling offence given they had usually been *intimi-* "*dated* or *dissolved,* they now found themselves pos- "sessed of new dignity and power; their consent " being necessary for raising *annual supplies.*

"No body of men, except in the simplest and "most virtuous times, ever found *themselves pos-* "*sessed of power,* but many of them would attempt "to turn it to their own private advantage. "Thus the parliament, finding themselves of weight, "and finding, at the same time, that the disposal of "all *lucrative employments* was vested in the crown, "soon bethought themselves, that in exchange for "*their* concurrence in granting supplies, and *for-* ^ *warding the measures of government,* it was but "equitable that the crown should concur in vesting "them or their dependents with the *lucrative employ-* "*ments* of state.

"If this was done, the wheels of government ran "smooth and quiet; but if any large body of claim- "antswas dispossessed, the public uproar began^ "and public measures were obstructed or over- "turned.

"William the Third found this to be the natural "turn, and set himself, like a *politician,* to oppose "it; he therefore silenced all be could by places "and pensions, and hence the origin of making of "PARLIAMENTS."

This *making of parliaments,* I contend, is *fundi nostri calamitas,* the origin of all our present political evil; it defeated the good purposes of the revolution, and tended to introduce the despotism of tbe Stuarts, under the. mask of liberty. It arose from

L 2

the corruption of the people, and has gone on augmenting it to this very day.

"Vanity, luxury, and effeminacy," proceeds Dr. Brown, "increased beyond all belief within these "thirty years; as they are of a *selfish,* so are they of "a craving and unsatisfied nature. The present rage "of pleasure and unmanly dissipation hath cre-"ated a train of *new* necessities, which in their de-"mands outstrip every supply.

** And if the great principles of religion, honour, "and public spirit are weak or lost among us, what "effectual check can there be upon the great, to "control their unwarranted pursuit of lucrative "employments, for the gratification of these un-"manly passions ?

"In a nation so circumstanced, it is natural to "imagine that, next to gaming and riot, the *chief* "*attention* of the great world must be turned on "the business of election jobbing, of securing "counties, controuling, bribing, or buying bo-"roughs; in a word, on the possession of a great "parliamentary interest.

"But what an aggravation of this evil would arise, "should ever those of the *highest rank,* though pro-"HIBITED BY ACT OP PARLIAMENT, insult the laWS, "by interfering in elections, by soliciting votes, or "procuring others to solicit them, by influencing "elections in an avowed defiance of their country, "and even *selling* vacant seats in parliament to the "BEST BIDDER."

Would not this be treason *against the constitution?* a more dangerous and heinous political crime than any that have, been prosecuted by attornies-general ? Does not this directly destroy the democratical part of the system, and establish a power independent both of the monarch and the people? Are no*t both,* therefore, interested in putting a stop to such gross violations of law and equity ?

"What," continues Dr. Brown, "can we suppose "would be the real drift of this illegitimate waste "(among the great) of time, honours, wealth, and "labour ? Might not the very reason publicly as-"signed for it be this: * That they may strengthen "themselves and families, and thus gain a lasting' "interest (as they call it) for their dependents, sons, "and posterity?' Now what would this imply but a "supposed *right or privilege of* demanding lucra-"tive employs, as the chief object of their views ? "We see then how the political system of self-inte-"rest is at length completed.

"Thus faction is established, not on ambition, "but on avarice: on avarice and rapacity, for "the ends of dissipation.

"The great contention among those of family and "fortune will be in the affair of election interest: "next to effeminate pleasure and *gaming;* this (for. "the same end as gaming) will of course be the ca-"pital pursuit; this interest will naturally be re-"garded as a kind of *family fund,* for the provision "of the -younger branches.

"In a nation so circumstanced, many high and "important posts, in every public and important "profession, must of course be filled by men, who "instead of *ability* and *virtue,* plead this *interest* (in "elections) for their best title.

"Thus, in a time when science, capacity, cou- "rage, honour, religion, public spirit, are rare, the "remaining few who possess these virtues will often "be *shut out* from these stations, which they would "fill with honour; while every public and impor- "tant employ will abound with men, whose man- "ners and principles are of the *newest* fashion.

"Is not the *parliamentary interest* of every power- "ful family continually rung in the ears of its "branches and dependents ? And does not this in* "evitably tend to relax and weaken the application "of tbe *young men* of quality and fortune, and "render every man, who has reliance on this prin- "ciple, *less qualified* for those very stations, which "by this very principle he obtains. For why should "a *youth offamily or fashion,* (thus he argues with "himself,) why should he submit to the drudgery "of schools, colleges, academies, voyages, cam- "paigns, fatigues, and dangers, when he can rise "to the highest stations by *the smooth and easy*
    A of PARLIAMENTARY INTEREST?

"Where effeminacy and selfish -vanity form' the "ruling character of a people, then those of *high* "*rank* will be of all others most vain, most selfish, "most incapable, most effeminate.

"Such are the effects of the prevailing principle "of self-interest in *high life.* But if we take into the "account all that *despicable train of* political mana- "gers, agents, and borougb-jobbers, which hang like

"*leeches* upon the great, nor ever quit their hold
"till they are full gorged, we shall then see this
"reigning evil in its last perfection. For here, to
"*incapacity* and *demerit,* is generally added inso-
"jlence. Every low fellow of this kind looks upon
"the man of genius, capacity, and virtue, as his
"*natural enemy.* He regards him with an evil eye;
"and hence *undermines* or defames him; as one
"who thwarts his views, questions his title, and en-
"dangers his *expectations."*

< In another -place, the same author very plainly deduces the corruption of the *youth of the nation,* the young nobility and gentry in particular, from *parliamentary corruption.*

"Notwithstanding the privilege vested in the com-
"mons of commanding the purses of their consti-
"tuents, it is not difficult to point out a situation
"where this privilege would be nothing but a *name.*
"And as in the last century the regal and demo-
"cratic branches by turns bore down the constitu-
"tion, so, in such a situation as is here supposed,
"the real danger, though hidden, would lurk in
"the *aristocratic* branch, which would be secretly
"bearing down the power both of the king and
"people.

"The matter may be explained in a small com-
"pass. Cannot we put a case, in which the *parlia-*
"*mentary interest* of the *great nobility* might swal-
"low up the house of commons? Members might
"be elected, indeed; and elected in *form* too. But
"by whom might they be *really* elected? By the
"free voice of the people ? No impartial man would

"say it. It were easy to suppose thirty-.orOForty
"men, who, if wanted, might go nigh to command a
"majority in the lower house. - The members of
"that house might *seem* to be. the representatives of
"the people; but would be, in truth, a great part
"of them, no more than the *commissioned deputies*
"of their respective *chiefs*, whose sentiments they
"would give, and whose *interests* they would
"pursue.

"Thus, while power would, in appearance, be
"centering in the lower house, it would in reality
"be lurking in the higher.

"This state of things might not perhaps result
"from any design in the aristocratic branch to de-
"stroy the constitution. They might have no farther
"views than those of *gain, vanity, or pleasure*. Not-
"withstanding this, their conduct might have those
"effects which their intentions never aspired to.
"Let us consider the most probable effects.

"The first fatal effect which offers itself to obser*
"vation is, that the consciousness of such an in-
"creasing and exorbitant power, which the lords
"might acquire in the house of commons, would
"destroy all honest ambition in the younger
"gentry. They would know, that the utmost
"point they could hope to arrive at would only be
"to become the deputy of some great lord in a
"county or borough. All the intentions of such a
"post can be answered by ignorance and servi-
"lity *better* than by genius and public spirit.
"People of the latter stamp, therefore, would not
"naturally be appointed to the task; and this, once

** known, would check the *growth of genius and "public spirit* throughout the nation. The few "men of ability and spirit that might be left, seeing "this to be the case, would naturally betake them- "selves to such *private amusements* as a free mind "can honestly enjoy. All *hope,* and therefore, by "degrees, all *desire* of serving their country, would "be extinguished.

"Thus **honest** ambition would naturally and "generally be quenched. But even where ambition "*continued,* it would *he perverted.* Not useful, but "*servile* talents would be applauded; and the ruling "pride would be, not that of freemen, but of "slaves."

The above remarks were made long before American independence was established, the French revolution thought of, or the discussions on the subject of parliamentary reform became general. The author wrote the pure result of impartial observation; and what be wrote deserves the serious attention of all **honest** *men,* all good members of the community. I will make no comments upon it, but leave it to operate on the mind with its own force.

SECTION XX.

On several Subjects suggested by Lord Melcombe's *"Diary particularly the Practice of bartering the Cure of Souls for the Corruption of Parliament.*

It is very desirable, that country gentlemen, who are often inclined to shew a blind attachment to ministers, as if loyalty were due to the *servants* of a court as well as to the master, would peruse, with attention, the Diary of Lord Melcombe. There they are admitted behind the curtain, and even under the stage, to see the machinery. There they behold filthy workmen, dirty wheels within wheels, every thing offensive to the eye, and all busy for hire to produce a specious, outside shew on the stage, for the amusement of the spectators, while the shewmen pocket the pence. It would have been worth the while of courtiers to have paid the price of a campaign in Flanders, and the subsidy of a German prince, to have suppressed the publication of Lord Melcombe's Diary. The secrets of the ministerial conclave are there laid open; and the sight and stench are no less disgustful than those which strike the senses on the opening of a common sewer. Nothing but the most selfish covetousness, the weakest vanity, the meanest, dirtiest, most villainous of the passions! No regard *for the happiness of the nation,* much less *for the hap-*

piness of mankind; one general struggle, by artifice and intrigue, not by honourable and useful exertions, for power, profit, and titles! It might be supposed* that the parties concerned were banditti, contending in a cave about the division of plunder. How are the words *lord* and *duke* disgraced and prostituted, when prefixed to persons warmly engaged in such transactions! Such men are truly levellers, the enemies of the peerage, the involuntary promoters of equality! In a greedy rapaciousness for themselves, they forget not only the good of their country and mankind, but the interest of their own privileged order.

When little and base minds, like the heroes of *Bubb Doddington's* Diary, bear rule, every thing, even religion itself, becomes an instrument of corruption. It is well understood by every body, that church preferments, even with *cure* of *souls,* have long been used to secure the interest of courts in venal boroughs; but the following passage contains a curious proof of it, under the hand of Lord Melcombe, and, under the authority of the then prime minister, the Duke of Newcastle.

"December the 11th, 1763," (says Lord Melcombe,)"I saw the Duke of Newcastle. 1 told "him, that in the election matters (of Bridgwater "and Weymouth) *those who would take, money I* "would pay, and not bring him a bill;»those that "would not take, *he must pay*; and I recommended "MY TWO PARSONS of Bridgwater and Weymouth, "Burroughs and Franklin:—he entered into it VERY "CORDIALLY, and assured me they should have the "first CROWN LIVINGS that should be vacant in "those parts, if we would look, out and send him "the first intelligence.—I said, 1 must think, that so "much offered, and so little asked, in such hands "as theirs, and at a time when BOROUGHS were "particularly MARKETABLE, could not fail of re-"moving, at least, resentments, and of obtaining par-"don.-... His Grace was very hearty and cordial.

"29th. Went to the Duke of Newcastle, and got "the living of *Sroadworthy* for Mr. Burroughs.

"March 21st. Went to the Duke of Newcastle "—told him I was come to assure him of my most "*dutiful* affection and sincere attachment to him, "having no engagements to make me look to the "right or the left.... 1 *engaged to choose two mem-*"*hers* for Weymouth, which he desired might be a "son of the Duke of Devonshire, and Mr. Ellis of "the admiralty. I supposed he would confirm that "nomination—*hut that was nothing to me** He "might name whom he pleased.—Mr. Pelham told "me tbe KING asked him if I seriously designed to "endeavour to keep Lord Egmont out of Bridg-"water. Mr. Pelham told his Majesty that he "thought I would; that I desired him *to lay me* "*at the king's feet,* and tell him, that as I found it "would be *agreeable to* his majesty, I would spare "neither pains nor expence to exclude him. The "Duke of Newcastle said he had seen how *hand-*"*some my proceedings had been;* that this was the

---

* i *Tutu, 0 dux magne, quid optes Explorare labor;* *umjutta capcttertfat est.*   Virg.

"MOST NOBLE that could be imagined ?... I said,
"What if I came into the place Sir Thomas Robin-
"son left? He considered a little, and said, Very
"well, pray go on. I said I would particularly
"support him in the house, *where* he would chiefly
"want it. He said he knew I would. I said, There
"is my old place—TREASURER OF THE NAVY; I
"should like that BETTER THAN ANY THING. But
"I added, Why should I enter into these things; I
"leave it wholly to your grace. He said the *direc-*
"*tion* of the *house of commons* was fallen upon him
"—therefore he could not chuse by affection, but
"must comply with those who could support him
"*there*. I said I understood so; and that I thought
"I might pretend to some abilities *that way*; that id
"the opposition, I was thought of some use Mere;
"that in court, indeed, f never undertook much,
"*because he knew I never was supported:* but now,
"*when I should be supported,* I hoped f might pre-
"tend to be as useful there as my neighbours. He
"said it was incontestably so. I said, that consi-
"dering that I chose *six members for them* at my
"own great expence, I thought the world in gene-
"ral, and even the gentlemen themselves, could not
"expect that their pretensions should give me the
"exclusion. He said, that what 1 did was VERY
"GREAT ! that he often thought with surprise at the
"ease and cheapness of the election at Weymouth!
"that they had nothing like it! I said, I believed,
"there were few who could give HIS MAJESTY *six*
"*members for* NOTHING. He said he reckoned five,
"and had put down five to my account.... I said

"I mast be excused from talking any more about "myself; that I left it entirely to him and to the "**KINO**; that I was fully determined to make this "sacrifice to his Majesty; that I knew I had given "no just cause of offence, but that I would not jus-"tify it with bis Majesty; that it was *enough* that "he was displeased, to make me think that I was "iu the wroog, and to beg him to forget it: I would "NOT EVEN BE IN THE RIGHT AGAINST HIM; and "I was very sure I would never again be in the "wrong against him, for which I hoped- bis Grace "would be my caution. He said be would, with "all his heart. HE took me up in his arms, and "kissed mb twice, withstrong assurances of aflec-"tion and service."

A few days after, this HONEST MAN went to Bridgwater to manage the election, and thus proceeds his Diary.

"April 14, 15, 16. Spent in the infamous "AND DISAGREEABLE COMPLIANCE WITH THE LOW "HABITS OF VENAL WRETCHES," the electors of Bridgwater.

If the men of Bridgwater, urged perhaps by want, were *venal wretches,* what must we think of tbe Duke of Newcastle and Lord Melcombe? I hope my reader will pause, and ponder the words of the preceding passage. They furnish a great deal of matter for very serious reflection to those who regard the true interests either of church or state.

Lord Melcombe's Diary was much read when it first came out; but it has since fallen into neglect. Events, however; have happened in the political wprld, which raider it extremely interesting at the present period. In consequence of the French revolution, much pains have been taken to decry the people, and extol the aristocratical part of society. The tide has run wonderfully, in consequence of *false alarms* and ministerial artifices, in favour of courts and courtiers. The people have been called, not only *venal wretches,* but the swinish multitude. Long and tiresome books have beat written to run down the people, as destitute of virtue, principle, of every thing honest and honourable, and that can give them any right to interfere with the grand mysteries of a cabinet. But he who reads and considers.duly the very in Lord Melcombe's Diary, will see, that, in order to find venality in its full growth, and survey sordidness in its complete state of abomination, it will be necessary to turn from low to high life.

The people are often turbulent and indiscreet in
their transactions, but they are always honest and always generous. They feel strongly for the cause of humanity and justice. They have a noble spirit, which leads them. to view meanness and sinister conduct with detestation. But is there any of this manly independence, this honest openness, this regard for the rights and happiness of man, among those whom Lord Melcombe, so unfortunately for the great vulgar, has introduced to public notice? There is all the deceit in his own character, which would denominate a man a swindler in the commercial walks of life. All the transactions of the junto are

conducted with the timidity, secrecy, duplicity of a nest-of thieves, mutually fearing and fawning, while they hate and despise each other from their heart's core.

On the practice of purchasing votes in boroughs, by bartering the cure of souls, the most sacred charge, if there be any thing sacred in human affairs, I shall expatiate more at large in a future section.

This Bubb Doddington, after selling himself, betraying the prince, and offering his six members to the best bidder, was made a lord. He was created Baron of Melcombe Regis, as a[1] reward for such prostitution of principles as ought to have caused him to. be branded in the forehead with a mark of indelible infamy.

But can we suppose that there has been but one Bubb Doddington in this country? one Newcastle?■ I wish the supposition were founded in probability. It would be the simplicity of idiotisin to suppose, that Bubb Doddington has not exhibited in his Diary a picture of parasitical courtiers, in all times and countries, where corruption is the main.principle of administration.

If *such men* should, in any country of Europe, influence the councils of princes, and manage the popular assemblies, would there not be reason to be alarmed for the best constitution ever devised by human wisdom ? *Such men* hate the people. They love nothing but themselves, the emoluments of places, the distinction of titles, and tbe pomp and vanity: of the courts: in which they flatter and are flattered. They will ever wish for a MILITARY government, to *awe* the saucy crowd, and keep them from intruding on their own sacred privileges and persons. The Herculean hand of a virtuous people can alone cleanse the Augean stable of a corrupted court, formed of miscreant toad-eaters like Lord Melcombe.

SECTION XXI.

On choosing rich Men, without Parts, Spirit, or Liberality, as Representatives in the National Council.

IT has been long observed, that none are more desirous of increasing their property than they who have abundance. The greatest misers are those who possess the greatest riches. None are fonder of the world than they who have engrossed a large share of it. If they should acknowledge that they have enough money, yet they cannot but confess, at the same time, that they think themselves entitled, in consequence of their property, to civil honours, power, and distinction. They have a kind of claim, in their own opinion, to court favour; especially as they are ready to use the influence, which their riches give them, in support of any minister for the time being, and in the general extension of royal prerogative. Are such men likely to be independent members of a senate, honestly following the dictates of their judgment or conscience, and consulting no interest but that of MAN in general, and the people in particular, by whom they are deputed ? There are no men *greedier* of gain than such men, and none more attached to those vain honours, which a minister bestows in order to facilitate the movements of his political machine. None will rake so deeply in the DIRT to pick up a penny as a rich miser; none will contend more eagerly for a feather in the cap, than, those < whose minds are weak, empty, and attached to the world by the consciousness of being, in great measure, its proprietors.

But what is it to me, as an ELECTOR, that the man who solicits my vote has, by great cunning, sordid arts, and insatiable avarice, accumulated great riches ? Has wisdom, has virtue, has knowledge, has philanthropy increased with his increasing fortune? Uncommon success, enormous wealth, acquired in the short space of half a human life, is a *presumptive evidence of little principle* in the means of acquiring, and as little generosity in the modes of giving or expending it. Perhaps he *inherits* his unbounded riches. What then ? His *ancestors* were probably knaves or muck-worms. In this case, he has not to plead the merit of industry. His ancestors have left him vast sums of money; when perhaps his own talents would scarcely have earned him a penny, or kept him out of the parish poor-house.

Nevertheless, because he is rich, though totally destitute of parts and virtue, he stands forward boldly as a candidate to represent a city or a county. He finds thousands ready to clamour on his side, and to give him their vote. He can treat bountifully, open houses, and give away ribands plentifully. Therefore he is constituted a senator, a national counsellor, commissioned to vote away the people's money, and to decide on the most, important questions of constitutional liberty.

What can he do but put himself into harness, and be driven his daily stage, by the political coachman, the prime minister ? He cannot go aloue. He has not sense enough to judge for himself in the smallest difficulty. He has not spirit enough to preserve his independence; therefore he will consider himself merely as a puppet, to be moved by the higher powers, at their will; a stop-gap, to fill up a place which might be occupied by an abler member, whose virtues and talents might serve the public indeed, but would render him troublesome to those who gladly dispense with all virtuous interference.

Let us suppose, for argument sake, four such *poor* creatures (such 1 call them, though *rich* in gold) chosen to represent the city of London, the grand emporium of the world, and, from its number of inhabitants, claiming a fuller representation than any part of the nation. 1 own the supposition is most disgraceful; for it can never happen, one would think, that such a city should not supply men of the first *abilities,* for a trust so important and so honourable. But let us suppose the CITY, from a system of manners favoured by, and favourable to, ministerial corruption, so far degraded as to choose four men of very moderate abilities and characters, merely because they happen to be rich contractors, and of sycophantic dispositions, likely to pursue, their *own* interest by servilely obeying the beck of a minister.

Suppose them once in for seven years. The taverns are now shut up, the *advertisements,* the canvassing all forgotten, and they commence as arrant courtiers as the meanest tool of power, *put*, by a paltry lord, into a rotten borough of 'Sussex, Wiltshire, or Cornwall.

But mark the mischief. As they nominally represent the first city in the world, the measures which *they,* vote, for, (because they are bidden, and hope for contracts and baronetages,) are supposed, by foreigners at least, to have the concurrence of the most important part of the British empire. Though the minister may despise them from his heart, - personally, yet he avails himself of that weight which tbe. place they represent gives them in the eyes of Strangers. "The GREAT *city* is *with* him," (in the only place he preteuds to know it, the house of representatives).

. Their ignorance, their meanness, and their sycophancy, have another effect, highly injurious to all plans of constitutional reformation. "Here" (says the courtier) "are four men sent by the first city "in the world. Are they better senators, or more "respectable men, than those who are sent from "Old Sarunij or any of the boroughs inhabited by "beggars, and purchased by lords, as a lucrative "speculation?" The probability is, (he will say of them,) that, with more *greediness after gain*, from the sordid habits of their youth, they have less of the accomplishments and liberality of gentlemen. Their eagerness to raise their families, renders them more tractable tools in the hands of a skilful minister, than those whose families are already raised, and who, however they may place themselves under the guidance of the peerage, have hadan education which ought to have given them enlarged minds and sentiments Of honour.

Thus the friend to despotic principles, and the opposer of parliamentary reform, draws an argument from the meanness of rich men, (sent by *great cities* to parliament merely because- they are rich,) against all improvement of the representation^ The boroughs, he alleges, send at least *gentlemen* and well-informed men, though in circumstances comparatively indigent; whereas these great commercial bodies, placing all excellence in the possession of superior wealth, depute men as senators, who are unqualified for any department beyond the warehouse or the counting-hohse, whose views are confined, and purposes *habitually* sordid and selfish. He uiges, that, from the specimens afforded by great cities, there is no reason to conclude that the extension of the right of suffrage would render the representative body more virtuous or enlightened. He doubts whether it would be favourable to liberty. If great bodies depute men only for their property, since they who *have* most usually *want* most, none will be readier to sell themselves and their constituents to a minister, for a feather or a sugar-plum, than the representatives of great bodies, delegated to parliament merely because they have inherited or acquired, *excessive riches,'* with scarcely ahy ideas beyond the multipficafioh-table. ' '

' Men 'deputed to parliament should certaihly be far above want; but I contend that riches, independent of personal merit, can never be a sufficient recommendation. It is the most important trust that can be reposed in man. It requires a most comprehensive education, strong natural abilities, and, what is greater than all, a just, honest, upright heart, with a manly firmness, and an enlarged philanthropy.

Can there be any difficulty in finding, at any lime, four men of such character in the city of London, or two such in any county of England ? Certainly not; especially when the corrupting idea shall be exploded, that PROPERTY is the best qualification for a national counsellor and lawgiver. *Able* and *honest* men are not the most inclined to thrust themselves forward, and to *obtrude* themselves, much less to enter into competition, when all the influence of riches and ministerial favour will be exerted to traduce their character, to frustrate their endeavours, and send them back to private life with their fortunes injured, and their tranquillity disturbed. The electors must *search* for such men, and draw them from their virtuous obscurity. Thus honoured, they will go into the senate with the pure motives of serving their country and mankind, and return, with *clean hands,* sufficiently rewarded by the blessings of the people.

The city of London, and all great cities, as well as counties, are to be most seriously exhorted, to consider the importance of the trust they delegate at an election, and to choose men of known abilities, and experienced attachment to the cause of the people. They should beware of men, however opulent and respectable in private life, who can have no other motive for obtruding on public life, for which they are *unqualified,* but to raise themselves and families to fortune and distinction, by *selling their trust* to a minister. Such men can never be friends to liberty and the people. They contribute, by means of their property, to the general system of corruption, and, perhaps without knowing it, (for they *know* but little,) promote, most effectually, the spirit of despotism.

SECTION XXII.

Of the despotic Influence of great Merchants over their Subalterns, of Customers *over their Tradesmen, and rich trading Companies over their various Dependents, in* compelling *them to vote for* Court *Candidates for Seats in Parliament, merely to serve* private Interest, *without the smallest Regard for* public *Liberty and Happiness, or the Fitness or Unfitness of the Candidate.*

The rottenness of corruption, originating from ministers, intoxicated with the love of power, and greedy after the emoluments of office, is sometimes found (especially under the influence of *false alarms*) to pervade the whole mass of the people, and to infect the very heart of the body-politic. The vitals of liberty become tainted, and, without great efforts, a *mortification* may be justly apprehended.

In this corrupt state, *little despots,* aspiring at court favour, hoping to draw the notice of the minister on their faithful endeavours to serve him, arise in almost every town and village of the country, and in every street of a great city. They claim and exercise a jurisdiction over certain vassals, as they think them, their tradesmen, their tenants, and nil others, who derive emoluments from them in the way of their business, or expect tbgir custom and countenance. If the vassals presume to act for themselves as men and freemen, they lose their business, their dwelling places, their farms, and all chance of acquiring a competency. The vengeance of the *little despots* pursues them; and frequently quits not the chace, till it has hunted them down to destruction.

Even in the City of London, opulent as it is, and *independent* as it might be, a city which used to be the first to stand up in defence of liberty, an overbearing influence can find its way to the obscurest district, and insinuate itself into the blindest alley. The great merchant or manufacturer, who is necessarily connected with many subordinate traders or workmen, considers the influence he gains from extensive connections in business, as a very valuable and vendible Commodity at the *market* of a *minister*. Naturally wishing to make the most of bis trade, he resolves to treat this connection as a part of his *stock,* and cause it to bring him an *ample* rettirn. At least he will *adventure.* It may be a prize 'to him,' as it has been to 'inany. Much depends on his 'own prudential "management of the Commodity. Tt may lead to a valuable *contract,* Especially if 'kind fortune should kindle the fiatnes **Of** war; it may **open** the path to court favours of various 'kinds'; it may ultimately confer' a seat in the hiJtlSe, and perhaps a baronetage. This last hOnotfr is highly desirable, as it removes'at once'the tfiLTH that'naturally attaches 'to the very name¹ of *'ditiz'en, 'd&tter,* find *thdpman.* '

In the city Of **London,** the majority of *electors,* who send the *OFew* members Of parliament allotted to it, are df the *middle,* and indeed of the inferior

OF DESPOTISM. 171

rank of shopkeepers, rarely rising to the dignity of merchants, who reside at the houses with *great gates*, or rather in the *new Squares*%, two or three miles north-west of the polluted and polluting *city:* for such is the insolence of little city despots who are in a very *great way*, that they commonly *despise* the *freedom* of the city where their counting-house stands, and where they gain their plums. They do not *condescend* to be free of the city. They Would consider it as a degradation from their *gentility* to be liverymen and members of a city company: Liverymen, indeed 1 'What! *great men*, as *ail* bankers are, *East India Directors*, usurious *motiey-lenders*, living'magnificently in Portland-place or Poriman-square, or the grand avenues 'to theth, to be LIVERYMEN! Horrid degradation! The very idea is shocking to the *spirit of despotism*. ! It is time enough to take up their freedom of the city, when it is necessary, as candidates, to possess that'qualification. There arC too *many voles* to make it *worth 'while* to be *A* voter. These *great* lhen, therefore, VieW the electors as Subordinate persons, whom¹ they may Send On fib errand to Guildhall to VOTE for the minister's 'candidate, just as they would diityatdh a clerk pr porter to the'CustOm-houseto take a Custom-'honse 'oath, 'Or t6 do any jOb connected with the *low* trade or riianufacture Which enables them t6 associate with the fine fdlk of St. James's.

The *elector* who goes to the hustings *must*, indeed, vote upon his *oath*, that he *has* received and *will* rec&iVe Wo BkfBE. He' dbes not cdtisider the-lucrative employments and the emoluments arising from the *great man's* custom, which would be lost on *disobedience, as* a *bribe,* and therefore votes against his judgment, conscience, and inclination, without a murmur; especially as his daily bread may perhaps depend on his obsequiousness, and very likely the comfort and security of a wife and a large family.

This conduct of the GREAT MEN is not only unconstitutional and affronting to the city, but as truly DESPOTIC in principle as any thing done by the Grand Seignior. It is *mean* also and base to the last degree; for the great men usually exert not their influence from friendship to the minister, or to a candidate, or from any regard to a cause which they think connected with the public good; but solely to serve themselves, to provide for poor relations, to enrich or to aggrandize an upstart family, already rendered wretched and contemptible by fungous pride.

. The glorious rights and privileges of Englishmen, of which we read and hear so much, are then to be all sacrificed to serve a man, who perhaps went out as a *writer* to the East Indies, and returned in five or six years, laden with riches; the injured widow and orphan in vain lifting up their hands, and uttering their lamentations over the deaf ocean, while the spoiler is hastening to Europe, with that treasure which, as it was gained by extortion, is to be expended in corruption.

Male parta male dilabuntur.

A prodigious recommendation this, as a representative in parliament of industrious citizens, who have toiled all their lives at the counter, or in the manufactory, for a bare competence!

When NABOBS, as they are called, perfect ALIENS, recommended only by riches and court influence, can *seat* themselves for *great* cities and *counties* as easily as they used for Coniish BOROUGHS, there certainly is reason to fear that the spirit of despotism has rapidly increased, and is proceeding to destroy all remains of public virtue among the PEOPLE. The* question naturally arises, if a NABOB, a perfect alien, should ever be elected for the city of London; whether, in so large a body as the free-born citizens, and among the livery of London, a man is. not to be found who has served a regular apprenticeship, gone through all the gradations of successful trade, and become a member of the. corporation, worthy to represent the first COMMERCIAL body in the universe? Is it necessary to IMPORT members, as we do tea and muslins, from China and Bengal? Honesty, virtue, independence, and abilities, must indeed be rare qualities, from Temple-bar to Whitechapel, if not enough of them can be found to constitute a representative in parliament. Must the English oak be neglected, for EXOTICS raised rapidly in warm climates; and from the hasty growth of which, very, little is to be depended upon, when the wind and weather assail them ? A sad encouragement this to the young merchants, traders, and manufacturers, who enter regularly on business, and become free--men and *liverymen,* to find that.the most industrious and successful trader, and the best, character, cannot secure the honourable appointments and important trusts,, in the gift of their fellow-citizens! to find, that persons, who never served apprenticeship, never-carried on trade, never became free, never were connected in the city companies, perfect *strangers to the corporation,* and avowed *despisers* of them all, shall be. made, by the influence of a minister, and the overbearing weight of oriental riches, legislators for the emporium of Europe! If such an event were ever to happen, it would discourage all *virtue\n.*the *rising generation* of merchants, traders, and manufacturers; and teach them, that every thing bows to almighty money, however obtained, and to court influence, always ready to favour overbearing and overgrown property. It would be a melancholy symptom of degeneracy among the people. It would shew that the.*manly spirit* begins to fade and wither, as it has long done in *Turkey* and *JEgypt,* under the spirit of despotism.

It is truly alarming to all true Englishmen, to see great *trading companies* using the influence which riches bestow, in seconding the views of a *minister,* without the least attention to the public good, the preservation of *liberty,* and the happiness of the human race. It is certain, that men united in corporate bodies will act in a maimer which they would be ashamed of in their *private* capacities; because, when sq united, the responsibility appears to be thrown from individuals on the aggregate, and so attaching, to *every one,* can be fixed on *none.* Such bodies may be truly dangerous, when, from the hope of titles;and other favours, the members who com-*

pose them, are servilely devoted to the *minister;* not indeed to the *man,* but to the *favourite at court,* who, from his office, has in his hands the means of corruption, contracts, loans, appointments in all the professions, and, above all, titles.

Such monopolizing fraternities attack liberty with the club of Hercules. They rise with gigantic force. Reason, argument, the law and the constitution, yield to them, as the chaff before the wind. If they should not receive a powerful check from the *people* at large, who have not yet fallen down worshippers of GOLD, they must go on to establish, on the banks of the Thames, *oriental* despotism: and it would not. be wonderful to see the two sheriffs riding up Cheapside on elephants, with the Lord Mayor borne in a *pabnquin,* on the, necks of liverymen, hastening to *prostrate* themselves at the feet of a *prime minis-'* **tor, now become** as great as the Emperor of China: it wonld Dot be wonderful to see BANKERS erecting an *filigqr.chy;* the great house in Leadeqhall-street, a *trnpk,* and a *golden calf* the GOD.

SECTION XXIII.

Of the. Pageantry of Life; that it originates in the Spirit of Despotism; and contributes to it, without advancing private any more than public Felicity.

THE proud despise the people, represent them as little superior to the brutes, laugh at the idea of their rights, and seem to think that the world was made for themselves only; yet the proud are never satisfied but when they attract the notice of this very people, by splendour, by ostentation, by tbe exercise of authority over them, and by insolent airs of self-importance. The people, it must be owned, in the simplicity of their hearts, gape with admiration' at the passing spectacle which insults them with its glare, and feel themselves awe-struck with the grandeur 6f the cavalcade, which would trample them in the dirt if they did not struggle to escape.

Politicians, observing this effect of finery and parade on the minds of the unthinking, take care to dress up the idol, which they themselves pretend to worship, and which they wish the people really to adore, in all the taudry glitter of tbe lady of Loretto. They find this kind of vulgar superstition extremely favourable to their interested views. Accordingly, in all despotic countries, great pains are taken to amuse and delude the people with the trappings of royalty. Popery prevailed more by the gaudiness of its priests and altars, and the pomp of its processions, than from the progress of conviction. The people, in such circumstances, have indeed the pleasure of fine sights; but they usually pay much more dearly for them than for exhibitions at the theatre; and have this mortifying reflection, as a drawback from their pleasure, that the payment is involuntary, and the sight a political delusion, ft insults their understandings, while it beguiles them of their rights; and takes from them the earnings of their industry, while it teaches them to feel their own insignificance.

But not only despots, courtiers, and public functionaries, think it proper to strike the vulgar with awe, by purchasing finery of the builder, the taylor, and the coach-painter; but the titled and the overgrown rich men, through every part of every community, where family aggrandizement is procurable without public services, or private or personal virtue. Riches, in such societies, confer not only the means of luxurious enjoyment, but of civil superiority. They assume a value not naturally their own, and become the *suecedanea* of wisdom, patriotism, valour, learning, and beneficence. The great object is therefore to make an ostentation of riches, and to keep the people at a distance, by dazzling their eyes with the blaze of equipage and magnificence. As all the minuter luminaries gravitate to the sun in our solar system, so all these aspirants at distinction and superior importance gravitate to royalty. The crown is the glittering orb round which they ambitiously revolve. They would all therefore contribute, if they were able, to add new brilliancy, new heat, new influence, and powers of attraction to their fountain of glory. They turn to it as the sunflower to the sun; and feel their colours brighter, and tbeir leaves invigorated, when a ray of favour falls upon them in a peculiar direction. They cannot turn a moment to the people. The popular climate chills them. The gales from this quarter are as the icy breezes from the frozen regions of the north, where the genial beams of solar influence can scarcely penetrate.

It may then be fairly presumed, that where all orders of the rich are vying with each other to make a splendid appearance, even above their rank and means of support, the spirit of the times, among these orders at least, is favourable to the increase of court influence, and therefore to the spirit of despotism* . ,

This rivalry in splendour is, in course, attended with great expence; an expence, which by reducing independent fortunes, diminishes independence of spirit. They who are ruined in seconding the purposes of a court, naturally think themselves, entitled to indemnity from courtfavour. They become then, merely tools of the minister, and dare not speak or act, in any instance, against him, lest they renounce all hope of the glittering prize, the secret *douceur,* the share of the loan, tbe contract, the place; the pension, fhe provision for aBon, a nephew, a cousin, or the clerical tutor of the family, who has perhaps grown grey in hungry; hope, fed only by tjie meagre diet of a ministerial promise.

OF DESPOTISM.

Thus the rage for outshining others in externals contributes to ruin both fortune and principle. Add to this, that the - prevalence of pageantry erects, in society, a false standard of human excellence. Money becomes the deity. Money is to give consequence, consideration, power. Money engrosses honour, which is< due, and has often been paid, to poverty, when adorned with art, virtue, knowledge, or any other kind of personal merit. The man becomes nothing, and money all. How must the human mind sink in such a conjuncture! Its noblest energies cannot give it that estimation with mankind, which money,' inherited by a fool, or acquired by a knave,[1] boldly claims';and obtains. Then what encouragement ■ to young men to pursue improvement with any singular ardour? Common attainments are perhaps the best adapted to facilitate the acquisition of money. Common attainments and superficial ornaments will form'the whole of education. In the mean ■ time, MIND is neglected, and human nature degenerates. Then steps in the *despot.* For the consequence,' take the map, and look over the countries which formed antient Greece.

..The'pageantry of life, considered in a political view, as designed by the *grandees* to awe the people, and 'keep them but of the pare of selfish happiness, which* the'grandees- have fenced with high pales, and guarded with spring-guns and man-traps, certainly may lay- claim to the praise of deep cunning or worldly wisdom; The pageantry of life may an-[1] swer the purpose; of ^fee scenery.0# the play-house, add keep the vulgar from beholding the grandees of the world, before they are dressed and *made up* for public exhibition. The galleries would certainly lose much of their veneration for the theatrical kings, queens, and nobles, if they were to see them behind the scenes, unbedizened. The pageantry of life is therefore highly efficacious in deluding the vulgar. Wheu not carried too far, and abused for the purposes of oppression, it may sometimes have its use. But is it, in general, conducive to the happiness of man; either of those who are the actors in the pageant, and gratify their pride by attracting the eyes of beholders; or of those who are led by it to a foolish admiration and a tame acquiescence ? Chains of gold and silver are no less galling than fetters of iron.

Pageantry has contributed perhaps more than any other cause to the prevalence of war, the bane of happiness, the disgrace of human, nature. The grand operations of war, the splendour of arms, the finery of military dress, have been the amusements which despots have chiefly delighted in, whenever they could behold them in perfect consistence with their own personal safety. The pageantry of war dazzles young minds, and supplies both armies and navies with willing victims. Tbe ugliness of slaughter, the desolation of fertile plains, the burning of peaceful villages, have all been unnoticed, amid the *pride, pomp, and circumstance of glorious war.* The taste for false glare and deceitful appearances of happiness and glory, has then been one of the mqst prolific parents of human calamity. It has palliated robbery, and covered foul murder with a glittering veil of tinsel.

All imposture is ultimately productive of evil. Pageantry, in a wretched world like this, assumed by infirm mortals doomed shortly to die, cannot but be deceitful. Its object is to put off false and counterfeit goods for true. There is nothing in human affairs that will justify or support that glare of happiness which the pageantry of the rich and great wish to display. The mask is too small and too transparent to conceal tbe face of woe, the wrinkles of decay and imperfection. In times of great ignoranee, when scarcely any could read, and very little communication was preserved among the different orders of society* the mummery of courts and courtiers taught the vulgar to believe that the internal organization of beings, so decorated externally, must be of a superior nature. Princes and priests dressed themselves in grotesque garbs, in a kind of masquerade habit, to carry on tbe delusion. But tbe reign of great wigs, fur gowns, hoods, and cloaks, is nearly at its close. Gilded coaches, horses richly caparisoned, gaudy hammer-clotbs, fine footmen, endeavour to supply their place; but they have lost much of their influence; and at last it will be found, that to obtain the respect of the people, it will be necessary to deserve it. No longer will the public admire the poor creature who rides *within* the coach, for a splendour which he owes entirely to the manufacturer of carriages, tbe painter, the carver, the gilder, the harness-maker, the horse-dealer, and the groom. No longer will men unjustly transfer the praise due to the taylor and bair-dresser, to the proud beau, who struts as if the earth were not good enough to tread. upon, nor the people whom he meets, to look at as he passes them.

The pageantry displayed by contractors, by placemen, by pensioners, by commissaries, by all who fatten on the public spoils, may justly be considered as an insult on the people. In times of great prosperity it might be winked at; but in times of distress and adversity, it is offensive. It answers no good end. It merely gratifies the vanity of those who make the ostentation. How can they find in their hearts to throw away sums that would maintain hundreds, in setting off themselves, and making a figure, during an hour or two every day, in.Bond-street and Pall-mall, while they pass hundreds who are ready to perish with cold and hunger, and cannot but know that the world abounds with instances of extreme want and misery ? The pageantry of the unfeeling great in France aggravated the sense of suffering under its despotism; but, on the other hand, in provoking the people by the insult, it accelerated and completed the glorious revolution.

It is probable that every little wretch who decorates himself, and all that belongs to him* with finery to the utmost of his power, would be a *despot,* if be could, and dared. He shews all the disppsitions to assume superiority without merit. He certainly has a narrow and vain mind. He cannot be a philosopher or philanthropist. With.all his style and splendour in eating, drinking, dwelling, dressing, and riding, we cannot admire him; then let us pity, or deride.

Mere folly might be laughed at and neglected; but the folly I describe is *mischievous.* It delights in oppression and war; and is one of the principal promoters of the *despotic spirit.*

SECTION XXIV.

Insolence of the higher Orders to the Middle Ranks and the Poor; with their effected Condescension> in certain Circumstances, to the lowest of the People.

PUBLIC corruption must produce private. When PRIDE is a ruling principle in the conduct of state affairs, it must display itself in every part of domestic life, accompanying its lordly possessor from the palace at St. James's and the levee in Downing-street, to the rural mansion in the distant province, to the convivial table, to the fire-side, to the stable, and to the dog kennel.

A due degree of self-respect, a dignified behaviour, a demand of what is due to oneself, attended with a cheerful payment of what is due to others, are highly laudable, and have no connexion with that senseless, sullen, cruel pride, which marks the spirit of despotism.

This latter sort of pride is totally destitute of feeling for others. It scarcely acknowledges the common tie of humanity. It stands alone, completely insulated from all human beings below it, and connected only by a narrow isthmus with those above it. It seems to think the world, and all that it contains, created for its own exclusive gratification. The men and women in it are merely instrunieots subservient to the will and pleasure of aristocratic insolence.

With this idea of its own privileges and claims, it is no wonder that it shews symptoms of extreme soreness and excessive irritation on the least opposition to its *will and pleasure.* Accordingly those of the human race, whose unhappy lot it is to be domestic or menial servants to persons of either sex who swell with the selfish pride of aristocracy, are kept in a state of abject servility, compelled to watch the looks and motions of the demigod or demigoddess, and spoken to with a severity of language seldom used to the horses in the stable, or the dogs in the kennel. No attendance by night or by day can be sufficient. Such superior beings cannot perform the most ordinary operations of nature without assistance, which degrades both the giver and receiver. They cannot put on their own clothes; but like eastern tyrants surrounded by slaves, stretch themselves on the couch of indolence, while their fellow-creatures, equals by nature, with trembling solicitude fasten a button, or tie a shoe-string. The slightest error, delay, or accident, draws down imprecations on the head of the offender, more terrible than the anathemas of a pope.

If the *little Mogul* affect spirit, then he talks, in his ire, of horsewhips, kicking down stairs, breaking every bone in the skin of the wretched operator, who, as human nature is prone to error, may have deviated, in adjusting a curl, from the standard of court propriety. When he has occasion to speak of one of his servants, he commonly says, "one of my.

rascalsdidthisor that;" and when he speaks to them, especially on the slightest neglect or mistake, his choler breaks out into oaths, curses, and epithets; expressive of bitterness and venom, for which language has not yet found adequate terms. The genius of Homer, which described the wrath of Achilles, can alone paint in colour black enough the atrocity of the *great man's* ire. If it were not for that vulgar thing *law*, which, on some occasions, makes no distinctions* the great man would trample the little man who has buckled his shoe awry, out of existence.

To maintain that accuracy of dress and splendour of appearance, which so superior a being thinks absolutely necessary, certain vulgar people, called tradesmen, must inevitably be employed; and in this country of plebeian liberty, they will no more work for a nabob, or a rich contractor, or a peer of the realm, without payment, than for a French *sans eulottes*. But woe betide them, if they have the insufferable insolence to present their bills uncalled, though their families are starving, and their landlords are ejecting them from their habitations. ** The "insolence of the rascals!" (exclaims the great man,) "let them wait, let them call again, and think "themselves well off if I do not-chastise them with "a horsewhip, or kick them down stairs, for knocking at my door, and bringing bills without order. "But, d'ye hear: pay the scoundrels this time, and "mind, I never deal with them any more!" Then follows a volley of oaths and curses on the heads of all such blackguards, low-lived wretches, scum of the earth, thieves, aqd pickpockets, that do not know how to keep their distance, and treat a *gentleman* with due respect. "Aye," (he adds,) "there we "see the spirit of the times, the effect of these cursed "doctrines, which those *miscreants*,# the pbilOso- "phers, have broached, to the destruction of all law, "order, and religion, throughout Europe."

The middle rapk of people, who reside in his vicinity, he takes no more notice of, than if they lived at the arctic or antarctic pole. He keeps them at a distance, because, though not so rich as himself, yet claiming and supporting the rank of *gentlemen,* they would be likely to approach too near, and perhaps presume upon something of an equality, hot only by nature, but by self-esteem and institution. He passes his next-door neighbours in his carriage or on horseback, in his daily rides, without condescending to turn his eyes upon them. He does qot recollect even their names. They may be very good sort of people, for any thing he knows to the contrary; but really he has not the honour of knowing them. A despot will not bear a rival uear his throne; and therefore he cannot bear any who, with inferior fortunes, might happen to equal him in spirit, in sense, in behaviour, and in education. But if there is any body in the neighbourhood very low indeed; so low, as to be removed from all possibility of clashing with his importance, such an one he will make a companion, and shew him most marvellous marks of hnmility and condescension. Indeed, for

* Lord Auckland's expression, when speaking of modem philosophers. *

the sake of obtaining a little popularity, he will notice cottagers and poor children at play, and make extremely free with clowns, jockies, grooms, huntsmen, and all who have any thing to do with dog and horse flesh. But keep your distance, ye little squires, parsons, and professional men, who make saucy pretensions to knowledge or ingenuity. However, he can never be at a loss for company, while he and his equals drive phaetons and four, to dine with each other at fifteen miles distance, and while officers are quartered in the vicinity. He is abjectly servile to his superiors, insolent and neglectful to the middle ranks, and free and easy to the humble sons of poverty, who will bear a volley of oaths whenever he thinks proper to discharge them, and who, if spit upon, will not spit again, because they are his workmen or tenants.

He who can eradicate such insolence from a neighbourhood, by treating it with the contempt and ridicule which it deserves, certainly contributes to tbe happiness of society. It is confined in its sphere of action; but it is the same sort of despotism which ravages Poland, and deluges the earth with human gore. In a free country like this, where law and liberty flourish, it is a vulture in a cage, but still it is a vulture; and the little birds, to whom nature has given the free air to range in, ought to unite in endeavouring to destroy it.

Does any sensible man believe that such persons, if their power were equal to their will, would suffer freeholders of forty shillings a-year, to vote for members of parliament; or juries of twelve honest plebeians to decide in state trials, where ministers are anxious (as they value their places) for a verdict' favourable to their administration? They would not permit, if they could help it, the middle ranks to breathe the common air, or feel the genial sun, which God has given to shine indiscriminately on the palace and the cottage. They are as much enemies to kings as to the people, because they would, if possible, be kings themselves; but as that is impossible, they crouch, like fawning spaniels, to the hand which has it in its power to throw them a bone.

This description of persons is peculiarly formidable to liberty, because they are insatiably greedy of *power*. -From their order chiefly arise the purchasers of boroughs, in which they traffic on speculation, like dealers in hops, determined to re-sell their commodity, as soon as they can, to tbe best bidder; They are also of that hardened effrontery which pushes its way to public employment,, stands forward at court, and, on all occasions, assumes that importance, which, from the general diffidence of the better part of mankind, is but too easily conceded to the most impudent pretensions. In consequence of this unblushing assurance, this arrogant, audacious presumption, this hardened temper, which can bear repulse without being abashed or dispirited, they oftenest rise to the highest posts;, and such as would be posts of honour, if they were, not filled by men who have not one quality of a beneficent nature, or which deserves the esteem of their fellow-creatures. But though they have no inclination to do good; they acquire the power, which they fail not to exercise, of doing much evil. They encourage arbitrary principles. They depreciate the people on all occasions; and add weight and confidence to 4he aristocratical confederacy. They 'may sometimes be men of parts. They are seldom deficient in the graces of Lord Chesterfield. But they are hard-hearted, selfish wretches, attached to the childish vanity of the world, and preferring a title; or a ribaind to the peace, the lives, the property, and the liberty of their fellow-mortals'; all which they are ready to sacrifice, even for the *chance* of pleasing a prime minister, and obtaining some bauble, which reason must ever despise, when it is not the badge of experienced virtue. "One 'of these" (says an i old writer*) "values being called His "Grace,, or Noble Marquis," {*unideal* names as they are,) "inorethan a million of. lives, provided that 'V ini. such a general destruction he can: save one; "and to., confirm themselves in their ill-gotten "honours, they generally hatch plots, subom rer V. hellions, or any thing. that they, think can create ".business, keep.themselves from being questioned, "mid THIN mankind, Whereby they lose so many of their enemies."

* Samuel Johnson; not the *Lexicographer,* whose *religion* was *qften* Popish superstition, and whose *loyalty* the most *irrational* Toryism. I venerate his abilities; but detest his politics. He Would have displaced the *firunsmck family* for the *Stuarts,* if his power hdd kept pace with his inclinations.

SECTION XXV.

Of a Natural. Aristocracy.

NOBILITY, according to the idea of the vulgar, both in high and low life, is nothing more than RICHES that have been a *long time* in *one* family: bnt it often happens that riches have beeu originally gained and preserved in *one* family by sordid avarice, by mean and dishonest arts; such arts as are utterly incompatible with true nobility, with superiority of intellects, united with generosity of disposition.

Most of the *titles* of *nobility*, and other civil distinctions, were taken from WAR: as a marquis, a duke, a count, a baron, a landgrave, a knight, an esquire. The inventors of arts, the improvers of life, those who have mitigated evil and augmented the good allotted to men in this world, were not thought worthy of any titular distinctions. The reason is indeed sufficiently obvious: titles were originally bestowed by despotic kings, who required and rewarded no other merit but that which supported them by *violence* in their arbitrary rule. In some countries they are *now* given, for the same reasons, to those who effect the same purposes, not by war only, but by CORRUPTION.

Persons thus raised to civil honours, thus enriched by the long-continued favour of courts, would willingly depreciate all dignity which is derived **from GOD and virtue only, unindebted to patents** royal. They would create au artificial preference to a distinguished few among the human race, which pature is for ever counteracting, by giving superior abilities to those who are pushed down among the despised and neglected many. This conduct is both unjust and unnatural. It cannot be favourable to human happiness, because it is adverse to truth, and does violence to the will of God manifested in the operations of nature. In France it was carried to that extreme which brought it to its termination. There is a tendency to carry it to extremes in all countries where courts predominate. The friend of reason and of man will therefore endeavour to convince the people, that an aristocracy, founded on caprice or accident only, without any regard to superior abilities and virtues, is a fertile cause of *war,* and all those evils which infest a great part of civil society.

That the BEST and *ablest* men should govern the worst and weakest, is reasonable: and this is the *aristocracy* appointed by God and nature. But what do we mean when we say the best and ablest men ? Do we mean men of the BEST families; that is, men in whose families riches and titles have long been conspicuous? By the ABLEST men, do we mean men who possess the greatest *power,* by undue influence, in borough and county elections, though the exertion of that *power* be strictly forbidden by the law and constitution ? Or do we mean men of honest, upright, and benevolent HEARTS; of vigorous, well-informed, well-exercised understandings? Certainly the latter sort, which forms the *aristocracy*

OF DESPOTISM.

established by God and nature. This is gold; the king's head stamped upon it may make it a *guinea*. The other is only copper; and though the *same* impression may be made upon it at the mint, it is still intrinsically worth no more than a halfpenny.:

But Mr. Burke has favoured mankind with a description of what he calls a *true* natural aristocracy.

The first *requisite* * according to him, is "*To be bred* in a PLACE of *estimation*." Mr. Burke is a good classical scholar, and often writes *Latin* in English.† PLACE here is the Latin LOCUS, which every polite, scholar has observed to signify FAMILY. If I were to translate this little sentence into Latin, 1 might venture to render it in this manner: *honesto oportet oriundus sit loco*—*you must,* as the common people would express it, be a *gentleman born.* The accident of *birth* therefore is placed at the head of the qualifications necessary to give a man *pre-eminence* in society. This dootrine is certainly consistent, with the whole tenor of the book; but whether it contributes to tbe general happiness of mankind, or tends to the spirit of despotism, let impartial observers determine. Mr. Burke had said a few lines before, *satis est equitem mihiplaudere*—"It is enough for me that *gentlemen or nobles* approve my doctrine and there is therefore little doubt but that he *is* satisfied; for their approbation must be secured by opinions so favourable to their *importance*

---

* See Appeal from the *new* to the *old* Whigs, page 128.

† Thus he uses the word VAST, which the common reader understands VERT GREAT, in its classical sense, for *desolate.* Many other instances might be given.

O

in society, independently of laborious, virtuous, and *useful* exertion.

The next *requisite* is, "to see nothing low or sordid from one's infancythat is, to be kept at a distance from the swinish multitude, so as not to know those *wants* which it is the business of superiors, or of a *natural* aristocracy, to supply or alleviate.

The third *requisite* is, "to be *taught* to *respect oneself.*" This seldom requires any great *teaching* among persons who have the two preceding *requisites.* Pride and selfishness are the very principles of despotism.

The fourth *requisite* to natural aristocracy, "is to "be *habituated* to the *censorial* inspection of the "public eye." Yes; so habituated as to be hardened by effrontery, and to say that *a king holds his crown* in contempt of the people;* and, *satis est equitem mihi plaudere,* which may be rendered, paraphrastically, "I care nothing for the *people's censo** "*rial eye* or tongue, if the great honour me with "their applause, for defending their exclusive privi* "leges from being trodden under the hoof of the "swinish multitude."

I pass over some very proper *requisites,* to proceed to the last. The last is, "to be among rich "traders, who, from their success, are presumed to "have *sharp* and vigorous understandings, and to "possess the virtues of diligence, order, constancy, "and regularity, and to have cultivated an habitual "regard to commutative justice.—These are the cir-

* Mr. Burke's doctrine.

"Cumstances of men who form what I should call "a natural aristocracy, without which there is no "nation. Without this," (the writer intimates, in a few subsequent lines,) "he cannot recognize the "*existence* of the people."

. Respecting Mr. Burke greatly, as I do, add agreeing with him in many particulars in this very passage, I cannot help thinking that he has laid too much stress on riches and birth, in pointing out the men intended by nature to take the lead in all human affairs, and to form what he calls a *true* natural aristocracy.

> Nam genus et proaros, et *qua nonfecimus ipsi,*
> Vix ea nostra voco.

I think it injurious to society and mankind at large to lavish honours and confer power on accidental qualities, which may exist in their greatest degree and perfection without the least particle of *personal merit,* without wisdom or benevolence. It discourages industry. It stifles all virtuous emulation. It makes riches the grand object of pursuit; not for their own intrinsic value, not for their power of supplying necessaries, and even luxuries, but for the *political consequence* they bestow, independently of the mode of acquisition or expenditure. I would have no idolatry. God has shewn his peculiar indignation against it. I would not worship a *cay',* though & *golden* one., KINGS LOG, and *Gods* made pf stocks and stones, can only command reverence from men *really* sunk to a state *below* the swine.

I know Xord Bolingbroke's doctrines of liberty

are disliked by those who see their own consequence*
increasing in the increasing spirit of despotism. But*
I will cite a passage from him, which > may counter-
balance the *servile* ideas which some men entertain
of the aristocracy constituted by NATURE.

"It seems to me," (says he,) "that in order to
"maintain the moral system of the world at a certain
"point, far below that of *ideal perfection;* but how-
"ever sufficient upon the whole to constitute a state
"easy and happy, or, at the worst, tolerable; I say,
"it seems to me, that the Author of Nature has
"thought fit to mingle, from time to time, among
"the societies of men, a few, and but a few, of
"those, on whom he is graciously pleased to bestow
"a larger portion of the setherial spirit, than is
"given, in the ordinary course of his providence, to
"the sons of men; * * *

"You will find that there are superior spirits,'
"men who shew, eVen from their infancy, though it
"be not always perceived by others, perhaps not-
"felt by themselves, that they were bom for some--
"thing more and better.' These are the men to
"whom the part I mentioned is-assigned. Their
"talents denote their *general designation.*

"I have sometimes represented to -myself the
"**vulgar,** who are accidentally distinguished by the
"titles of **king** and **subject,** of **lord** and **vassal,**
"of nobleman and peasant; and the pew who are-*
"distinguished by nature so essentially from the-
"herd of mankind, that (figure apart) they seem to
"be of another species. The *former* loiter or trifle-
"away their whole time; and their presenee or

"their absence would be equally unperceived, if "caprice or accident did not raise them often to "*stations,* wherein their stupidity, and their vices "make them a **public misfortune.** The latter, "come into the world, or at least continue in it, "after the effects of surprize and iuexperience are "over, like men who are sent on more important ** errands. They may indulge themselves in plea-"sure; but as their industry is not employed about ^{M} trifles, so their amusements are not made the busi-"ness of their lives. Such men cannot pass unper-"ceived through a country. If they retire from the "world, their splendour accompanies them, and en-"lightens even the obscurity of their retreat. If "they take a part in public life, the effect is never in-"different. They either appear like ministers of "divine vengeance; and their course through the "world is marked by desolation and oppression, by "poverty and servitude; or they are the guardian "angels of the country they inhabit, **busy** to avert "even the most distant evil, and to maintain or pro-"cure **peace,** plenty, and the greatest of human "blessings, **liberty.**"

Such men, when they take the latter course, and become the guardian angels of the country they inhabit, are the *aristocracy* appointed by God and nature. Such men, therefore, should be selected by kings for civil honours, and public functions of high importance. If kings were *republicans* in the proper sense, all the people would be royalists. But when brilliant honours and ministerial employments are bestowed on fools and knaves, because they were begotten by ancestors whom they disgrace, or possess riches which they abuse, government becomes a nuisance, and the people feel an *aristocracy* to be little better than an *automaton machine*, for promoting the purposes of royal or ministerial despotism.

SECTION XXVL

'The excessive Love of Distinction and Power which prevails wherever the Spirit of Despotism exists, deadens some of the finest Feelings of the Heart, and counteracts the Laws of Nature.

IN a system of manners, which renders the possession of riches more honourable than the possession of virtue, which attaches a degree of merit to hereditary rank and nominal distinctions, above all that personal exertions can possibly acquire, the natural ideas of right and wrong are confounded; and man, become a depraved, artificial animal, pursues preeminence in society, by *counteracting nature*, as well as by violating justice.

That he *counteracts nature*, under such a system, will be evident, on considering the present slate of conjugal union among those who appear to place the chief good of man in riches, splendour, title, power, and courtly distinctions. LOVE is every day sacrificed, by the loveliest of the species, on the altar of PRIDE.

The fine sensibilities of the heart, if suffered to influence the choice of a companion for life, might lead to family degradation. "Nature, then, avaunt," (exclaims Aristocracy). "Love is a vulgar passion. "The simplest damsel, that slumbers under the roof "of straw, feels it in ail its ardour. Daughter, you. have, nobler obje

"Remember your birth. You must make an al-
"liance 'which may aggrandize the family, which
"may add title to our riches, or new brilliancy to
"our title."

In vain have the Loves and the Graces pioulded her shape and face with the nicest symmetry. In.vain hi nature. Poor **Iphigenia** must be sacrificed. Her heart, peradventure, has chosen its mate, and happy would she be, if she could renounce all the embarrassments of high fortune, and emulate the turtle-dove of the vale. But no; she must not tell her love. Perhaps the object of it is only a *commoner;* perhaps he is only a younger brother; perhaps he has little to recommend him but youth, beauty, honour, and virtue. He cannot keep her an equipage. He has no mansion-house. Yet her heart inclines to him, and both God and nature approve her choice; but neither her heart, nor God, nor nature, will be heard, when pride and aristocratical insolence lift up their imperious voice, and command her to. remember her rank, and keep up the family dignity.

Lord ***** is introduced as a suitor, under the father's authority. Lord ***** influences five or six boroughs, and the junction of such an interest with that of the family must, in all human probability, secure a riband, and perhaps a marquisate.

His lordship is ten years older than poor Iphigenia. His life has been spent, from infancy, in the midst of luxuries and pleasures, to speak of it in the softest terms. He has a lively juvenile pertness about him; but his face is that of an old man—pale,

/or rather yellow, except his nose, which is decorated with a settled redness, and his forehead, which is •variegated with carbuncles.

Behold, then, the suitor, alighting from a high phaeton, beautifully adorned with coats of arms, not only on the sides and back, but on the lining, drawn by four cream-coloured ponies, and followed by two £ne figures of men in white liveries, with horses richly caparisoned, and displaying, in every part, where it is possible, coronets of silver.

Iphigenia appears delighted at the honour of his proposal, though her heart, when she reclines on her pillow, feels a pang of regret which no language can describe. The struggle between love and pride is violent; but it passes in secret. She hears of nothing among her companions, but of the great alliance she is going to make with an ancient and illustrious family. Splendid mansions, glittering carriages, birth-day dresses, flit before her imagination. Above all, tbe delightful idea that she shall take precedence of those who now think themselves her equals and superiors, dispels every thought of love. As to the man, the husband, he is scarcely considered at all, or he must be considered with disgust, But his title, his house in town, his mansions and parks in the country, his parliamentary interest, the favour in which he stands at court, the brilliant appearance he makes in the realms of fashion; these, added to a father's influence, determine Iphigenia at once to forget the object of her love, and give bet hand to deformity, and folly. She marries: the fa-, mily estates and influence are united, and the buttered, worn-out bridegroom becomes, in time, a **Marquis.**

The puny offspring of such connubial alliances are trained in the same idolatrous veneration of rank, title, and grandeur; and **woman,** formed to love and be loved, sacrifices her happiness to family pride, and lives and dies a legal prostitute, without once tasting the exquisite and natural delight of virtuous, equal, and sincere affection.—Taught from the era?die to believe herself a superior being, she is cheated of the happiness which falls to the lot of those who view their fellow-creatures as one great family, and are not too proud to partake of the Common banquet of life, and to choose a *partner* like the *turtle of the vale.*

■ Now mark the consequence. In no rank of society is conjugal happiness more rarely found than among those who have imbibed most copiously the aristocratical principles of selfish pride. The prersent age abounds with public and notorious imstances of infelicity of this sort in the highest ranks of society. It would be painful to dwell upon them. I drop a tear of pity, on the lovely victims to despotism, and let the curtain fall.

But surely that degree of **pride,** nursed by ill-constructed systems of society, which leads to the violation of the first law of nature^ and produces misery of the severest kind, ought to be disgraced and reprobated by all who have hearts sufficiently tender to sympathize with the sufferings of their fellow-mortals. Love, and the natural affections between human creatures, are the sweet ingredients which Providence has thrown into the cup of life, to sweeten the bitter beverage. And that state of society, which divests man of his nature, which renders him a factitious creature, which hardens his heart with selfishness, and swells him with the morbid tumours of vanity, deserves execration. It increases all the natural misery of man, and withholds the anodyne.

Something may be said in excuse for the more amiable part of the species, when they discard love from their bosoms to indulge pride. Their haughty fathers too often inculcate the lesson of pride from the earliest infancy; and teach them to think nothing really beautiful and lovely, which is not marked by fashion, or varnished by titles, riches, and heraldic honours. The *men* in general set them the example.. They lavish their *love* on the courtezan, and follow *prudence* in the choice of a wife; that is, they seek, not a heart that beats in unison with their own, but a legal connexion which increases their fortune, or aggrandizes their situation. A marriage of love, at an age when the heart is most prone to it, is considered as a folly and a misfortune, unless it advances the man in society. The women learn to retaliate* and to give their.hands without their hearts; gratifying pride at the expence of love.

When truth, justice, reason, and nature are little regarded, in competition with the desire *of distinction,* which is the case wherever the spirit of despotism has insinuated itself, all true.and solid happiness will be sacrificed for the *appearance* of superiority in birth, in possessions, in houses and carriages, and above all, in court favour. The tenderest ties of consanguinity, affinity, and friendship, snap asurp der when opposed to the force of any thing which is* likely th contribute to personal splendour or family pride, political consequence, influence at elections, and Anally, to the honours conferred by royalty. The little aspirants at subordinate degrees of despotism, are continually crawling up the hill, ever looking at the brilliant object on the summit, and leaving below, all that love and nature teach them to embrace.

From this principle, unnatural as it is, arises the anxious desire of aristocratical bigots to *make*, as they express it, an **eldest son**; to starve, or at least to distress, a dozen sons and daughters, in order to leave behind them one great representative, who may eontinue to toil in the pursuit of civil pre-eminence, for the gratiAcation of *family pride*. The privileges of primogeniture establish petty despots all over the land, who are interested and sufficiently inclined, from pride as well as interest, to promote the spirit of despotism. They would have no objection to the feudal system, in which the only distinction was that of lords and vassals. Not contented with engrossing the property which ought to be shared among their brothers and sisters, they claim privileges in conse-: quence of their property, and would *appropriate* the birds of the air and the beasts of the forest for their recreation in the Aeld, and their luxury at the table.

When the laws of nature, and eternal truth and justice^ are violated, no wonder that despotism advances, and man is degraded.

SECTION XXVII. *

On the Opinion that the People are annihilated or absorbed in Parliament; that the Voice of the People is no where to be heard but in Parliament; and on similar doctrines, tending to depreciate the People.

There is no doctrine so absurd but pride and selfishness will adopt and maintain it with obstinacy, if it be conducive to their gratification. Alexander, it is said, *really* believed himself a god. The vilest of the Caesars demanded divine honours. Many instances are on record of wretched beings, with hardly arty thing worthy of *man* about them, forgetting, in consequence of a little elevation above others, that they were mortals; behaving with the wickedness and cruelty of devils, and at the same time arrogating the power and dignity of the celestial nature. It is related of Hanno, the Carthaginian, that be taught starlings to say *"Deus Hanno;"** and that when a very lafge number had learned their lesson, he turned them loose into the woods, hoping that they would teach the wild birds on the trees to repeat the same words, and that thus the divinity of Hanno might be wafted into the remotest regions, and become the worship of the universe. Such conduct appears to resemble the ravings of the poor lunatic, who crowns himself, as he sits in his desolate cell, with a crown- of straw, and imagines,, while he

' *   * Hanno is a God.   '

sways a sceptre of the same materials, that he is an emperor. But iu truth, the pride of despots, I mean those who have all the dispositions of despots, though they may not have the diadems, displays many of the symptoms of downright lunacy. Pride is allowed by the physicians to have a powerful effect in turning the brain; and though it may not always fit the unhappy sufferer for Bedlam, yet commonly renders him unfit for the offices of social life.

Shocking as madness is, it sometimes behaves in a manner, which turns pity into laughter. Can any thing be more ridiculous, than the inso ence of some person^ who having adopted high aristocratical no* tions, to. correspond with their high birth, high titles, and high rank, declare that they know not what is meant by the people out of parliament; that they do not acknowledge the political existence of the people, but on the benches of St. Stephen's chapel ? Individuals of low degree they may know, and. employ in. their service, but they know nothing of the *people,&% millions* of MEN, possessing rights or power. "The constitution" (say they) "knows nothing of

the people considered as individuals." King, lords, and commons, constitute the nation; but what is meant by the people they cannot divine.. A mob they know, and would always have them dispersed by the military, as soon as two or three are gathered together; but the people, as a part of the constitution, they never could discover.-

Mr. Burke, the great Coryphams of aristocracy, says,As a *people* can have no right to a corporate "capacity without *universal consent,* so neither have "they a right to hold exclusively any lands in the "name and title of a corporation. On the scheme "of the present rulers in our neighbouring country, "regenerated as they are, they *have no more right to* "*the territory called France,* than I (Edmund Burke) "have. *Who are these, insolent men, calling them-* "*selves the French nation,* that would monopolize "this fair domain of nature? Is it because they "speak a certain jargon ? is it their mode of chat- "tering? The crowd of men on the other side of the "Channel, *who have the impudence to call themselves* "*a* people, can never be the lawful exclusive pos- "sessors of the soil." How truly laughable to hear an individual, Mr. Edmund Burke, taxing twenty-six millions of humamcreatures with impudence, for presuming to call themselves.a people ! I must smile at such absurdity, while I sincerely lament that this ingenious man has missed tbe opportunity of raising his family to the peerage, the grand object of so many years indefatigable labour, by a loss never to be repaired, and in which every feeling heart must sympathize. Ambition, what art thou to the feelings-of a father* exclaiming, like David, "O Absalom, my son, my son!" The great teacher Death shews the vanity of all human aspirations at sublunary glory. He who loses[1] a son in the prime of life and the career of honour, may learn to. weep over the thousands, whose dearest, relatives have been cut off by the sword of war* in consequence of dootriues which he maintained by a gaudy display of his eloquence, without foreseeing on regarding the calamities they had a tendency to produce...

The subtle Writer goes on and observes, that "When the multitude" (from the context he means a **majority** *of the people)* "are not under the habi-"tual social discipline of the wiser, more expert, "and more *opulent,* they can scarcely be said to **be** "in civil society.... When you separate the *com-*"*mon sort of men* from their proper chieftains, so as "to *form them* into an adverse army, I no longer "know that venerable object called the **people,** in "such a disbanded race of deserters and *vagabonds.* "For awhile they may be terrible indeed; but in "such a manner as wild beasts are terrible. The "mind owes to them no sort of submission. They ".are, as they have always been reputed, rebels. "They may *lawfully be* **fought with** and *brought* "*under,* whenever an advantage offers."

What gave rise to these elucidations he has told us a few pages before. "The factions now so busy " amongst us, in order to divest men of all love of "their country, and to remove from their minds all "duty with regard to the state, endeavour to propa-"gate an opinion that the **people,** in forming their "*commonwealth, have by no means parted with their* "*power over it !"* Horrendum dictu !

"Discuss any of their schemes—their answer is "—it is the act of the **people,** and that is sufficient; "—The people are masters of the commonwealth! "because in substance they are the commonwealth!

The French revolution, say they, was the act of "the majority of the people; and if the majority of any other people, the people of England for in* "stance, wish to make the same change, they have "the same right.—Just the same, undoubtedly. "That is, **none at all.**"

Such is the doctrine of this warm partisan of aristocratical distinction. But what say seven or eight millions of good people, who wish nothing, in their interference in politics, but to secure and extend their own happiness, and to make all others happy within the sphere of their influence? Let them say what they please, their remonstrance must not be heard. They are political *non-entities;* they are, as pride commonly calls inferiors in private life, **nobody,** or *people whom nobody knows.*

But now comes the tax-gatherer. These non-entities must find *read* tangible money to pay for the salaries of places, to pay pensions, and the interest of money advanced for the waging of wars, said to be in defence of law, order, and religion. It will not do to plead that they have no political existence. A very considerable part of their property, the produce of their labour, must be annually paid for the support of those who have the effrontery to say they are not *visible,* as a majority of individuals, in the eye of the constitution.

At a general election, would any candidate for a considerable city or county dare to advance such opinions respecting the insignificance,'or rather non-existence, of the people, as have been advanced by borough members, in their zeal for power and prerogative? The *People* would deny the doctrine with a voice loud enough to silence the most obstreperous declaimer.

Mr. Burke will make no new converts to this opinion. The Tory party had adopted it previously to the instruction of their sanguine advocate, ft was always one of their principles. The people themselves will certainly reprobate ideas which lead to their, political *annihilation*, in *every* respect, but in the privilege of contributing to the public revenue. But one cannot be surprised at any wild assertions of a man who writes under the impulse of passion. Anger, inflamed by mortified pride, seems to animate almost every sentence of his late invective. And wbat are we to think of the whiggism of one, who, in the commencement of the alarm concerning French principles, is said to have proposed to Mr. Fox to join together (these are the very words of the proposal) in "FROWNING DOWN THE DOCTRINES OF LI-"berty."* The proposer must have no small opinion of himself, when he imagined that, assisted by *one* more, he could *frown down the doctrines of liberty*. Jupiter shook Olympus with a nod; and Bufrke was to discountenance liberty, mid annihilate the political existence of a people, with a Erown.

<blockquote>Divisum imperium cum Jove, Burk us babet.</blockquote>

I revere the private virtues of the man. I feel and admire his excellence as a writer. I deplore the mistake which has led him to gratify the *few* in power, at the expence of millions of his fellow-creatures, who would have rejoiced in such an advocate against the influence of the despotic spirit. Imperial power has means enough to maintain itself Genius should ever espouse the cause of liberty, and

. * See Mr. Wyvill's Letter to Mr. Pitt, page 108.

of those who have no standing armies, no treasury, no' tribe of dependents, nothing to stand their friend, but a good cause, which, in a corrupt state of society, is too often defeated by a bad one..

May the people, in all climates which the sun views in his daily progress, prove their political existence by their public virtue! May despots learn to fear thp power of those whose happiness they have dared to destroy. In our own country, we have a king who rules in the hearts of his people, and who would therefore be the first to reject the doctrines of Mr. Burke, which tend to sink the people, as a majority of individuals, into a state of insignificance. May the people claim and preserve their rights, in defiance of all over-ruling influence, and all sophistical declamation. But let them pursue their philanthropic ends with steady coolness. Let them-respect themselves, and act consistently with their dignity. Let not a single drop of blood be* shed, nor a single mite of property unjustly seized, in correcting abuses, and recovering rights. Let them pass a glorious act of amnesty, and generously forgive the Pitts, the Burkes, the Loughboroughs, the Aucklands, the Mansfields, the Wyndhams; proving to an admiring world, that a great **people** can be gentle and merciful to frail, erring individuals, while it explodes their errors, and calmly evinces, by virtuous energies, its own *political existence* and supreme authority.

SECTION XXVIII.

The fashionable Contempt thrown on Mr. Locke, and his Writings in Favour of Liberty; and on other Authors and Books espousing the same Cause.

IT is an infallible proof of great abilities in a writer who espouses the cause of the people, when he is cavilled at, written against, and condemned by the persons whose despotic principles he has endeavoured to expose and refute. It is a sign that he has touched them to the quick, and left a sore place, the smart of which is continually urging them to murmur. Their affected derision and contempt of him are but transparent veils to hide the writbings of their tortured minds; an awkward masque to cover the ugly features of impotent revenge, struggling, through pride, to conceal the painful emotions of rage..

It is amusing to observe what mean and little arts are used by these angry persons, to lower the character of any writer, whose arguments they cannot refute. They hire a venal tool to write his life, and crowd it with every falsehood and calumny which party malice can invent, and popular credulity disseminate. They relate, without examination into a single fact, and decide, without the smallest attention to candour or justice. The man is to be hunted down. The minister and his creatures cry havoc, and let slip tbe vermin of corruption. The newspapers, in daily paragraphs, discharge the venom of abuse on his name. *Venal critics* pour their acrimonious censure, in general terms, on his compositions, which they could not equal, and dare not examine with impartiality. Nicknames are fastened on him; and whenever he is spoken of, all additions of respect are omitted, and, in their place, some familiar and vulgar abbreviation of his Christian name is used to vilify his surname.. Poor artifices indeed ! for while they expose the malice and weakness. of those who use them, they leave the arguments and doctrines of the writer rather confirmed than shaken by an attack so feeble.

It is not surprising, indeed, that *contemporary* writers in favour of the people, whatever their abilities^ and however convincing their arguments, are treated with affected contempt, as often as they excite real admiration. Envy always strikes at *living* merit. The policy of the aspirants at arbitrary power unites with envy, to depress all who are rising to public esteem by personal exertion, by their own virtue, independently of court patronage and hereditary distinction. But it might be supposed that *departed* genius, elevated, by the conspiring voice of nations, to the highest rank, would be surrounded with a sanctity which would defend it from profanation. It is not so. The love of power, in the hearts of mean and selfish men, acknowledges no reverence for genius. It has no reverential feelings beyond the purlieus of a court. The false brilliancy of what is called high and fashionable life, is preferred by it to the permanent lustre of all solid personal virtue.

' Mr. Locke, therefore, one of the chief glories of English literature, is to be depreciated, for be wrote on the side of liberty. Possessing *reason* in greater perfection than most men, he naturally inclined to espouse the cause of man, without confining hiB regard to those who boasted adventitious honours, the fantastic distinctions of birth, or the fortuitous advantages of fortune. These are few, compared with the millions who constitute the mass of a commonwealth..His understanding, greatly elevated above the ordinary standard, clearly saw, that the purposes of real philanthropy can be accomplished solely by improving the condition of the many. *They* must be taught to know and value their rights. They must learn to reverence themselves, by feeling their importance in society. Snch an improvement of their minds will lead them to act consistently with their dignity as.rational creatures, and as members of a community which they lOve, and the welfare - of which they find to depend on their own virtue.

Mr. Locke was certainly stimulated to write his book on government by these philosophical and philanthropic ideas. In pursuance of those ideas, he wished to support, by doctrines favourable to general liberty, the Revolution. Let us attend to his own words in his Preface.

"These papers," (says he,) "1 hope, are sufficient "to establish the throne of our great Restorer, our "present King William; to make good his title, in

V tbe CONSENT OF THE PEOPLE, which BEING THE.
"ONLY ONE OF ALL LAWFUL GOVERNMENTS, he.has
"more fully and clearly than any prince in Christ-
"endom; and to justify to the world the people of
"England, whose love of their just and natural
"rights, with their resolution to preserve them,
"saved the nation when it was on the very brink of
"slavery and ruin."

Mr. Locke's book then tends directly to strengthen the foundation of the throne on which the present royal family is seated. It is equally favourable to the king and the people. Yet because it is *at all* favourable to the people and the general cause of liberty, it is the fashion, in the aristocratical circles, to revile it. It is said to contain the elements of those, doctrines which the philosophers of France have dilated, which gave independence to America, and rendered France a republic. It is. said, very unjustly, to contain the seminal principles of Mr. Paine's matured and expanded tree. Mr. Locke, therefore, the great defender of the Revolution and of King William, is reprobated by Tory courtiers, and numbered, by the aspirants at enormous power and privileges, to which they have no just and natural claim, among Lord Auckland's, *"miscreants "called philosophers"*

Men who undertake to defend any thing contrary to the common sense and common interest of mankind, usually hurt the side they intend to defend, by promoting a *discussion,,* and calling forth common sense, excited by the common interest, to defend its own cause. Thus. Sir Robert Filmer's book gave rise both to Sydney's and Locke's defence of liberty. Thus Mr. Burke's Reflections on France drew forth Mr. Paine's Rights of Mao, in which is much excellent matter, mingled with a blameable censure of limited monarchy. Thus Salmasius's mercenary invective against the republicans of England in the last century, provoked the great Milton, scarcely less eloquent in prose than in poetry, to defend the right of the people of England to manage, in their own country, their own concerns, according to their own judgment and inclination.

Milton and Locke are great names on the side of liberty. But Milton has been treated contemptuously; and some have shewn a spirit illiberal enough to detract from his poetry in revenge for his politics.. His last biographer, Dr. Johnson, who had many early prejudices which his most, vigorous reason, could not to the last subdue,, was, by early prejudice, a violent Tory and Jacobite. I think, there is. reason to believe, that he would have been easily made a convert to popery. I venerate his abilities, and virtues; but I cannot help remarking, that his high-church and high-prerogative principles, led him: to speak less honourably of Milton than he must have done if he had viewed him through a medium, undiscoloured. Milton was a greater man than Johnson; and though I think he went too far.in his hatred to monarchy and episcopacy, yet, in extenuation, let it be considered how much monarchy and episcopacy had been abused in his time, and how much more friendly to freedom they both are in our happier age. Milton discovered a noble spirit of independence, and his writings contain some of the finest passages that ever were written in vindication of civil liberty. They contributed to raise that spirit which afterwards produced our happy revolution; and I have no doubt but that Milton would have rejoiced under a *limited* monarchy. It is to writings and to a spirit like his, mankind are indebted for the limitation. If honest and able minds like Milton's had not appeared on the part of the people, it is probable that no such thing as a limited monarch would have been found on the. face of the earth; and the family now on the British throne wonld have been known only in the petty dynasties of the German empire.

JFree spirits are therefore to be pardoned in some errors which the propensity of human nature to err must ever render *venial;* and the general tendency of their writings to make the mass of mankind free and happy, ought to secure attention to their doctrines, and honour to their names. The enemies to the spirit of despotism have seen, with pain, the attempts to lessen these great men in the eyes of the world extended to writers of less renown, but of more recent date. They have seen men *good men in private life,* and philosophers, whose discourses and letters have gained the notice and esteem of every enlightened country, reproached, vilified, persecuted, and almost destroyed, because, in consequence of that fine understanding which had done so much in philosophy, they made some discoveries in politics which must for ever militate powerfully against the spirit of despotism. Voltaire, Rousseau,

Raytial, Price, Priestley, Paine, however different their characters, attainments, and abilities, are all vilified *together,* (because they have written admirably on the side of liberty,) all involved in one indiscriminate torrent of obloquy. The partisans of unlimited power would persuade us, not only that they were knaves, but fools. Some of them have very exceptionable passages in their, works; but where they treat of civil liberty, they plead the cause of human nature. They have not pleaded it unsuccessfully. Political artifices cannot stifle truth and common sense.

The independent part of mankind, who detest parties and faction, and mean nothing but the happiness of their fellow-creatures, will do well to be upon their guard against the misrepresentations of those who would vilify a Locke, a Milton, a Sydney. Let them read and judge for themselves. The men who are anxious to withhold or extinguish the light, may fairly be suspected of intending to do evil.

SECTION XXIX.

Of the Despotism of Influence; *while the Forms of a free Constitution are preserved.*

•The words of a great lawyer, instructing the youth of a nation at a celebrated university, must be supposed to be well considered. Blackstone, the grave commentator, after expatiating on the advantages derived from the Revolution, proceeds to remark, that "though these provisions have *nominally* and in ap-"*pearanee* reduced the strength of the executive "power to a much lower ebb than in the preceding "period; yet if, oh the other hand, we throw into "the opposite scale the vast acquisition of force "arising from the riot act, and the anuual expe-"dience of a standing army; and the vast acqui-"sition of personal attachment, arising from the "magnitude of the *national debt,* and the manner of "levying those yearly millions that are appropriated "to pay the interest; we shall find that the Crown "has gradually and imperceptibly gained almost as "much influence as it has apparently lost in pre-"rogative."

Blackstone, consistently with the habits of his profession, expressed himself cautiously. He says the Crown has gained *almost* as much influence as it has apparently lost in prerogative. There are men of great political judgment who think that it has gained more. The House of Commons has, in an auspicious hour, resolved, and it can never be too often repeated, that the influence of the crown has increased, is increasing, and ought to be diminished. Influence is more dangerous than prerogative. It is a subtle poison that acts unseen. Prerogative can be resisted, as a robber; but influence is an assassin.

Lord Bolingbroke tells us, that "we have lost the "spirit of our constitution; and therefore we bear, "from little engrossers of delegated power, what "our fathers would not have suffered from true pro- "prietors of the royal authority."

Such suggestions are certainly alarming. They come from high authority, and are abundantly confirmed by recent transactions. The magnitude, of the national debt, and the share that.almost every family in the kingdom, directly or indirectly, possesses in the public funds, contribute, more than all other causes, to increase the influence of the Crown among the mass of the people.. But the debt, is still increasing, in consequence of war. Property in the funds is still more widely diffused; the influence, in consequence, more extended. Liberty may be more effectually invaded by the influence of the *stocks,* than it ever was invaded, in the days of the Stuarts, by the abuse of prerogative. _   .

We are happy in a king, who, making the happiness of. the people his first object, certainly would not avail himself of any advantages afforded by circumstances, to intrench upon their liberty. But.be it remembered, that *ministers* in this country,.with their favourites, often constitute an oligarchy.

OF DESPOTISM.

This ministerial oligarchy may certainly abuse the influence of the Crown, so as to render itself virtually superior to the limited and constitutional monarchy. Should such ever be the case, the *oligarchy* will be a species of despotism, the more formidable as the more insidious; possessing the power, but denying the form. By a judicious distribution of favours, by alluring all the rich and great to its side, either by hope or by fear, it may erect a rampart, which the independent part of the people, acting from no system, and disunited, may vainly seek to demolish. The monarch and the people may join, hand in hand, without effect, against a *ministerial oligarchy,* thus buttressed by a faction composed of rank and wealth, artfully combined, in the meanest manner, for the basest purposes. False alarms may be spread on the danger *of property* from the diffusion of new principles, so as to drive all who possess an acre of land, or a hundred pounds in the public funds, within the ministerial pale. *Religion* may be said to be in danger, in order to bring in the devout and well-disposed. *Order* may be declared in jeopardy, that the weak, the timid, and the quiet, may be led, by their fears, to unite with wealth and power. Plots and conspiracies are common expedients of delusion. They have been used, by profligate ministers, with such a total disregard to truth and probability, that they now begin to lose their effect. But how dreadful, if influence should ever prevail with juries, to gratify the inventors of false plots, treasons, and conspiracies,- by bringing in verdicts favourable to the views of the villainous fabricators! English, juries are indeed still uncorrupted. They are unconnected with courts and ministers. And the uncorrupt part of our system, in cases of state trials, is able to prevent the mischief which would be caused by the corrupt part of it. The honest juries, in the late trials for treason, have not only done honour to our country and to human nature, but added great strength to the cause of truth, justice, and the constitution.

But it is truly alarming, to hear the verdicts of juries obliquely impeached by great men in the *legislative assemblies*. There has appeared no stronger symptom of the spirit of despotism, than die attempts of courtiers and crown lawyers, in the public senate, to vilify juries and their verdicts, given after a more solemn and longer investigation than ever took place on similar trials. Persons acquitted after such an ordeal, have been said to be no more innocent than *acquitted felons*. That the people have borpe such an insult on their most valuable privilege, with patience, is a proof that a tame acquiescence has been produced among them, unknown to. their virtuous ancestors. It is to be hoped the insult will stimulate future juries to preserve their rights with jealous vigilance, and render them impregnable by ministerial influence, directly or indirectly applied. If the men who disapprove the verdicts of the vir-' tuous juries, on the late occasions, had themselves been the jurors, they would have given different verdicts, pronounced the prisoners guilty, and as> signed them over to the resentment of irritated, aristocratic pride. So mighty is the despotism of influence, that neither justice nor mercy can check it in the breast of a proud parasite.

There is every reason to believe, (and the belief is highly consolatory,) that juries will, long continue to preserve their integrity; because they are indiscriminately selected from the *middle* rank and the mass of the *people.* Influence cannot reach every individual in the millions that constitute a great nation. But we must remember that influence is *increasing;* and that its nature is to diffuse deadly poison, without giving alarm. Like the air loaded with infection, it silently and secretly wafts disease into the strongest abodes of health, and penetrates the castle, which is impregnable to the sword of the open invader. Therefore, as influence increases, the jealousy and vigilance of the uninfected part of the community should increase in proportion. Though undue influence may never operate on juries, yet is there no danger lest it should, at some distant period, contaminate the minds of judges and *crown lawyers,* for whose obsequious interpretations of law may be held up prizes most glittering in the eyes of imagination, and most alluring to avarice and vanity?:

But granting that the foul stain of corruption should never spot the white robe *oijustice;* that the religion of an oath should still be revered, and com science hold the balance with an even hand; yet is there no danger lest the *despotism of influence* should destroy the vitals of a *free constitution,* and leave nothing behind but the form, the *exuvite,* the name? There was a *senate* under the vilest of the Roman emperors. The British house of commons might become, under a *ministerial oligarchy,* the mere levee of a prime minister. They might meet merely to *"bow and bow,"* receive their orders and *douceurs,* and then depart in peace.

The *present* state of the house of commons cannot be too generally known; and I therefore transcribe the following passage from the proceedings of the Society of the Friends of the People.

• "The condition of the House of Commons is *"practically* as follows:

"Seventy-one *peers* and the *Treasury* nominate "ninety members, and procure the return of *seventy-* "*seven,* which amount to one hundred and sixty- "seven. Ninety-one commoners nominate eighty- "two members, and procure the return of fifty- "seven, which amount to one hundred and thirty- "nine."

So that the peers, the *Treasury,* and *rich* commoners with influence equal to peers, return three hundred and six members out of five hundred and thirteen, which is the whole number of *English* representatives in the House of Commons. The *Scotch* members are not considered in this part of the Report.

The Society give the names of the different patrons at full length, 'to authenticate their statement; and I believe its accuracy and authenticity have never been controverted.

After observing that *seventy-one* peers and the *Treasury* nominate or procure the return of one hundred and sixty-seven members of parliament;

who may vote away the *people's* money, and make laws, with the other branches, to bind many millions, let us remember, that at the commencement of every session, the following resolutions are entered on the Journals:

"Resolved, that no peer of this realm hath any "right to give his vote in the election of any member. "to serve in parliament. Resolved that it is a high "infringement upon the liberties and privileges, of "the Commons of Great Britain, for any lord of "parliament, or any lord-lieutenant of any county, "to concern themselves in the elections of members "to serve for the Commons in parliament."

The committee of the Friends of the People say, "they have been the more disposed to take notice "of these resolutions, because the power of the "House of Lords, in matters of election, has been "prodigiously increased, within the *last ten pears,* "by the creation of *nine peers,* who return, by no- "mination and influence, no less than twenty-four "members to the House of Commons. If, there- "fore, the interference of the Lords in the election "of the Commons be, as the latter uniformly de- "clare, a *high infringement* of their liberties and "privileges, the Committee must report those liber- "ties and privileges to have been of late subject to "the most alarming and frequent attacks."

After producing facts that defy denial, I confidently leave every honest and sensible man in the kingdom, unblinded by prejudice, unwarped by interest, to determine whether the cause of liberty is not on the decline, and the spirit of despotism likely

Q

to avail itself of the general corruption of the aristocracy, and the tame acquiescence of the people.

I leave the question to be determined by such men, whether it is not possible that influence may create a complete *despotism* in a country, even while the *forms* of a free constitution are preserved inviolate?

SECTION XXX.

The Spirit of Despotism delights in War or systematic Murder.

"The *people* of England are industrious, they are "peaceful, they wish to enjoy the fruits of their in-' "dustry without a *war,* and to recover their lost "weight in our mixed frame of government, without "the hazards of a *revolution.* '

"It is from the prevalence of *Mr. Burke's poli-* "*tics* alone, among the *upper classes* of society, that "the rise of any *dangerous disaffection* in this coun- "try is to be apprehended. To the plain sense of "Englishmen, a war commenced with France, on "*his* principles, must appear to be a war on French "liberty, to beat down the equitable claims of refor- "mation *het'e,* and *eventually to destroy every valu-* "*aMe right of the 'people.*

"Such will be the suspected motives for plunging "this country in a war, in which our *fleets* may be "victorious, but in which even our successes must "be rUinous. For views thus 'wild and Chimerical, "the nation, whose wounds received in the late war "with AmCrica are hardly ^et closed up, must prepare to bleed afresh. For[1] objects thus odious "and detestable, *the industrious clc^ses of the people inust forego their cdmforts;* the shoulders, already "galled with'taitekj the pernicious consequence of "*former* injustice and folly, must submit again "to new and heavier impositions.

"They will be cheerfully voted, no doubt, by the "*faithful Commons;* but the Commons will no "longer enjoy the confidence of the public. Every "vote of credit or supply will then increase the ge-"ueral disgust; and should no greater disaster be-"fall us, the mere protraction of the war must ex-"haust the patience of a disabused people..

"But what may be the contagious effect of French "opinions on a nation *sick of the war of kings,* "groaning under an intolerable load of taxes, and "hopeless of redress from men, *whom they will cease* "*to consider as representatives,* it is needless to state. "To foresee it, is easy; to prevent it, may be im-"possible." ....

Thus far the excellent Wyvill, in a letter to Mr. Pitt, in which he wisely dissuaded, him from the unfortunate and disgraceful war, of which that minister must soon repent, though power and repentance do not usually unite. No dissuasion could cool Mr. Pitt's heroic ardour, or check his juvenile impetuosity. War was hastily commenced. The consequences were foretold, and the prediction is fulfilled.

But to an accurate observer it is an alarming proof of the spirit of despotism, when the great are eager to rush into *war;* when they listen to no terms of accommodation, and scorn to negociate, in any mode or degree, previously to unsheathing the dreadful instrument of slaughter. If war, instead of being what it has been called, the *ratio ultimo,* becomes the *ratio prima regum,* it is a proof that *reason* has lost her empire, and force usurped her throne.

Fear is the principle of all despotic government, andtherefore despots make war their first study and delight. No arts and sciences, nothing that contributes to the comfort or the embellishment of human society, is half so much attended to, in countries where the spirit of despotism is established, as the means of destroying human life. Tigers, wolves, earthquakes, inundations, are all innocuous to man, when compared with the fiercest of monsters, the oory despots. Fiends, furies, demons of destruction ! may the day be near, when, as wolves have been utterly exterminated from England, despots may be cut off from the face of the whole earth; and the bloody memory of them loaded with the execration of every human being, to whom God has given a heart to feel, and a tongue to utter!

Wherever a particle of their accursed *spirit* is found, there also will be found a propensity to war. In times of peace, the *grandees* find themselves shrunk to the size of common mortals. A finer house, a finer coach, a finer coat, a finer livery than others can afford, is all that they can display to the eye of the multitude, in proof of their assumed superiority. Their power is inconsiderable. But no sooner do you blow the blast of war, and put armies under their command, than they feel themselves indeed great and powerful. A hundred thousand men, in battle array, with all the instruments of destruction, under the command of a few *grandees,* inferior, perhaps, in bodily strength, to every one of the subject train, and but little superior in intellect or courage, yet holding all, on pain of death, in absolute subjection; how must it elevate the *little despots* in their own opinion!. "This it is to live," (they exclaim, shaking hands with each other,) "this is to "be great indeed. *Now* we feel our power. Glory "be to us on high; especially as all our fame and "greatness is perfectly compatible with our per- "sonal safety; for we will not risque our precious "persons iu the scene of danger, but be content "with our *extended patronage*, with the delight of "commanding the movements of this human ma- "chine, and with reading of the blood, slaughter, "and burnt villages, in the Gazette, at our fire-side."

All the expence of war is paid by the people, and most of the personal danger incurred by those, who, according to some, have no political existence; I mean the *multitude, told bp the head,* like sheep in Smithfield. Many of these troublesome beings in human form, are happily got rid of in the field of battle, and more by sickness and hardship previous or subsequent to the glorious day of butchery. Thus all makes for the spirit of despotism. There are, in consequence of a great, carnage, fewer *wretches* Jeft to provide for, or to oppose its will; and all the honour, all the profit, all the *amusement,* falls to the share of the *grandees,* thus raised from the insignificance and inglorious indolence of peace, to have their names blown oyer the world by the trumpet of Fame, and recorded in. the page of history..

But a state of war not only gives a degree of personal importance to some among the great, which they could never obtain by the arts of peace, but greatly helps the cause of despotism. In times of jpeace the people are apt to be impertinently clamorous for reform. But in war, they must say no more On the subject, because of the public danger* It would be ill-timed. Freedom of speech also must be checked. A thousand little restraints on liberty are admitted, without a murmur, in a time of war, that would not be borne one moment during the halcyon days of peace. Peace, in short, is productive of plenty, and plenty makes the people saucy. Peace, therefore, must not continue long after a nation has arrived at a certain degree of prosperity. This is a maxim of Despotism. Political phlebotomy is necessary in a political plethora. "Bleed "them *usque ad deliquium,"* (says the arbitrary doctor,) "and I will undertake that in future the patient "shall be more tractable."

Erasmus, the friend of man, the restorer of civil and religious liberty, has the following passage in a Dissertation on War, lately translated into English under the title of *Antipolemus* •• •.

'There are kings who go to war for no other rea-
"son than that they may with greater ease establish
"*despotic authority* over their own subjects at home.
"For in time of peace, the power of parliaments,
"the dignity of magistrates, the vigor of the laws,
"are great impediments to a prince who wishes to
"• exercise arbitrary power. But when once a war
"is undertaken, the chief management of affairs de-
"volves on a *few,* the ministers of executive *govern-*
"ment, who, for the general safety, assume the pri-

"vilege of conducting every thing according to their "own humour, demanding unlimited confidence. "The prince's favourites are all exalted to places of " honour and profit. Those whom he dislikes are "turned out and neglected. *Now*—(the time of "war) is the time for raising as much money upon "the people as the despot's heart can wish.—In "short—now—the time of war, is the time that they '** feel themselves despots in very deed and truth, not "in name only, but despots with a vengeance. In "the mean while, the grandees play into one ano- "ther's hands, till they have eaten up the wretched V people, root and branch. Do you think that men "of such dispositions would be backward to seize "any the slightest occasions for war, so lucrative, "so flattering to avarice and vanity?"*

Language has found no 'name sufficiently expressive of the diabolical viilany of wretches in high life, who, without personal provocation, in the mere wantonness of power, and for the sake of increasing what they already possess in too great abundance, rush into *murder!* Murder of the innocent! Murder of myriads! Murder of the stranger! neither knowing

---

* "*Sunt qui non aliam ob causam* bellum *movent, nisi ut hdc via fa-*
"*cilius in* suos tyuannidem *exerceant. Nam pacis temporibus,* senatus
"*auctoritas, magistratuum dignitas, legum vigor, nonnihil obstant, quo*
"*minus liceat principi, quicquid libet. At,* bello suscepto, *jam omnis*
"*rerum summa ad paucorum* libidinem *devoluta est. Evehuntur quibus*
"*bene vult princeps; dejiciuntur quibus infensus est. Exigitur pecunia*
"*quantum libet. k Quid multis?* Tum demum sentiunt se vere mo-
"narchas *esse. Colludunt interim duces, donee infelicem populum usque*
"*ad radicem arrosennt. Hoc animo qui sint, an eos putas gravatim*
"*arreptaros, oblatam quamcunque belli occusionem?"*—Erasmus.

nor caring bow many of their fellow-creatures, with rights to life and happiness equal to their own, are urged by poverty to shed their last drops of blood in. a foreign land, far from the endearments of kindred, to gratify the pride of a few at home, whose despotic spirit insults the wretchedness it first created. There is no greater proof of humau folly and weakness than that a whole people should suffer a *few worthless grandees,* who evidently despise and. hate them, to make the world one vast slaughter-house, that the grandees may have the more room to take their insolent pastime in unmolested state. A man, a reasonable being, a Christian, plunging the bayonet, without passion, into the bowels of a man, for hire! The poor creatures who actually do this (in despotic countries) are but mechanical instruments of knaves in power. Their poverty, and not their will, consents. May Heaven's sweet mercy, then, wash off the blood-stains from their hands, and reserve its wrath for those whose thirst of power, which they never had a wish to use for the good of man, leads them to wade to it through seas of human gore!

Let any dispassionate man, uninfluenced by placemen, pensioners, contractors, and expectants of court favour, impartially consider, from the earliest ages to the present, the history of war. He must observe that scarcely any wars have been *just* and *necessary;* though they almost all have claimed these epithets, with a persevering formality which would excite ridicule, if ridicule were not lost in abhorrence. He will find that folly, extreme folly, wearing a crown instead of a fool's cap, has, in many countries, from the mere wantonness of mischief, icried " Havoc, and let slip the dogs of war." He will find that in most countries (Our own, of course, always-excepted) war has been eagerly sought, from *policy*, to divert the people's attention from domestic abuse, to aggrandize those who build the fabric of their grandeur on the ruins of human happiness, and to depress, impoverish, and humble the people.

There is uothing from which the spirit of liberty has so much to fear, and consequently the spirit of despotism so much to hope, as from the prevalence of military government, supported by vast standing armies, and encouraged by alliances with military despots on the continent of Europe. The whole energy of the sound part of our free constitution should be exerted in its full force to check a proud minister, who rashly runs into a. war, and notwithstanding accumulated disasters, perseveres in its prosecution. He cannot hope for victory. He. must have some other motive for persevering against all rational hope. Let the people investigate the, motive; and if it be inimical to liberty, let ithem succour her in distress, by calling in her best auxiliary, PEACE.

SECTION XXXI.

On the Idea that we have arrived at Perfection in Politics, though all other Sciences are in ₁ a progressive State.

Those who have been fortunate enough to have gained possession of honours and profits, under a corrupt system, well pleased with *things as they are,* boldly contend that they cannot be better. But these, compared with the mass of the community, are few, and ultimately of little consequence..Their opinion therefore must not weigh against any improvement which is likely to promote the melioration of human affairs. Let them enjoy unmolested the luxuries of the table, the splendour of equipages, large houses, and every other external advantage, which makes *little man* swell into fancied importance. In tbe mean time let every honest, benevolent member of the community, who is satisfied with being happy himself, without desiring to entrench on the happiness of others, endeavour to reform abuses, and promote every improvement which can render human life (short as it is, and full of calamity) more comfortable, and less exposed to the injuries and contumelies of the proud oppressor.

Rewards are offered for the discovery of the longitude at sea. Men are not only allowed but encouraged to prosecute their inquiries into all other arts and sciences. But the grand art, the art of government, that is, the art of securing the civil happiness of millions, is to be considered as sacred and inscrutable. Those very millions whom it more immediately interests, dare not, if the despots could prevail, to lift up the awful veil. Racks, gibbets, bowstrings, chains, and prisons, are prepared, in most of the kingdoms of the world, to awe the curious, and check the spirit of political improvement. Optimism has long been established in the courts of despotic princes. *Whatever is, is right,* say they; for knowing that they stand on a rotten foundation, they fear that the very fixing of the 'scaffold for repair would precipitate the downfal of the whole fabric.

Mankind might, at the close of this century, justly celebrate a general jubilee; for arbitrary government, in Europe at least, has received its death-blow by the revolution in France. And it is devoutly to be wished, for their own sakes, that in limited monarchies, the voice of truth and virtue, calling for the reform of abuses, existing evidently as the meridian sun, will never be silenced by the terrors of the law in the hands of crown lawyers, or the sabre of dragoons, under the command of a despotic minister.

Is it to be believed that governments were brought to *perfection,* in early and dark ages, when the minds of the great as well as the little were enveloped in the mists of ignorance, and shackled by the chains of superstition ? Is it reasonable to suppose that they who were narrow-minded, ill-informed, childish,, and barbarous in all other parts of knowledge and of conduct, were liberal, wise, and illuminated in the science and practice of government; so liberal, so wise, so illuminated, as to strike out at once a system *complete* in all its parts, and such as could in no subsequent age, in no variety of circumstances, admit of correction, addition, or melioration ? Did this wonderful sagacity, approaching to inspiration, produce any thing else, in any other department, which defies all improvement, and challenges the respect and veneration of the latest posterity? Reasoning from analogy, we must conclude, that men, capable of establishing at once a perfect system of government, must have produced *other* inventions fi>r the accommodation and security of life, worthy to be preserved inviolate, and handed down unaltered, till '■ time itself be absorbed in the ocean of eternity. But where shall we look for it? The very question implies a doubt of its existence; for singular excellence, such excellence as approaches to perfection, cannot be concealed, but will shine with its own lustre, and force observation and wonder ? Is the *architecture* of these paragons of wisdom superior to the modern, in beauty or convenience? Let us only walk the streets of London, and mark those houses which were spared by the great fire, and which may fairly be supposed improvements on the more antient fabrics. We see them, contrary to every principle of common sense, with stories projecting over each other. We see them ugly, mean, inconvenient. Let us proceed to the north-west parts of that great town. Take a view of Portland-place. ■ Contrast the symmetry, the accommodation, the magnificence, with the old edifices of Holborn or Aldersgate, and be persuaded that modern improvements in government might be as much superior to the work of antient bunglers; as.the elegant buildings of an Adam or a Wyat to the old mansions now converted into inns, in the dirtiest streets, in the most decayed districts of. the metropolis.   J

Man is a progressive animal, and his advance towards improvement is a pleasurable state. Hope cheers his path as be toils up the hill that leads him to something better than he has yet experienced, on its gay summit gilded with sunshine. The labour of the ascent is a delight. But if he cannot -help conceiving, from a sense of grievances which he feels, something excellent, to which he is prohibited by coercion from approaching, hope sickens; and ill-humour succeeds to complacency. Hence arises a disagreement between the governed and the governors; and the governors being possessed of present power, use force and rigour to stifle the murmurs of complaint. Coercion! but increases the ill humour, Which often lies latent, like the fires of a volcano, for a considerable time, but at last bursts forth with irresistible fury. It is wise, therefore, as well as just, in all governors, who have a regard for any thing but their present and private interest, to entourage discussion, to seek improvement of the system, and to reject no reform proposed by great numbers, without a cool, a temperate, and a long deliberation. The reasons for rejection should be clearly stated, with the utmost regard to open and irtgehttotia behaviour; and those who remain unconvihced, after all, should not be treated with asperity. Every individual, in a free country!, has a right to approve or disapprove the system under which he lives, without peril or control, while he preserves the peace. His peaceable deportment and acquiescence in the opinion of others, contrary to his own conviction, renders him a very meritorious character. He may be won over by gentleness; but force only tends to excite the violence which it would imperiously repel.

But to tell a man of sense, reading, and reflection, that he must not venture to entertain an opinion on political matters, or the existing government, different from that of the minister and the herd of courtiers, is an impotent endeavour to exercise a despotism over his mind, against which nature revolts, and a manly spirit must rebel. Such a man ·can usually judge of governments, and all the institutions of social life, better than mere men of business, however high their rank or important their employments; far better than courtiers, occupied in vain ceremonies, and usually as little able as inclined to enter into deep disquisition.

Indeed it is difficult to avoid laughing at the extreme ignorance of crowned heads. themselves, in despotic countries, when one contrasts it with the importance they assume, and the pomp and splendour with which they transfer, their rdyal persons from place to place. The sight is truly ludicrous. Are these the men, occupied, as they <ufttrally are, in: the- meanest trifles and the most degradirig pleasures, who tell us that the. go'ternmeut over which

they preside, is a perfect system, and that the wisest philosopher knows not how to govern mankind; that is, to consult. their happiness and security, so well as themselves, neglected as they have been in youth, and corrupted in manhood by panders to their vices, and flatterers of their foibles, their pride, and their ambition ? There is reason to believe that many kings, in despotic kingdoms, have been less well educated, and possess less abilities, than a common charity-boy, trained in a parish school to read and write. Yet these are the men who, with their upstart creatures, presume to call philosophers wretches, and to condemn the Voltaires, the Rousseaus, the Sydneys, the Harringtons, and the Lockes.. -

There are persons, even in countries where limited royalty is established, who are for ever extolling the constitution, with all the abuses that have insinuated themselves into it, in terms of extravagant and unqualified praise. They talk against better knowledge, and may therefore be suspected of some sinister motive. They can see defects as well as others; but they assume the worst of all blindness, that which is voluntary.

The truth is, these men, for the most part, are such as would not like the *constitution in its purity*, because in its purity the constitution is really excellent, and highly favourable to the liberty which they hate. The constitution, in its purity, renders the people of *consequence,* whose political existence they are inclined to controvert or deny. But the constitution, in its state of corruption, is favourable to prerogative, to aristocratical pride and influence, to Tory and jacobitical principles; therefore it is, in their eyes, criminal to handle it, to hint at its im*provement, to remove a grievance, or reform an abuse. The whole together, though violated every day by corrupt influence, they affect to consider as a written charter, dropt down from heaven, like the old Roman *Ancilia*, and therefore scarcely to be viewed by vulgar eyes, and certainly not to be touched by the hand of the profane People.

Despotism is so ugly in its form, and so hostile, in its nature, to human happiness, that no wonder those who wish to diffuse its spirit are inclined to check and discourage among the people all political investigation. But let it be a rule among those who — really value liberty and the constitution, to use the more diligence in political discussions, in proportion as courtiers and ministers display a wish to suppress political writings and conversations, and disseminate the doctrine, that things are so well constituted as neither to require nor admit any improvement.

SECTION XXXII.

On Political Ethics; *their chief Object is to throw Power into the Hands of the worst Part of Mankind, and to render Government an Institution calculated to enrich and aggrandize a few, at the Expence of the Liberty, Property, and Lives of the many.*

In the *schools* of early discipline, where youth is usually initiated in the studies of humanity, men are taught to believe that virtue is founded on *eternal ttuth,* and that the distinctions of right and wrong are as clearly definable as those between the meridian sunshine and the midnight shade. They are told, from the highest authority, that happiness is to be found in rectitude of conduct; and that'under all circumstances, whatever may be the consequence, nothing can justify the dereliction of integrity. The sacred scriptures, the antient philosophers, parental authority, the laws of their country, and the pro*clamations of kings, all combine to convince them that morality is founded on the rock of truth, and that governments are *sincere* in their professions to encourage those who do well, and be a terror only to the evil.

Why was a national *church* instituted and supported at a great expence, but to enforce among the people the laws of God, as paramount to all human laws, and superseding the wretched devices of state policy? Government, by entering into a strict alliauce with the church, certainly engages to support the doctrines of Christian morality; and it is no less impious in a king or a minister to promote or increase any public measures repugnant to Christian morality, than it would be in the bench of bishops.

When we enter our *libraries,* we find ourselves surrounded with authors, celebrated for ages by the most enlightened part of the world, who teach the immutability of truth, enforce the purest doctrines of morality, and endeavour to found the dignity and happiness of human nature on the basis of virtue.

But let us leave a moment the school, the church, the library, and enter a court and a cabinet. There *Machiavelian* ethics prevail; and all that has been previously inculcated appears like the tales of the nursery, calculated to amuse babes, and lull them in the lap of folly. The grand object of counsellors is to support and increase the power that appoints to splendid and profitable offices, with little regard to the improvement of human affairs, the alleviation of the evils of life, and the melioration of human narture. The restraints of moral honesty, or tbe scruples of religion, must seldom operate on public measures so as to impede the accomplishment of this primary and momentous purpose. A little *varnish* is indeed used, to hide the deformity of Machiavelism; but it is so very thin, and so easily distinguished from the native colour, that it contributes, among thinking men, to increase the detestation which it was intended to extenuate.

Thus, for instance, treaties between nations commence with a most solemn avowal of good faith, in the name of the Father, the Son, and the Holy Ghost. Great and mighty nations, professing Christianity, maintaining a church, and united most intimately with the church, enter into agreements, under this awful sanction, and break them without the least reluctance, whenever a *cabinet* minister finds it in his inclination, or imagines it his interest to' cause a rupture. The Father, the Son, and the Holy Ghost are little thought of; but the great object is to strike a blow with advantage, before the adverse nation is on its guard, and while it is relying on the treaty.

Another instance of *political religion* is conspicuous in the prevailing practice of rendering the emoluments of the church subservient to the *minister,* \n securing him a majority, and facilitating what is called his principal duty, the *management* of the SENATE.

The Roman pontiffs, while in the rank of inferior clergy, and even of cardinals, have exhibited the appearance of great piety, and a religious regard to truth and justice; but when advanced to the *triple mitre,* and become, in fact, kings, they have usually become perfectly secular in their public conduct at home, and in their connections with surrounding nations, and have pleaded, in excuse, state necessity. But can any *necessity* arise to violate the eternal laws of truth and justice ? Is religion a leaden rule, in the *hands* strong enough to bend it to their various purposes? Pope Julius the Second appears to have been one of the very worst princes that ever reigned. He delighted in war, while he professed to be the representative of the Prince of Peace. lie was guilty of oppression and injustice; and while he pretended to be feeding the *sheep* of Christ, gave himself no other concern but how he might secure the fleece. Yet all his conduct was palliated,'by the politicians around him, from, the plea of state necessity. Morality and religion gave way to the system of political ethics; and he, who ought to have blessed mankind, and to have preached peace, became their oppressor, despot, and unrelenting murderer. I mention Julius only as a striking instance, and hundreds may be adduced, of the depraved system which rules cabinets, and which, for the gratification of the few, renders the many miserable. No Machiavels can ever justify, in the eyes of God, or of *men* uninfluenced by corruption, any politics, however subtle and able, which, for the sake of aggrandizing a *nation*, (an *abstract idea,)* much less of gratifying a court, renders all the individuals of the *nation* so to be aggrandized, poor, wretched, insecure, and slavish.

Let us suppose a nation entering most eagerly, and without listening one momeut to terms of accommodation, into a most dangerous war, *professedly* to exterminate the bad *principles* and morals of a neighbouring people, and to defend *law, order,* and *religion.* It is impossible to imagine but that a nation acting in this manner, and with this profession, *must* regulate all its *own* public conduct, especially in a war of this kind, according to the *strictest* law, order, and religion.

Will that nation oppose an armed *nentrcdity,* instituted to prevent the interruption of *neutral* commerce ? Will she maintain her reputation for *justice,* if she should be the first and most violent in destroying this neutrality? Will she break the law of nations, by insulting ambassadors ? Will she take up arms, and actually fight in defence of popery, after professing herself at the head of protestantism, and the opposer of all intolerant superstition ? Will she, after declaring herself the friend of order, religion, and liberty, enter into alliances with and subsidize the plunderers and oppressors of Poland? Will she, pluming herself upon the love of order and religion, and detesting the cruelty of the nation with whom she is at war, suffer Asia to be pillaged, and its inhabitants to.be slaughtered by her own sons; or encourage the Indians to attack her brethren in North America; or hire mercenaries ' of German princes to do the work of death, in a contest in which they have no immediate concern? Will she endeavour to *starve* a *whole* nation, with whom she is at war, not only the rulers and warriors, but infants, women, and old people, by preventing the importation of *com?* Will she forge assignats? Will she continue the slave trade ?

A conduct like this appears to be not only inconsistent with the pretended defence of *law, order,* and *religion,* but at once proceeding from the spirit of despotism, and promotive of it. It is certain that a man in, private life, acting in this manner, would be thought a bad man, a man destitute of principle^ and with whom it would be scarcely less dangerous to be' on terms of professed friendship than of open enmity. Bnt actions do not alter their nature with the paucity or multiplicity of the actors; and a *nation* may be guilty of perfidy, as atrocious and contemptible in its nature as an individual, and infinitely more mischievous. Certainly the advisers and abettors of such conduct do not take the most effectual means of recommending to mankind that *monarchy* which they wage war to reestablish. They are hurting the cause of kings in the minds of independent men and of posterity, while they blindly appear to themselves to be promoting it with the greatest energy.

Whatever may be urged by sophists or politicians,; it is certain that the great eternal laws of truth and justice cannot be violated with impunity. The violation may answer some sordid and temporary purpose; but in the end, it must be injurious, if not fatal. Truth, like the sun in the heavens, is one. The clouds indeed are variegated; but then they are insubstantial, and of momentary existence. So is falsehood. It can assume any colour. But time causes the hues to fade; and truth bursts forth with new effulgence. We see despotism gradually withdrawing from the finest countries of Europe. It must depart, at last, from all, for it is opposed by reason and nature. They who endeavour to render it permanent, labour in vain; but at the same time, they may detain it a while, and cause, in the interval, misery and carnage.

Let us reject all Machiavelism, all *political ethics,* that contradict the acknowledged principles of truth and moral honesty. There can be no legitimate government which is not founded and supported by systems of conduct favourable to the happiness of human creatures,—the great mass of the people. Good government cannot be formed on the basis, of falsehood and chicanery. Let the government of England ever stand on the square, solid, upright pedestals of truth and justice, and it must defy every shock, but the convulsion of the world's dissolution.

SECTION XXXIII.

On trafficking with the Cure of Souls, *(Cura Animarum,)/or the Purposes of political,* i. e. moral, *Corruption.*

THE parish priests of a protestant country, when they are, what they ought to be, and what they would usually be, if it were not for political influence, CHRISTIAN ORATORS and CHRISTIAN PHILOSOPHERS, are the most useful body of men, considering their numbers and their power, in tbe whole community. The good they are able to do is beyond all estimate; but unfortunately, it is a sort of good not always taken into the account of those who are in pursuit of more palpable advantages, solid gold, high station, and dominion over their fellow-creatures. The proper business of the clergy is to mortify this very, pride, the indulgence of which is, to their courtly patrons, the *summurn bonum,* the chief good of existence.

. These persons, not having time or inclination to attend to religion, or any thing but the pomp and vanity of the world, idolizing themselves, and unwilling to acknowledge any other Deity, consider religion and the church merely as state engines; powerful engines, in conjunction with military force, to press down the elastic spirit of the people. They think, indeed, the emoluments attending ecclesiastical functions *too much,* if considered as recompences for religious services, which, in their minds, are no services at all, but *scarcely enough,* when converted into *douceurs* for the business of corruption, the grand object of modern ministers. •

Ambitious noblemen, therefore, buy boroughs, and, like Lord Melcombe, send their myrmidons to the senate; and ministers pay the expence of the purchase, by conferring the highest ecclesiastical dignities, with stipends of many thousands a-year, designed originally to be spent in charity, on the younger brothers, the cousins, the tutors, or the agents of these patrician boroughmongers. It is in-* deed deemed *politic,* now and then, to raise a very ingenious, learned, and pious man to the hither but seldom without contriving to promote, at the same time, the grand business of corruption.:. This ingenious, learned, and pious man, *un kvtque de.la fortune,* is highly satisfied with the dignity and emolument of his office. What need has he of the *patron-t age* appendant to it? In this age, it were a childish weakness, something similar to the simplicity re* commended in the gospel, to give away good things to modest merit. But, though *he* has no. need of the patronage, there are those, to whom he is bound,: by every tie of -gratitude, who want it all.: He therefore understands that the cure of souls is to be given to persons whom: the prime minister may recommend; as the Duke of Newcastle recommended Burroughs and Franklin, whom he had never seen or known, to the patronage of the lord chancellor. A *translation* may be impeded, if scruples of conscience should prevent an obsequious compliance

OF DESPOTISM.

with a minister's *conge delire.* "As to fitness or unfitness," (cries the friend of corruption,) "any "man that can read is *sufficient,* for both prayers "and sermons are ready made; and even if it were "supposable that a man could not read, a parish, "that pays the rector a thousand a-year, may be ** supplied with an ingenious curate for forty."

Formerly learning was scarce among the laity. The clergy engrossed what little there was in the world, and made themselves necessary to the state, not only in ecclesiastical, but political offices and employments. "Before the Reformation," (says a learned writer,) "the canon law was in great use "and esteem, and of great use; and while the laity "were in general unlettered, or employed in a mili- "tary life, the king made use of clergymen, skilled "in this law, in the offices of the chancery, privy "seal, secretary of state, in the courts of justice, "and in embassies. The king rewarded men thus "qualified to do him service, with benefices and "other ecclesiastical preferments; and the Lord "Chancellor or Lord Keeper, in particular, was "furnished with many advowsons, to which, as they "became vacant, he might present worthy masters "and clerks in Chancery, who were *then all clergy-* "*men;* which advowsons still continue in his gift, "though the reason thereof hath long since ceased." But *one* reason having ceased, *others* may have risen still more weighty. We have already remarked, more than once, how that prime minister the Duke of Newcastle used the advowsons in the gift of the Chaucellor. We know how preferment is bestowed in Ireland as well as England. We remember the *old manner* of appointment to the provostship of Trinity-college, Dublin.

The excellent divine from whom the last quotation was taken, speaking of clergymen honoured and enriched with *two cures of souls,* proceeds thus: "I "do not deny but there are *pluralists* of great ecclesiastical merit; but I do deny that in general "*pluralists* have greater merit than unalists, or than "many in orders who have no living at all; or that "pluralists in general, become pluralists for their "ecclesiastical merit.

"Read over the list of pluralists in Englaud, and "see whether this sort of merit be universally, or "generally, or commonly, regarded in the *dispensations granted* them to hold pluralities. See whe-"ther the *judge* of this sort of merit hath power, if "he were ever so well inclined, to regard it univer-"sally, or generally, or *commonly:* see whether the "motive of the patron to present a clerk to a second "living, hath, in one instance out of twenty, been "his eminent ecclesiastical merit; or whether the "same favour would not have been bestowed on "the *same* person, had his merit *been inferior;* nay, "in many cases, upon the *same* person, although "instead of merit there had been demerit; and very "often also, if not the more likely, if instead of want "of a competence, there had been affluence. See "whether the merit, which hath been *sometimes* "considered in this case, hath not instead of ec-"CLESIASTICAL MERIT, been POLITICAL OPINIONS, "SERVICEABLENESS IN ELECTIONS, private treaties,

"domestic negotiations, and other *mean offices,* be-
"low the consideration and interposition of ecclesi-
"astics, and hurtful to the ecclesiastical character.

With some patrons, there is not one of these qua-
"lifications that is not a stronger motive than parts,
"and learning, and piety, and prudence, and virtue

put together." Thus said Dr. Newton, the foun-
der and head of a college in Oxford, at a time when
the *cure of souls* was not considered as so trifling a
care as it has been by more recent ministers, who
have seemed ready to sacrifice both soul and body
to the gaining of a majority in the senate. The
church once preserved her own dignity with a noble
independence; but now she must bow, like a lac-
quey, to the vilest minister of state.

But what is this *cura animarum,* this office of
watching over the spiritual state of populous districts ? Is it not, on the hypothesis that the Christian religion is true, the most important office that
can be undertaken by man on this side the grave?
Is not the power of appointing to that office a trust
most sacred, if there be any thing sacred here below? What is sacrilege ? the stealing of a cushion
or silver chalice from a church? And is it no sacrilege to steal the church itself, and all its emoluments,
designed to *prevent* the increase of corruption, in order to reward and to promote corruption? Is the
cura animarum to be the last consideration in the
patron's mind, though the first in the eye of reason
and religion? And is all this injustice, sacrilege, impiety, and blasphemy to be endured, because the gift
of the stipend, the endowment, the tithes, the fees,

buy cm elector, who *swears,* at the time of giving his[1] vote, that he has not received a bribe? Is it to be wondered, if, under such abuses, religion should be on the decline? Do the writings of infidels, or the venal practices of patrons, contribute *most* to exterminate Christianity ? What has a similar system in France effected, carried indeed to still greater lengths, but still similar ? The greedy rapaciousness of court sycophants in England is doing the work of antichrist, and destroying civil liberty.

But I am chiefly concerned at present to consider the using the church, or the *cure of souls,* for the corruption of the *state* and the *violation* of the *constitution,* as a political enormity. It certainly contributes to the spirit of despotism. It naturally tends to make all the youth in the nation, who enter on this sacred profession, look up to court favour, and not to depend on their own merit or exertions, for promotion. It prevents them from voting freely at elections. It prevents them from preaching freely from the pulpit. Its natural tendency is to make them what they ought particularly to avoid, adulators, worldly wise, parasitical, and *acceptors of metis persons for the sake of advantage.* They must know^ under such a system, that if they vote according to conscience, or preach or write according to the truth as it is in Jesus, they must forego all those prospects of rising in their profession, which,, if merit were rewarded, are a stimulus to every thing that can benefit human nature. Clerical men, infirm, like others, often sink under this temptation. Few can renounce great temporal advantages for the sake of promoting public good, especially when they are sure of persecution as well as neglect. Now, what must be the consequence to liberty, of a whole national clergy rendered expectant on the favour of a court, and a proud aristocracy ? May we not hear again from the *pulpit*, the doctrines of divine right and passive obedience; the same doctrines in effect, under names less offensive to the people? Have we not *lately* heard them?

There is no mode of promoting the purposes of corruption, and the aggrandizement of those who already engross the pomp of grandeur, more injurious to liberty, and more villainously base, than that of seizing the appointments and rewards of piety and virtue, to bestow them ou those, whose worldly wisdom is their chief recommendation, and who seem ready to worship God only in the *second* place, if they worship him at all.

The Tindals, the Collinses, the Bolingbrokes, the Humes, the Gibbons, the Voltaires, the Yolneys,' the *miscreant* philosophers of France; never did so much injury to the cause of Christianity, as those English ministers of state, who, while they shed the blood of thousands for the sake of law, order, and *religion,* prostitute the church and the cure of souls to the corruption of the senate.

SECTION XXXIV.

Of Mr. Hume's *Idea, That* absolute Monarchy *is the easiest Death, the true* Euthanasia *of the British Constitution.*

The very ingenious speculatist, Mr. Hume, seems to wish as well as think, that as death is unavoidable by the political as well as the animal body, the British constitution may die in the arms of despotism. His words are, "I would much rather wish "to see an absolute monarch than a republic in this "island. Absolute monarchy is the easiest death, "the true *euthanasia* of the British constitution."

His opinion that our free government will terminate in despotism, seems founded on the following argument, which he has inserted in his Essay on the British Government.

"The British spirit and love of liberty, however "great, will never be able to support itself against "that immense property which is now lodged in the "king, and is still increasing. Upon a moderate "computation, there are near three millions annu-"ally at the disposal of the crown. The civil list "amounts to near a million; the collection of all "taxes to another million; and the employments in "the army and navy, along with ecclesiastical pre-"ferments, to above a third million. A monstrous "sum! and what may fairly be computed to be "more than a thirtieth part of the whole income

"and labour of the kingdom. When we add to this
"immense property the increasing luxury of thena-
"tion, our proneness to corruption, along with the
"great power arid prerogatives of the crown, and
"the command of such numerous military forces,
** there is no one but must despair, without extra-
"ordinary efforts, of beipg able to support onr
"free government much longer, under all these.dis*
"advantages."

But why should no*t* "*extraordinary- efforts^-* be made, when the object is - extraordinary——no less than the preservation of human happiness, by < the preservation of civil liberty? No efforts should be declined in such a cause; nor should men, sensible of their blessings, and desirous of handing them down as. they received them, sink, with dastardly indolence, into a state-of despair.   -   .:

Mr. Hume,, with all his penetration, could not foresee the revolution in France;.and.how much the - establishment of liberty,, in that extensive aud enlightened, country, would contribute to defeat the purpose of despots in all the nations of Europe. It is. certain that- the minds of the *people* in all.countries are opened Jo the light of truth, by the emancipation of four or. five and twenty millions of meu, from the slavery of prejudice and arbitrary dominion. There is now very little occasion for that despair, of pre- serving the freedom-of the British government, if the people will but be true to their own cause. Despo- tism, in its last struggles, may make great efforts; but,even.they will exhaust.its strength, and accele- rate-its dissolution. Firmness.and perseverance "in

s

the people will ultimately triumph over the unnatural exertions of. despotism, driven to madness by despair.

The spirit of liberty, it has been said, is a spirit of jealousy. It ought to be ever-waking and circumspect; for the spirit of despotism never slumbers; but watches every opportunity to increase prerogative, and diminish popular authority. During those late alarms which cowardly and selfish aristocracy laboured to diffuse, in its panic fear for its own privileges, many instances occurred of men who would willingly have sacrificed all the boasted freedom of Englishmen to the security which they flattered themselves grandeur, titles, and riches would enjoy under an absolute government. Their pride was stung to the quick by. the idea of equality, while their avarice trembled for their property, and their cowardice for their personal safety. They saw spectres in the shapes of Truth, Justice, and Liberty; triumphing over an enslaved and deluded world; they knew that they had little interest.or connexion with such *personages,* and shuddered at their fancied approach. They shrieked with terrors; and would gladly have hastened to thegreatest despot on earth for protection. England bad no despot on the throne to afford them an asylum; and therefore,they placed all their hopes on the *military* arm. War was the ery; victory was sure. Bastilles were already built in imagination, and chains fabricated for the (millions that people the provinces of Gaul.

Had it been possible for these men to prevail, in the moment of their consternation, the sceptre *of*

England would have been converted by them into an iron rod, and its king into the *grand monarque* of the old French tyranny. Despotism} expelled from France, would have crossed from Calais to Dover, and been received with open arms by devoted ▼assals, the slavish alarmists of an Epglish aristocracy. The free government of England might have found at this period, as Mr. Hume prophesies it will hereafter do, an easy death in absolute monarchy.

But though the high *church and king alarmists* did not succeed at that time, which seemed auspicious to their designs, yet. still., they continue on their posts, watching opportunities to infringe on liberty, to seduce the people from their love of it, and gradually to reconcile them to arbitrary rule.

Strange as it is, as a moral phenomenon, that men should wish to be slaves, yet it is certain, that the tribe of persons devoted to the pomp and power of uncontrolled royalty, whom I call Tories or Aristocrats, for want of a,,more appropriate and precise appellation, are still extremely zealous to make our kino a far superior potentate,than he is allowed to be by that Revplution, which gives him all the royal rights he possesses, and places him on the throne.   :

Many circumstances favour the wishes of these persons; and nothing opposes them so much as the French revolution, and those liberal opinions on the rights and happiness of man which begin to prevail, wherever courts and ministers have little influence. Among the circumstances which flatter them most with thé extension of royal power, the elevation of themselves, and the depression of the people* is the interest which almost every man and woman in the natron possesses in the public funds, and which they are all taught to believe would be depreciated, or even annihilated, if the parliament were reformed, the people reinstated in their rights* and the influence of the crown diminished. This has communicated the *panic* of the alarmists among multitudes too remote from courts, and too inconsiderable in station, to be influenced by ministerial bribes; who, Otherwise, could not but have sided with the cause of'justice and humanity. The terror of anarchy, occasioned by the *ill-judged*, impolitic, as well as cruel conduct of some among the first leaders of the emancipated French, has increased the number of ministerial partizans and favourers of *extended* power and prerogative.

Were it possible that a *panic* could be permanent, or falsehood and artifice ultimately victorious over truth and justice, there might be reason to fear, from the spirit which the *alarmists* diffused, that English liberty might soon sicken, and at last die *paralytic* in the arms of despotism. But notwithstanding a temporary lethargy, the mass of the people, those who are quite out of the reach of courtiers and grandees, still retain the healthy vigour of their fathers'virtue, and Would rouse themselves effectually to prevent the accomplishment of Mr. Hume's prediction. They must indeed be lulled with the Circéan cup of corruption to sleep on, and take **their** rest, when the giant Despotism is at their doors, teddy to crush, with his mace, all that, readers, life valuable'to MEN; to men who have learned to. think that, mere vegetation is•,, not life. But Circus cup is not- Capacious enough to contain opiate for a whole people. All the douceurs of a minister, all the patronage in the professions, all the riches of the east 'and the west, are insufficient to bribe the obscufe *millions'*, who constitute the *base* of the political fabric, into complete acquiescence under the pressure of despotic power, or under the apprehension of it. The light of reason and of learning is too widely diffused to be easily extinguished. There is every reason to believe that it will shine more and more unto *a perfect day.*

But as popular commotion is always to be dread* ed, because bad men always arise to mislead its efforts, how desirable is it that it may be prevented, by conciliatory measures, by a timely concession of rights, by redress of grievances, by reformation of abuses, by convincing mankind that governments have no other object than faithfully to promote the comfort and security of individuals, without sacrificing the solid happiness of living men to *national* glory, or royal magnificence. True patriotism and true philosophy, unattached to names of particular men, or even to parties, consider the happiness of man as the first object of all rational governments; and, convinced that nothing is more injurious to the happiness of man than the spirit of despotism, endeavour to check its growth, at its first and slightest appearance.

If the free government of England evinces, by its

conduct, that the happiness of the people is its sole object, so far from dreading the late Mr. Hume's prophecy that it will die in the arms of despotism, we may •venture to predict that it will never die. My orisons shall be offered for its perpetuity; for I, and all who think with me, on this subject, are its *true* friends; while the *boroughwwngers,* under the cloke of loyalty, are enemies both to the king and the people.

SECTION XXXV.

The Permission of Lawyers *by Profession, aspiring at Honours in the Gift of the Crown, to have the greatest Influence in the Legislature, a Circumstance unfavourable to Liberty.*

When advocates address each other at the bar, they always adopt the appellation of *learned* brother. There certainly is a necessity for great learning in the profession of the long robe. But of wbat *kind* isthe (earning required ? It is undoubtedly of a kind very-little connected with philosophy or enlargement
* of the mind. It is, in its widest range, confined to local customs, and the statutes of a single nation. It pores upon thp.letter of the law, and scarcely dares to contemplate the spirit. It is for the most part emr ployed; inmmute disquisitions, in finding exceptions, in seeking subterfuges, and often in making the great eterpal rules of equity give way to the literal meaning of ^a narrow and unjnSt statute^ framed by ignorant'then in times little removed from barbarism^ and certainly both slavish and superstitious.

Is the *education* of professional and *practising* lawyers' particularly calculated' to expand the intellect, or. to fill the heart with sentiments of peculiar honour and generosity; such sentiments as alone can. constitute a* worthy lawgiver, and an all-accomplished statesman ? Is it not confined to particular and Uuniite objects, instead of taking hi the whole horizon of human concernments? Many of those who have risen to the first honours and emoluments, have not had a truly liberal education, but have been traiued either in the office of an attorney, or in studies and exercises that contribute no more to liberalize or improve the heart, than the copying of instruments, the perusal of statutes, the knowledge of *forms*. Some of the finest faculties of the human constitution, the imagination and sentimental affections, have little-room for play, where the eye and memory are chiefly concerned; and where the mind is obliged to labour in the trammels of dismal formalities, like the horse io harness; dragging a heavy vehicle in the wheel-ruts made by those, who have gone before, without the liberty of; deviation. A hard head, a cold unfeeling heart, with a tenacious memory, are likely to succeed -best in such toil; which requires less of speed than of -patient, plodding perseverance.

A dull man, trained in this dull manner, may become a very useful *lawyer,* and certainly deserving of all the *fees* and emoluments of his profession; Put does it follow that he must be a statesman, a senator, a cabinet counsellor, fitted to determine on questions of peace and war, and to cdnsult and pro? mqte the happiness of human nature? A lawyer, by singular felicity of genius and disposition,; may be fit for the momentous task; and I only ask wher ther his *education,* and the studies and employments of his profession,:are such as to render him *pre-emir yently* a statesman, and director of the measures; of government? Because he may, for a fee, plead suecesrffully on any side, conduct a trial,, sod assist a jury in determining a question of *meum* and *tuum,* or may be. able to expound a. statute, is he *therefore* nlore likely than all others to *frame*laws of the most *beneficent* kind, having a view, not to particular cases only,- but to the general welfare? All his studies of jurisprudence have been *merely* for the sake of lucre, and not free and disinterested, like, those of the general scholar, the philosopher, and philanthropist.

. The lawyer has, however, better opportunities for *displaying* his knowledge and abilities than the members of. other professions. Men have recourse to him on matters very dear to their hearts; matters of property. With the sagacity of a very moderate intellect, and a knowledge acquired by dint of mere labour and long. practice, he may be able to trans-, act their *pecuniary* business with skill and success; He becomes, therefore,;a favourite with *men of property* in the nation, which, whenever corruption prevails, will contribute much to push any.aspirant upr the:ladder of promotion. He soon pants for re-, wards extraneous to his profession. It js not enough to be a judge or a;chancellor; he must be a. peer of the realm, a counsellor of state, a chief director in; the *upper* house. It is painful to behold all the old nobility^ educated, as they have been, at the greatest expence, improved by private tutors and by travel, crouching to a man, who has acquired effrontery in the courts below, and whose, unblushing audacity may **have** been the chief cause; qf the elevation, at which himself is surprised., , '. ; '

Men like these, emboldened by success, and ac» customed, from their earliest entrance into active life, to browbeat and overbear, assume a' right to guide the opinions of the senate and the council in the most important measures of state;.They become, in feet, the rulers of the nation *of* but owing their elevatiom to the favour of a *court,* and placing all their expectations of fortherhonours on its continuance, they become devoted to its purposes. They are, in fact, still ATTORNIES AND SOLICITERS, ready to exert all their powers of sophistry, and' to exhaust all their stores of chicanery, to defend the measures of the minister, by rendering law, as far as they can, a leaden rule. The old peers sit in silent admiration; while men, furnished with all the subtleties of practising lawyers, long hackneyed and hardened in the paltry business of private individuals, presume to dictate peace or war, to impede or prevent salm tary reform, and' keep the church, the army, and die navy, under their[1] supreme control. Such is their habitual volubility and confirmed assurance, that men of more liberal minds, but of less self-conceit and less notoriety, stand in awe of them, and suffer thenM, With abject acquiescence, to *domineer.* Bat however they may oppose the people's right, -and the happiness of the public, they are 'sure to espouse the cause of those from whom comes their promotion; They therefore contribute to diffuse the spirit of des-* potism, more than any other profession.

"But" (Says the minister) we cannot do without
"them. We must' have *able* men in the House of
"Lords; therefore we must have new men; and

"they must be selected from a profession accustomed "to public business, and which gives those who be- "long to it opportunities of making an open display "of their abilities." This is a sad compliment to the hereditary nobility; as it seems to argue that they are totally unfit to conduct the business that' comes before them, without *attondes* and *solicitors* from below, who are ennobled merely to save the credit of the peerage. But the truth is, the minister wishes to have some *sharp* and tractable *tools,* by which he may do his dirty 'work, uninterrupted by the interference of those who, possessing a-constitutional *right* to examine it, would perhaps often censure it, if they Were not overawed and overborne by those who pretend to be initiated in the *mysteries* of law.

In consequence of thi$ management, a *whole profession,* with few exceptions, extremely, busy both with tongue and pen, is constantly eplisted in the service of a minister. A great number of *attondes* and *solicitorsy* besides the gentlemen *ojfficially* honoured with those names, are constantly *reiamed* on the side of the court, and consequently lean, for their own sakes, and with a hope of making their families, to the extension of crown influence and prerogative. A set of men, so subtle, so active, so attentive to interest, must serve any cause which they choose to espouse; and there is no doubt but that they greatly serve (in the hope of serving *themselves)* the cause of despotism. -

Let any one who is unacquainted with the pains taken by modem ministers to retain the lawyers on the side of prerogative, inspect the *court calendar,* and remark how great a portion of the modern peer have owed their coronets entirely to their profession as lawyers, to their qualifications as mere'men of business in *detail,* with very scanty knowledge [of apy thing else, and with small claims to excellence as patriots, philosophers, or philanthropists. MenC men of business commonly fix their eyes on objects of private lucre or temporal elevation *alone.* They are apt to laugh at the names of patriotism, liberty, and disinterested virtue. They have commonly been too long hackneyed among the lowest of mankind, not perhaps in rank only, but:in.spirit, knowledge^ liberality,, to. retain any very *scrupulous* delicacy in their own. bosoms, or to believe its existence in others. They consider the good things of the world as a scramble, where, every man is to get what he can by.address, and bold pretension, since the law will not allow the use of violence. Certainly there can he ho hope of reform, or what the French call a *regeneration* of human affairs,, while men so versed in [corruption,, so enriched by it, and so well pleased with'it, bear sway in senates, and direct tbb. councils of princfes.*

. # Several of the crown lawyer* concerned in the prosecution of Hardy, &c. in which ao, much, pain* was taken to sbed innocent blood, were, put into parliament by peers, or *grandees,* as their mem, bers.or agents, contrary to law and the constitution.

" The Marquis of Bath nominates Sir'John Scott, (the *Attorney General,)* to represent his Lordship in the House of Commons. '

. Lord Beverley nominates Sir John: Mitford, (the Solicitor General,) to represent him.

. Earl Fitzwilliam nominates Serjeant Adair.

The *Earl of Lonsdale* nominates Mr. Anstruther.'

Mr; Bulier nominates Mr. Bearcroft[

> See"Petition presented to the House of Commons, 6th of May*, ... r; 1?93.:t   _ V. • [. [; i

SECTION XXXVI.

Poverty, when not extreme, *favourable to all Virtue, public and private, and consequently to the Happiness of human Nature; and* enormous Riches, *without Virtue, the general Pane.*

Superfluity of riches, like superfluity *of* food, causes sickness and debility. *Poverty,* or mediocrity of fortune, is the nurse of many virtues; of modesty, industry, sobriety. But, in this age, the very name of poverty is odious. Poverty is a haggard phantom that appals half the world, and drives them over seas, into torrid zones, to disease and death! Life itself is thought by-many a gift fit to be thrown back again into the face of the Almighty Donor, if it is not accompanied with the *means* of luxury, the means of making *a figure* beyond *others;* in a word, the means of indulging the *spirit of despotism.* Things are so managed, in a state of deep political corruption, that the honours due only to virtue are paid exclusively to **money**; and those who want not riches for the sake of indulgence in pleasure, or from the love of money itself, grow complete *misers,* in the hope of obtaining, together with opulence, civil *honours,* seats in the senate-house, and **royal favour.** They hope to make themselves of *consequence* enough to be *corrupted,* or rather *purchased,* by the state.

What is the consequence to the *people,* the labourer, the manufacturer, the retail trader, to poor families with many children, women with small patrimonies, annuitants, dependents, and all the numerous train of persons who are compelled to live, as the common phrase expresses it, from *hand to month?* Their gains or means are *fixed*, and by no means rise with the rising price of necessaries. But, in consequence of this rage for riches, the necessaries of life become not ouly dearer, but worse in quality; less nourishing, less commodious, and less, durable. *Landlords* raise their rents to the utmost possible extent; each determining to make his rent-roll as respectable as some opulent neighbour, favoured by a lord lieutenant for bis influence. They will not let their forms in little portions, to poor industrious tenants; but to some *overgrown monopolizer,* who is in as much haste to grow rich as the *landlord* himself; seeing that as he becomes rich he becomes a *man of consequence* in the *county,* and that not only esquires, but even lords, take *notice* of him at the: ■—former, and will breed but few of the animals of the form-yard, and those only for his own family comsumption. His children are too proud to carry the productions of the hen-roost or dairy to the market. He scorns such *little* gains. He deals only in a *great way;* and keeps up the price by withholding his stores when the market is low. The neighbouring rustics, who used to be respectable, though little formers, are now his day-labourers, begging to be employed by the great man who has engrossed and consolidated half a dqzen farms. The old form-houses are pulled down. One *capital mansion* is sufficient for a large territory of meadow and arable land, which used to display smoking chimnies in every, part of. a cheerful landscape, with a healthy progeny of children, and tribes of animals, enlivening, the happy scene. The *tenant* now reigns over the uninhabited glebe, a solitary despot.; and something of the ancient *vassalage* of the feudal *system,* is restored, through the *necessities* of the surrounding cottagers, who live in hovels with *windows stopt up,* hardly enjoying God's freest gifts, light and air. A murmur will exclude them even from the hut, compared with which the neighbouring dog-kennel is a palace.

. The *little tenants* of former times were too numerous and too inconsiderable to become objects of *corruption.* But the *great tenant,* the engrosser of farms, feeling his consequence, grows as ambitious as his landlord. He may have sons, cousins, and nephews, whom he wishes to provide for by places; and therefore it becomes a part of his *prudential* plan, to side, in all county elections, and at all public meetings, with the *court party,* the lord lieutenant, and the aristocratical toad-eaters of the minister.

In like manner, the great *manufacturer,* finding that riches tend to civil honours, and political cpusequence, as well as to plenty of all good things, cannot be contented, with the *slow progress* of his grandfathers, but must *whip and spur,* in his. career from the temple of Plutus to the temple of Honour. His workmen therefore, are paid, not by the *day,* in which case they would endeavour to do their work *well,* though slowly, but by the *piece.* The public, perhaps, *must* of necessity purchase his commodity, however bad; and it is probably as good as others fabricate, because <?//are pursuing the same glorious end, by similar means. The materials, as well:as the workmanship, are of inferior quality. For, the great monopolizers and dealers can *force* a trade, and get *vent* among the little retailers, by giving credit, and by various other contrivances, for the most *ordinary* ware. The *great man,* whose, forefathers felt little else but *avarice,* now burns with ambition; and,; as *city honours* and rural dignities, senatorial consequence, and even magistracy, are bestowed by ministerial favour, he must.be devo/ed to a minister, and carry all the little traders and artisans to second the views of a court at the general election, or. at public meetings, appointed for the promotion of a minister's project to *keep himself in place.*

These, and a thousand similar causes, visible enough in the various departments of manufacture, commerce, agriculture, are at this moment urging on the great machine of corruption, and diffusing the spirit of despotism. The revolution of France will indeed check it, throughout Europe, by the in* fluence of principles, favourable to the freedom and happiness of man; but at present, even that event is used by short-sighted politicians, to increase arigtocratical arrogance, to depress popular spirit, and to give unnatural influence to the possession of money, however acquired and however abused.

OF DESPOTISM.

An indignant writer of ancient Rome exclaims:

' Nullum crimen abest, facinusque libidinis ex quo
     Paupertas Romana perit.*   Juvenal.
   Prim a peregrinos obsccena pecunia mores
 Intulit, et turpi fregerunt secula luxu
   Divitise molles.—

The virtuous ancients, by the light of nature and the evidence of experience, were taught that, when riches obtained a value and esteem beyond their *proper use,* merely for the sake of splendour, ostentation, and aristocratic oppression, a fatal blow was given ito liberty. The human race, they thought, degenerated under the *despotism of money.* In such a corrupt, system there was no encouragement given in the state to excel in virtue for its own sake: even generals and admirals went on *expeditions,* not even for false and vain-glory, far less from motives of patriotism; but to fill their coffers with plunder, and render war a cloke for pillage.

Cauponantes bellum, non belligerentes.

They made a *trade,* and a *sordid* trade, of *legal bloodshed,* not conducting it with the disinterested spirit of soldiers, animated with the love of their country, but with the cunning and. avarice of Jew usurers in Duke's Place.

And have we had no instances of generals or admirals making war a trade, in recent times, and in

* Since Poverty, our guardian god, is gone, -
  Pride, laziness, and all luxurious arts,
  Pour like a deluge in from foreign parts, f
     &c.   DRYDEN.

  f *Viz.* The *East Indtes* at present.

Christian nations; using the sword, to which the idea of *honour* has been attached, as an implement of lucre, and rendering it far less *honourable* than the knife of the butcher, exercising bis trade in the market of Leadenball? If it should ever be true, that ships of war are made merchantmen in the vilest merchandize, *the barter of human blood for gold,* will it not prove, that the attaching honour to the possession of *money,* is destroying, not only the national virtue, but its honour and *defence?* Have towns in the East Indies *never* been given up to plunder, contrary to the law of nations as well as justice and humanity, to make the fortune of European officers?

It is a noble and virtuous struggle, to stand up in defence of the rights of nature, true honour, liberty, and truth, against the overbearing dominion of *pecuniary* influence. Man will shine forth in his genuine lustre; when *money* can no longer *gild* the base metal of folly, knavery, pride, and cruelty.^ While the corrupt Ganges flows into the Thames, it will contaminate its waters, and infect the atmosphere of freedom. When British freeholders, yeotnen, merchants, manufacturers, generals, admirals, and senators, become slaves *to pelf* only, forgetting or despising the very name of *public virtue* and disinterested exertion, nothing can oppose the spirit of despotism but *the spirit of the common people. That* spirit, indeed, may at once rescue human nature from misery, and perpetuate the blessings of a pure and free constitution. But when they who fatten on the blood of their fellow-creatures, are also permitted to *domineer* by the influence of their ill-gotten money, over free countries, to command majorities at elections, and drive all opposition before them, what chance of happiness can remain to virtuous independence? What, in such circumstances, can preserve liberty, but a *convulsive struggle,* attended, perhaps, with the horrors of the first French revolution, which God, in his mercy, *avert!*

SECTION XXXVII.

OH the natural Tendency of making Judges and
■ *Crown Lawyers, Peers; of translating Bishops and annexing Preferments to Bishopricks, in what is called,* coinuiendam.

IF there is any part of the constitution of England, in the praise of which eloquence may employ her most glowing colours, without entrenching upon the confines of truth, it is the JUDICIAL part of it. The purity of public justice in England is unequalled in any country which the sun illuminates in his diurnal progress. The reason is obvious. The *verdict* is given by juries of men usually beyond the reach of corruption. No ministerial influence can descend to all the individuals, in middle and humble life, who may be called upon to sit in judgment, and ultimately decide, as jurors, on the property, the fame, and the life, of their fellow-citizens. We have lately had a most glorious instance of the virtue of private citizens, exercising this most important office. The *verdicts* given in the state trials, in one thousand seven hundred and ninety-four, do *more honour* to the British character, than all the military exploits in the reign of George the Third. Such verdicts make our constitution truly enviable to the nations of Europe. Twelve honest men, on each of these trials, proved to the world, that no power, no authority, no terror, not even the factitious rage of aristocratical principles, which had been artfully fostered, could lead them to swerve from the right line of justice. They *feared God, but not man;* and posterity will *honour* them, when the names of subtle politicians, clothed with a brief but lucrative authority, if mentioned at all, shall be mentioned with detestation. It was well observed by a zealous and honest advocate on the occasion, that he could not *despair* of the case, when it was brought from the corrupt to the uncorrupt part of the constitution. The days of acquittal were the jubilees of truth, the triumphs of virtue; and, in a time of dejection, revived the hopes of patriotism and philanthropy.

Official judges, not having the final determination of the cause, but feeling the check of the JURIES, commonly conduct themselves, even in *state trials»* with some degree of candour and moderation. Indeed, we are so happy as to see men appointed to this office, in our time, whose tried integrity gives reason to believe, that, if they were not thus wisely checked, they would, with *few* exceptions, preserve impartiality.

Nevertheless, though much has been said on the independence of judges, and though great praise is due to our king, who placed them in their offices for life, and not removable at his pleasure, yet it must be confessed, that there still remain temptations, which might have great influence on men less virtuous than our *present* judges are. It is observed, that PEERAGES, in modern times, have been bestowed, with peculiar bounty, on lawyers; and some have ventured to say, that the expectation of this splendid reward may frustrate all endeavours to secure, especially in *state trials*, the perfect independence of the judges who preside. It is not enough that they do not fear *removal* from their dignified office. Their *hopes* may influence, more than their *fears*. They may *hope* to add to opulence the dignity of family distinction, escutcheons, coronets, and hereditary seats in the legislature. If themselves have seen too much of the vanity and folly of worldly pomp to admire it, (which, however, is not often the case with men who may be great lawyers, without any philosophy or religion,) yet they may have sons, wives, daughters, relatives, and friends, to whom the splendour of life, (as *they* have, possibly, little *solid* merit,) is valuable in the *highest* degree. A peerage is therefore, for the most part, a very powerful allurement, I will not say, to disguise the truth or pervert the law, but obsequiously to seek ministerial favour.

When peerages are lavished on lawyers high in place, it is a circumstance viewed with some degree of jealousy by those who are willing to guard constitutional liberty with unwinking vigilance. Perhaps it might afford satisfaction to such men, if judges were by law *excluded* from all higher elevation; if they were indeed *most amply* paid and most respectfully revered; but, for the sake of preventing the possibility of a wrong bias, where the happiness of the people is most intimately concerned, were prevented from viewing a brilliant dazzling coronet, suspended as their *reward,* over the scales of justice.

But here an objector will urge, with serious solicitude, that, as the House of Lords is a court of judicature, in die last resort, a court of appeal from every court in the kingdom, it is necessary that it should be well supplied with lawyers of eminence.

On this subject Mr. Paley says; "There appears "to be nothing in the constitution of the House of "Lords; in the education, habits, character, or pro- "fessions of the members who compose it; in the "mode of their appointment, or the right by which "they succeed to their places in it, that should "qualify them for their arduous office; except, *per-* "*haps,* that the elevation of their rank and fortune "affords a security against the offer and influence "of small bribes. Officers of the army and navy, "courtiers, ecclesiastics; young men who have just "attained the age of twenty-one, and who have "passed their youth in the dissipation and pursuits "which commonly accompany the possession or in- "heritanee of great fortunes; country gentlemen, "Occupied in the management of their estates, or in "the care of their domestic concerns and family "interests; the gbeater part of tbe assembly *born to their station,* that is, placed in it by chance; "most of the rest advanced to the peerage for ser-*ʃ* vices and from motives *utterly* unconnected with *ⁱᶜ* iegal erudition;—*these men* compose the tribunal "to which tbe constitution entrusts the interpretation "of her laws, and the ultimate decision of every "dispute between her subjects!"

jFrom this *very degrading* representation of the House of Lords, the Reverend Archdeacon proceeds to justify the practice of constantly placing in it, some of the most eminent and experienced lawyers in the kingdom. He would, I think, with more propriety have argued against rendering one part of the *legislature* a court of justice, designed both to make and execute the laws; because every solid politician has agreed in the propriety of keeping the legislative and judicial powers as separate and as distant from each other as it is possible.

I leave this point for the discussion of future political writers, and satisfy myself with suggesting, that it is necessary to the perfect conteutmeut of a people jealous of their liberty and the purity of judicial proceedings, that all temptations whatever should be removed from the sight of frail human beings, sitting in the seat of judgment, which may lead them to court the favour of ruling powers at the expence of justice. It is not **money** alone which **bribes**. Title and rank have more influence on the universal passion, *vanity;* especially when avarice has been already gratified with ample salaries and the emoluments of a lucrative profession.

The consideration of the *possible* rewards which may diminish the independence of *judges,* naturally leads to the consideration of those which may *secularize* the *bishops,* and injure the cause of religion, for *which alone* episcopacy itself could be established.

But, as this is a subject of some delicacy, I shall use the authority and words of Dr. Watson, the present Bishop of *Llandaff*, who, having been in the minority at the time he wrote upon it, ventured to speak the *whole* truth, with that freedom which be*

comes an honest man in every rank, and is particu*
larly expected from a Christian bishop.

"I know," says Bishop Watson, "that many will
"be startled, I beg them not to be offended, at the
"■surmise of the bishops not being independent in
"the House of Lords; and it would be easy enough
"to weave a *logical cobweb*, large enough and strong
"enough to cover and protect the conduct of the
"Right Reverend Bench from the attacks of those
"who dislike episcopacy. This, I say, would be
"an easy task; but it is far above my ability to era-
-ᵛ dicate from the minds of others (who are, notwith-
•"standing, as well attached to the church establish-
"ment as ourselves,) a suspicion that the pros-
"pect of being translated *influences the minds*
"of the bishops too powerfully, and induces them
"to pay too great an attention to the beck of a m»-
"*nister.* The suspicion, whether well or ill founds
"ed, is *disreputable to our order;* and, what is of
"worse consequence, it hinders us from doing that
"good which we otherwise might do; for the laity,
"while they entertain such a suspicion concerning
"us, will accuse us of avarice and ambition, of mak-
"ing a *gain of godliness,* of *bartering the dignity of*
"*our office* for the *chance* of a translation.

"Instead then," proceeds the Bishop, "of *quib-*
"*bling* and disputing against the existence of *minis-*
"*ters' influence over* us, or recriminating and retort*
"ing the petulance of those who accuse us on that
"account, let us endeavour to remove the evil; or,
** if it *must not* be admitted that this evil has any

"real existence, let us endeavour to remove the *ap-*
"*pearance* of it.

"The disparity of income and patronage might
"be made so small, or so apportioned to the la-
"bours, that few bishops would be disposed to wish
"for translations; and consequently the bishops
"would, in *appearance* as well as in *reality*, be in*
"DEPENDENT.

"But, in rendering the bishops independent, you
"will reduce the power of the crown in the House
"of Lords.—I do not mean to deny this charge;
"nay, I am willing to admit it in its full extent.—
"The influence of the crown, when exerted by the
"cabinet over the public counsellors of the king, is
"a circumstance so far from being to be wished by
"his true friends, that it is as dangerous to the real
"interests and honour of the crown itself, as it is
"odious to the people, and DESTRUCTIVE OF PUBLIC
**LIBERTY.

"It may contribute to keep a *prime minister* in
"his *place, contrary to the sense of the wisest and
"best part of the community;* it may contribute to
"keep the king himself unacquainted with his peo-
"ple's wishes, but it cannot do the king or the state
"any service. To maintain the contrary is to sati-
"rize his majesty's government; it is to insinuate,
"that his views and interests are so disjoined from
"those of his people, that they cannot be effectuated
"by the *uninfluenced concurrence of honest men.*

"I cannot admit the circumstance of the bishops
"being rendered *independent* in the House of Lords,

* uoosle.

"as any real objection to tbe plan proposed; on the "contrary, I think it a very strong argument in its " favour; so strong an one that, if there was no "other, it would be sufficient to sanctify the mea-*■' sure."

The corruption of the church for the purpose of corrupting the legislature, is an offence far more injurious to tbe general happiness of mankind and the interests of a Christian commubity, than any of those which have banished the offenders to Botany Bay, or confined them for years within the walls of tbe prison-house. Both the corruptors and the corrupted, in this case, are more injurious to Christianity than all the tribe of sceptics and infidels; than Tindal, Toland, Bolingbroke, Hume, Rousseau, Voltaire, and Gibbon. The *common people* do not *read* them, and perhaps could scarcely *wnderstand* them. But the common people *do* read tbe newspapers daily, and see the names and qualities of those who divide in the senate-house, on questions of the last importance. They must therefore entertain a suspicion, as the Bishop of Llandaff expresses it, that religion itself, as well as its official, opulent, dignified supporters, is but an instrument of state, a tool in the hand of a minister. They must naturally consider *venality* as *doubly* base, when clothed in the sanctified robes of religion. What has happened in France, in consequence of the corruptions of the church by the state, ought to afford a striking admonition.

I wish to point out, in *these times, writings* of LIVING BISHOPS in favour of Christianity^ because they would be opposed with the best grace against the writings of living Infidels. But, to the reproach of my want of intelligence, I know not the' names of the majority, till I find them in the Court Calendar. The printed works of even this *majority* I cannot find, either in the shops or the libraries: the few I do find, even of the *minority*, are not adapted to the wants of the people at large. Their *occasional* sermons, after they have served their *day*, become, like almanacs, out of date: a collection of old *court calendars* would be nearly as edifying and more entertaining to the multitude.

It is indeed certain, that the archiepiscopal mitres received more lustre than they gave, from the sermons of Dr. Tillotson and Dr. Seeker. It would give me pleasure to place the sermons of living Archbishops by their side; and I would mention them had they come to my knowledge. The sermons, however, of the *few* living, bishops who are *known* at all to the public will, I hope, prove to mankind, that some among the bishops, in this happy isle, do not think it a sufficient return for princely revenues, to *vote always with a minister,* or to increase, with lawn sleeves, the pageantry of a birthday. To perform the occasional duties of ordination, confirmation, and visitation, cannot satisfy the minds of men who receive the honours and emoluments of Durham, Winchester, York, or Canterbury. That it is so, is happy; for if ever the prelatical clergy should be suspected of becoming merely ministerial instruments; if, for instance, they should ever be supposed so far secularized, as to

OF DESPOTISM. 285

concede to the minister that made them bishops, the right of nominating to all the most valuable preferments in their gift, in order to enable *him* the better to corrupt that parliament in which themselves also have engaged to give a venal vote; from that time, they would contribute more to the downfal of the church, than all the writings of all the unbelievers, from Frederic, late King of Prussia, to.the American Republican, Thomas Paine. The *sin of simony* in a private man, who pays a *fair price* for a profitable appointment, with his *own* money, honestly earned by virtuous industry, and *does the duties of it,* is as nothing when compared to the *simony* of him who buys a high and important station, greatly lucrative, with a corrupt vote and a base dereliction of those rights of patronage, which were intended to encourage merit only, and to prevent that very corruption which he feeds and cherishes, to gratify his own sordid avarice and childish vanity.

The bishops, in their charges, are now sounding an alarm. They very justly affirm, that the existence of Christianity is now in danger. They wisely urge the inferior clergy to the most vigilant activity. Thus far they certainly do honour to the episcopal function. But still, while, the public suspects the bare possibility of the bench being, as Bp. Watson says, at the *heck of the minister,* they will consider all this zeal as little better than that of Demetrius, who made silver shrines for Diana.

When indeed we add to the *probable* effect of *translations* from a poorer to a richer bishopric, the holding of rich *pluralities with* bishoprics, under the name of commendams, it is difficult not to think with Bishpp Watson, that episcopal independence is endangered, and that we must look rather in *cathedrals*, than in the House of Lords, for episcopal integrity. Conscientious dissenters are shocked, and libertines and infidels *laugh,* when they view the bench, as if they were spectators of a solemn mummery, or a mock-heroic farce. All this danger, offence, and reproach, might possibly be prevented, if *translations* and *commendams* were utterly prohibited.

But, setting aside the effect of translations and commendams on the state of *religion,* let us seriously consider them as they operate on the increase of prerogative and the spirit of despotism. These things influence not only those who have attained mitres, but a numerous tribe of expectants; and those expectants possess the ear op the people. Is it reasonable to suppose that the doctrines of the pulpit will not, under these circumstances, be fashioned to the inclinations of the minister? What can contribute more to diffuse the spirit of despotism, than the employment of many thousand pulpits, at least once in each week, in obliquely preaching doctrines^ that favour its prevalence, under the *sanction* of divine AUTHORITY ?

SECTION XXXVIII.

That all Opposition to the Spirit of Despotism should he conducted with the most scrupulous Regard to the existing Laws, and to the Preservation of public Peace and good Order.

Tmc frailty of human nature is one of the com*monest of common-places. The wisest and best of men are desirous of palliating their errors, by claiming a share, as men, in human infirmity. One of the infirmities most acknowledged and lamented is a tendency to rush from one extreme to another; a proneness to fall into a *vice,* in the desire of escaping an *error.* Thus the detestation of despotism, and the love of liberty, both of them rational and laud*able, have led many to factious and violent conduct* which neither the occasion justified, nor prudence would *precipitately* adopt, even if the occasion might appear to justify them.

From faction and violence in the cause of liberty, which disgrace the cause itself, and give advantage to the favourers of arbitrary power, I *most anxiously dissuade* all who love mankind and their country. Faction and violence are despotic in the extreme. They bring all the evils of tyranny, without any consolation, but that they are usually transient; whereas tyranny is durable. They destroy themselves, or are destroyed by force in the hands of a superior power. In either case, much is *lost* to the cause of liberty; because the persons who have been betrayed by their passions into excesses, were probably *sincere;* and if they had been also *discreet* and moderate, would have been effectual as well as zealous promoters of the public good. It is certain, that very honest men are very apt to be betrayed into violence by their warmth of temper. They mean good, and do ill. They become the instruments of dispassionate knaves; and are often led into extravagancies by the very party against whom they act, in order that they may be exposed, and become obnoxious to censure.

Wisdom is gentle, deliberate, cautious. Nothing violent is durable. I hope the lovers of liberty will shew the sincerity of their attachment by the wisdom of their conduct. Tumultuary, proceedings always exhibit some appearance of iusanity. A blow struck, with blind violence may inflict a wound or a bruise, but it may fall in the wrong place; it may even injure the hand that gives it, by its own ill-directed force.

Man being a reasonable creature, will always submit to reason, if you give time for his passions to cool, aud wait for the *mollia tempora fandi,* the proper opportunities of addressing him. A FEW, in the great mass of mankind, may be corrupted by views of interest, by expectations of preferment, by bribes, and by titles. But there are not rewards enough of this kind to corrupt the whole body of any people.: The great body of the people will follow that which: appears to. them right, and just, and true. Let it be clearly laid before them, and left for their calm consideratiori. If it should so happen, Which is very unlikely, that they should not adopt it, after understanding it, and duly weighing its importance,' then they must be left to the error of their ways. *Si p<h pulus vult decipi, decipiatur.* If the people will be deluded, they must be so. Force cannot eradicate error, though it may destroy life. Riot, tumult, turbulence, may do great mischief, but they carry no conviction.*

Inflammatory language at popular meetings is to. be avoided; and indeed multitudes *oi the lowest* of the people are not to be wantonly convened. Without in the least impeaching their rights, it must be allowed that their passions are too violent when heated, by collision with each other, and their judgments too weak, when not previously informed by reading and edncation, to act wisely when met in a large body, without authorized guides, and without strict regulation. A man who is a sincere patriot, and not a *mere demagogue* for sinister purposes, will be cautious of assembling crowds of the lowest of the people. Lord George Gordons unfortunate conduct has left a lasting lesson. He, I firmly believe, intended none of that mischief which ensued; but who can say to the waves of a troubled sea,"thus "far shall ye go, and no farther?" I know, and have already commented on, the advantage taken from those riots by the friends of high-prerogative doctrinies, for disparaging the *people* at large, notwithstanding the people certainly had no concern in them.

. Though decidedly a frieud to the reform of the House of; Commons, I cannot agree with the Duke of Richmond in the propriety of universal suffrage. I think his idea perfectly Utopian. Sir Thdmas More, never wrote any thing more visionary in his celebrated fiction; Sir Robert Filmer nothing more adverse *to real* liberty. Universal suffrage, I fear, would cause universal confusion; and the friends of mankind would be inclined to fly for temporary re* fuge even to the throne of a despot. Persons in a state of *servitude* could never be expected to give a *free* vote; and vagabonds and paupers would Use their **liberty for a cloke of maliciousness,** i wish the right of suffrage to be extended **as far as it possibly can,** without endangering public order and tran* quillity; but *extreme* ignorance and *extreme* penury cannot with prudence be trusted with a power which both requires *knowledge* and commands *property.*

But whatever politicians may determine upon this point, 1 think it certain, that debates upon it cannot be held in very large assemblies, into which, not. only the lowest but the vilest of mankind are allowed ad' mission, and all the privileges of counsellors, *de* sum* *ma rerum,* on matters of the highest importance, without extreme danger of violating law, and dis* turbing that order which is necessary to comfortand security.

I wish, therefore, that all preliminary consultation on this point, and all points like this, may be con* ducted by *writing,* by appeals to reason in the *clo* set,* and that a considerable time may be allowed to cool all intemperate heats; and give *solidity* to the materials of the intended repair. At county meetings or associations, I would have tbe civil power in fail force; but never the military.. The staff of the constable should be more coercive than the sabre of the dragoon for the constitution admits the one as its own, but certainly looks at the other with horror. Every tumult, productive of mischief, gives the friends of arbitrary power an opportunity for introducing the military, of arguing against all *popular.* interference iu that very government which the *people* support by their industry, and which, according to the law of God, nature, and reason, they have a right to control by their supreme authority. There may be cases Of the last necessity, which I shudder to think of, in which nothing but the power of the people, acting by force, can maintain or recover their Usurped rights. Such must occur but seldom. May Our country never experience them!

There can be no good reason assigned why government should not be, like every thing else, continually advancing to all the perfection of which it is capable. Indeed, as the happiness of mankind depends more upon well-regulated and well-administered government, than on any thing subordinate in life or in arts, there is every reason for bestowing all the time which every passing generation can begfow, in bringing government t<? its utmost point of attainable perfection. It is the business and the **duty** of those who now live, as they value their own happiness and the happiness of their posterity, to labour in tbe reform of abuses, and the farther improvement of every improveable advantage. Would any man be listened to with patience who should

say, that any useful art or manufacture ought not to be improved by ingenious projectors, because it does *tolerably* in its present state, satisfies those who are ignorant of the excellence of which it is susceptible, and cannot be altered, even for the better, without causing some *trouble,* for a *time,* among those who have been accustomed to the present imperfect and erroneous methods of conducting it? No; encouragements are held out for improvement in all arts and sciences, conducive to the'comfort and accommodation of human life. What, then, in the *first* art, the art of diffusing happiness throughout nations, shall he who attempts improvement be stigmatized as an innovator, prosecuted as a seditious intermeddler, and persecuted with the resentment of those who find their advantage in the continuance of error, and the diffusion of abuse and corruption? However courtiers - may patronize silly establishments, which claim a prescriptive right to folly, inutility, and even mischievous consequences, the common sense of mankind will revolt against them, join in demanding reform, and in saying of old customs, when become nuisances by alteration of circumstances, that instead of being *sanctified* by long duration, they are uow more *honoured in the breach than the observance.*   '   ■ ■   i ....

But let the reformation be gentle,- though - firm; wise, thougli bold; lenient to persons erring, though severe against error. Let her not alarm the friend of LIBERTY by sudden violence, but invite all to the cause of truth and justice, by shewing that *she* is herself guarded, not only by truth and justice, but by MERCY. Let us shew ourselves, in seeking political reformation, what we profess to be, a nation of Christians, if not philosophers; and let not a groan be heard amid the acclamations of triumphant liberty, nor one drop of blood sadden the glorious victory of philosophy and Christianity over PRIDE.

SECTION XXXIX.

The Christian Religion favourable to Civil Liberty, and likewise to Equality *rightly understood.*

You seldom meet with infidelity in a cottage. You find evil and misery there, as in palaces; but you do not find infidelity. The poor love the name and religion of Jesus Christ. And they have reason to love them, if they only considered the obligations they are under to them for *worldly* comfort, for liberty, for instruction, for a due consideration in civil society.

The rights of man, to mention which is' almost criminal in the eyes of despotical sycophants, are plainly and irresistibly established in the gospel. There is no doubt but that all his creatures are dear to the Creator and Redeemer; but yet, from motives of mercy and compassion, there is an evident predilection for the POOR, manifested in our Saviour's preaching and ministry. These are very striking words: "The blind receive their sight, and the lame "walk; the lepers are cleansed, and the deaf hear; "the dead are raised up, and the POOR HAVE THE "GOSPEL PREACHED TO THEM." The instruction, the consolation, the enlightening of the POOR, are placed with the greatest of his miracles,' the resuscitation of extinguished life. Who, indeed, did trouble themselves to care for the *poor*, till JESUS CHRIST set the glorious example? It was a *miraculous* thing,

OF DESPOTISM. 295

in the eye **Of** the *world,* that a divine *teacher* should address himself particularly to those who could not reward him with a worldly recompence. But he came to destroy that INEQUALITY among' mankind, which enabled the rich and great to treat the poor as beasts of burden. He himself chose the condition' of poverty, to shew the rich and proud of how little estimation are the trifles they doat upon, in the eye' of him who made them, and who can destroy them at his pleasure. ■

Let us hear him open his divine commission. Tbp; words are very comfortable, especially after reading the histories of the tyrants who have bruised mankind with their rods of iron. We find them in the fourth chapter of St. Luke.

" *And there was delivered unto him the book of the*
" *prophet Esaias; and when he had opened the booh,*
" *he fownd the place wherein, it. was written*

"The SPIRIT OF THE LORD IS UPON ME, BECAUSE "HE HATH APPOINTED ME TO PREACH THE GOSPEL. "TO THE POOR; HE HATH SENT ME TO HEAL THE "BROKEN-HEARTED, TO PREACH DELIVERANCE TO "THE CAPTIVES, AND RECOVERY OF SIGHT TO THE "BLIND; TO SET AT LIBERTY THEM THAT ARE' "BRUISED;

"TO PREACH THE ACCEPTABLE YEAR OF THE LORD.

"And he closed the book, and he gave it again "to the minister, and sat down, and the eyes of all: "them that were in the synagogue were fastened, on "him..

"And he began to say unto them, This day is the "iscriptare fulfilled in your ears.

■"And all bare him witness, and wondered at the "gracious words which proceeded oiit of his mouth: "and they said, Is NOT THTS JOSEPHVSON?"

—And soon after, "All they in the synagogue "were.filled with wrath, and rose up, and thrust "him out of the city, and led himunto the brow of "the hill, (whereon their city was built,) that they* "might cast him down headlong." ■

: Thus their *aristocratical* prejudices prevailed over the first strong feelings of gratitude and grace. The spirit of aristocracy displayed itself here in its genuine colours; in pride, cruelty, and violence. Many of the scribes (the lawyers) and pharisees were probably, in the synagogue, and their influence soon prevailed on the people to shew their impotent malice against their best friend and benefactor. In all ages, something of the same kind is observable.' The proud supporters of tyranny, in.which they hope to partake, hav.e always used.false alarms, false plots, cunningly-contrived' nicknames and watchwords, to set the unthinking people against those who were promoting their greatest good. '■

When Christ began to preach, we read in the, seventh chapter of. St. Luke, that the multitude: and the publicans heard him; but the scribes and the pharisees *rejected* the counsel of God towards them. They, like all persons of similar temper and rank, flourishing by abuses, could not bear *innovation*.

The most powerful argument. they used against him was this question:---------- HAVE ANY OF THE RULERS AND THE PHARISEES BELIEVED IN-HIM? In modern times the question would have-been, Have any per-sods of fashion and distinction given countenance to him ? Does my lord—or my lady—or Sir Harry go to hear him preach?—Or is he somebody whom nobody knows?—Such is the language of the spirit of despotism, in all times and countries.

. THREE HUNDRED YEARS elapsed, in consequence of these prejudices, before the gospel was recognized and received at COURT. And I am sorry to say that the COURT soon corrupted its simplicity. The pride of life, always prevalent among those who assume to themselves good things enough to support and comfort'hundreds of individuals equally deserving; could never brook the doctriues of Christ, which favoured liberty and equality. It therefore seduced the Christians to a participation of power and grandeur; and the poor, with their rights, were often forgotten, in the most splendid periods of ecclesias-' tical prosperity. Many nominal Christians have been and are as aristocratical as Herod and the chief priests and pharisees of Judea. . •

■ But the authority of Jesus Christ himself must have more weight with Christians, than all the pomp and parade of tbe most absolute despots in Europe, at the head of the finest troops in the universe. He taught us, when we pray, to say, *Our Father.* This alone is sufficient to establish, on an immoveable basis, the^ equality of human beings. All are bound to call upon and consider God as their Father, if they are Christians; and, as there are no rights of primogeniture in Heaven, all are equal brothers and sisters, coheirs, if they do not forfeit their hopes, of a blessed immortality. But these are doctrines which the great and proud cannot admit. This world is theirs, and they cannot bear that the beggar, the servant, the slave, should be their equal. We can hardly suppose, in imagination, the Empress of Russia, the King of Prussia, the Emperor of Germany, or any *grandee* with a riband, a garter, or a star, kneeling down, and from his *heart* acknowledging, in bis *prayer*, a poor private in a marching regiment, a poor wretch in a workhouse, or the servant that rides, behind his carriage, a *brother*. So void of reason and religion is a poor helpless mortal, when dressed in a little brief authority by the folly of those who submit to be trampled under foot by their equal; a man born of a woman, like themselves, and, doomed, like themselves, after strutting on the stage a few years, to the grave. Our Saviour, with a wisdom far above all the refinement of philosophy, frequently inculcated the vanity of riches and power, and the real pre-eminence of virtue.

And what say the *apostles?* Po they favour those. who usurp an unnatural and unreasonable power over their fellow-mortals, for'the sake of gratifying their own selfish vanity and avarice? Let us hear them.

St. Paul, in the first chapter of the First Epistle to the Corinthians, says, "You see your calling, "brethren, how that not many wise men after the "flesh, (worldly-wise men,) dot many *mighty*, not "many *noble,* are called."

In the second chapter of the Epistle of St. James, we read,

"Has not God chosen the poor of this world to "be heirs of his kingdom ?" To which is added,..

" The RJCH MEN blasphemer that- worthy name by *? Ivhieh ye are called." . , yr
.r These passages afford a. very strong argument of the truth and divinity of the Christian religion, for they contain the very doctrines, which were foretold several hundred years before the appearance of Christianity. ISAIAH, in his twenty-ninth chapter, speak*ing of the gospel, and its doctrines 'and effects, expressly says,

"The *meek* shall increase their joy.ift the Lord; "and the POOR AMONG MEN SHALL, REJOICE IN; THE "HOLY ONE OF ISRAEL."

' The inference 1 would draw from all that has preceded, is, that the middle ranks and the poor, that is, the'great majority of mankind, should place a due value on the gospel, not only for its religious, but also its civil and political advantages. It is the GRAND CHARTER OF THEIR FREEDOM, their indepemdence, their equality. All the subtilty of lawyers* all the sophistry of ministerial orators, all the power of all. the despots and aristocrats, in the world, can? not annihilate RIGHTS, given, indeed, by *Nature,* but plainly confirmed by the *Gospel.* The wbrdsalready cited are top clear and explicit to admit of misconstruction. JESUS CHRIST came to put an end to unjust inequality in this world, while he revealed the prospect of another, where *the wicked cease from troubling, and the weary are at rest,* O ye people, give not the tyrants such an advantage as to part with your gospel. Preserve it, watch over it, as the pearl of great price. It is your security for present and future felicity. Other Herods, other Neros

may arise, who will rejoice to see you voluntarily renounce a system which militates against their diabolical rule; rejoice to see you give up that which all the persecution of the ancient Herods an d Neros in vain attempted to abolish by shedding blood.'
- I think it may be depended on as indisputable, that men who endeavour to suppress all works in favour of truth,* liberty, and the happiness of the middle and poor classes of the people, would, if they had lived about one thousand seven hundred and ninety-five years ago, have joitied with the *high priests* and rulers to *crucify* JESUS CHRIST. They would have prosecuted and persecuted him for sedition and high treason. They would have despised and rejected the friend of Lazarus; and taken the part of DIVES, even in hell.. The spirit of pride is of the devil, and those who are actuated by that spirit, in all their conduct, would have fallen down and worshipped him, if he would have put them on the pinnacle of the temple, and promised them the kingdoms of the world, 'and the glory of them. >

* " *That make a man an offender for a* word."

Isaiah, xxix. 21.

SECTION XL.

The Pride which produces the Spirit of Despotism conspicuous even on the Tombstone. It might be treated with total Neglect, if it did not tend to the Oppression of the Poor, and to Bloodshed and Plunder.

DEATH is the great teacher and censor of human vanity; but even death cannot repress the pride of aristocracy, or the insolence of riches, endeavouring to make wealth and grandeur triumph over the law of nature, and outshine others even from the coffin and the grave. If we look into the churches and church-yards, we see tbe most insignificant of mankind honoured with the most magnificent monuments of marble, the proudest trophies, sculptured urns, a flattering inscription, and a gilded lie. The' walls of the sanctuary are hung with banners, escutcheons,' helmets, and spurs, which display the emptiness- of that pre-eminence which they are intended to:emblazon. The poor body, which all this paint and finery attends, lies mouldering in the vault; and give it but a tongue to speak, would exclaim, at the gaudy sight, "Vanity of vanities ! Mock not my humili-"ated condition with the contemptible pageantry "that misguided my feet from the path of reason " and happiness, during my mortal existence." The only means of being honourably distinguished. is to promote most effectually the general happiness of human nature, and to seek private good in public beneficence.

The spirit of despotism is remarkably visible in the *mausoleum*. There are families who seem to think that their precious bones would be contaminated, even if deposited in the consecrated cemeteries of the church, where plebeians sleep, and therefore they erect proud temples in their private domains, where their fathers may rot in state, unapproached by the vulgar. If they were illustrious inventors of arts and benefactors to mankind, the distinction might be a just compliment to their memory, and a useful incentive to emulation. But the persons thus magnificently interred are usually the most insignificant of the human race; whose very names would not be known a year after their decease^ if they were not deeply engraven on the marble.

Many an *aldemum,* notorious for the meanest avarice, as little distinguished for beneficence as abi-> lities, is decorated with the most sumptuous memorials which the *stone-cutter* can raise for money; while *MUton,* the glory of the nation, a man elevated above the rank of common humanity, had no monumental marble. But. all that the herald's office Can effect* all that can be done by painting, gilding, and marble, eannot ennoble the greatest favourite of a court, the most successful adventurer in the East Indies, or the most opulent contractor and money-lender, like a Paradise Lost; The nabobs find their influence cannot secure the *esteem* of a few eon temporaries, though it may commaud their votes, piuch less of whole nations, and of late posterity. Money, the only god which worldlings worship,.loses its omnipotence after the death of its possessor; land even the inheritor often despises the mauwho acquired it. The uhdertaker, the escutcheon painter, and the feculptor, are however employed to keep up the false pageantry of insignificant opulence; and a hearse, covered over with coats of arms, is used for the purpose of impressing the vulgar with a veneration for rank and riches, while, in the minds of men of sense, it excites ridicule, and converts a funeral into a farce.

Indeed the empty parade of pride, and the self-importance of despotism itself, might furnish a laughable entertainment, if it were not productive of mischief misery, and bloodshed. To support the vanity, exclusive privileges, and high pretensions of those who have little personal merit or services to recommend diem to society, it is necessary to have recourse to military force and corruption. A system of terror and coercion canalone keep down the people, and compel a tame acquiescence under usurped power, abused for the purposes of oppression.

Standing armies are therefore the glory and delight of all who are actuated by the spirit of despotism.* They would have no* great objection to military government and martial law, while power is in their own hands, or in the hands of their patrons. The, implicit sub the military system favours, that men in subaltern stations are to act as they are bidden, and never to deliberate on the propriety of the command, is perfectly congenial with the spirit of despotism. The glitter, the pomp, the parade and ostentation of war are also! highly pleasing to minds that prefer splendour and pageantry to solid and substantial comfort. The happiness, which must ever depend on the tranquillity of the people, is little regarded, when set in competition with the gratification of personal vanity. Plumes, lace, shining arms, and other habiliments of war, set off the *person* to great advantage.; and as to the wretches who are slain or wounded, plunged into captivity and disease, in order to support this finery, are they not *paid* for it ? Besides, they are, for the most part, in the lowest class, and those whom *nobody* knows.

. Such is the love of standing armies, in some countries, that attempts are made to render even the national militia little different from a standing army. This, circumstance alone is a symptom of the spirit of, despotism. A militia of *mercenary* substitutes, under officers entirely devoted to a minister, must add greatly to a standing army, from which, in fact, it would differ only in name. Should *the people* he entirely *disarmed,* and scarcely a musket and bayonet in the country but under the management of a minister, through the agency of servile lords lieutenant and; venal magistrates, what defence would remain, in extremities, either for the king or the people?

The love of pomp and finery, though ridiculous in itself, may. thus become injurious to liberty, and therefore to happiness, by increasing the *military order* in the time *of peace,* and when ministerial arts have contributed to render that; order devoted to purposes of selfish aggrandizement or borough in-

OF DESPOTISM.

Alienee. JMifids, capable of being captivated with the silly parade of war, are of too soft a texture to grasp tbe manly principles of true patriotism. They will usually prefer the favour of a court, which has nahy *shining* ornaments to bestow, to the esteem of a people. A heart deeply infected with the spirit of despotism, despises the people too much to be in the least solicitous to obtain popular applause. Praise is but breath; and often, like the wind, veers about inconstantly; and certainly will desert a man who has deserted the virtuous and benevolent conduct which first excited it. But. ribands, stars, garters, places, pensions, usually last for life; and titles descend to the latest posterity. Honour, once gained by royal smiles, is a part of the family goods and chattels, and goes down, from generation to generation, without requiring, to the day of doom, any.painful exertion, ing its happy possessors to the free enjoyment of idleness and luxury; No wonder, therefore, that where the selfish spirit of despotism prevails, a bauble bestowed by a court shall outweigh a whole people's plaudits. A coat of arms makes a figure on the escutcheon and the tombstone; but not a scrap of gild ad and painted silk—not even a *Moody hand,* can be bestowed by the most cordial esteem of the low multitude.

Heraldry *itself,* though a childish, is a harmless
vanity; but, as conducing very much to the spirit of despotism, it becomes not only ridiculous, but mischievous. It makes a distinction, on which men plume themselves, without merit and without ser-

x

vices. Satisfied with such a distinction, they will be less inclined to acquire merit and to render services. They can inherit a coat of arms; or they can buy one; or, which is more compendious still, they can borrow or invent one. It is enough that they are separated from the *canaille.* The coach, the hall, the church, is crowded with their *achievements;* there is no occasion for arduous exertion. They are now raised above the vulgar. The work is done. Their name is up; they may slumber in the repose of useless insignificance, or move in the restlessness of mischievous activity. The coat of arms is at once a shield for folly, and a banner in the triumph of pride.

But both pride and folly should be permitted for me to enjoy their baubles unmolested, if they did not lead to CRUELTY. But pride and folly are the causes of war.; therefore I hate.them from my soul. They *glory* in destruction; and among the most frequent ornaments, even of our churches, (the very houses of peace,) are hung up on high *trophies* of war. Dead men (themselves subdued by the universal conqueror) are represented, by their surviving friends, as rejoicing, even in their graves, in the implements of manslaughter. Helmets, swords, and blood-stained flags hang over the grave, together with the escutcheons and marble monuments, emblematical of human ferocity; of those actions and passions which Christianity repudiates; for as well might oil and vinegar coalesce, as War and Christianity.

Spirit of Despotism ! 1 would laugh at all thy extravagancies, thy solemn mummery, thy baby baubles, thy airs of insolence, thy finery and frippery, thy impotent insults over virtue, genius, and all personal merit, thy strutting, self-pleasing mien and language ! I would consider them all with the eye of a Democritus, as affording a constant farce, an inexhaustible fund of merriment, did they not lead to the malevolent passions, which, in their effects, forge chains for men born free, plunder the poor of their property, and shed the blood of innocence.

SECTION XLI.

CONCLUSION.

) To meliorate the condition of human nature can be the only rational end of government. It cannot be designed to favour one description of men, a minority of men, at the expfeoce of all others; who, haring received life from him who alone can give it, received at the same time a right to enjoy it in liberty and security. This was the charter of God and nature; which no mortal, however elevated by conquest or inheritance, can annul or violate without impiety. All government which makes not the advancement of human happiness, and the comfort of the individuals who are subject to its control, the *prime* purpose of its operations, partakes of despotism: and I have always thought that, in governments which boast of a free constitution, the views, even of statesmen and politicians who espoused the cause of liberty, have been too circumscribed. They have been attached to names and families. They seem not to have opened either their eyes or hearts to objects truly great and affections sincerely catholic and philanthropic. 1 hate to hear public men, who certainly can have no right to their pre-eminence but for the public good, professing themselves of the Rockingham Party, the Shelburne Party, the Portland Party, and appearing to forget, in their zeal for a few distinguished houses, the great mass of the

OF DESPOTISM.

People, the Party of human nature. The majority of men are poor and obscure. To them ail party attachments to names and families, little known as public benefactors, must appear at once absurd and injurious. They are the persons who stand in most need of protection and assistance from the powerful. The rich, under all governments, have a thousand means of procuring either comfort or defence. It is tbe mass, the poor and middling ranks, unknown to and unknowing courts or kings, who require all the alleviation which men enlightened hy knowledge, furnished with opulence, elevated by rank, can af> ford to lessen the natural evils of life, aggravated by the moral and artificial. Government possesses the power of alleviating, and sometimes of removing, that moral and physical evil which embitters existence. How deplorable, when government becomes so perverted as to increase the evil it was designed to cure. Yet this has been, and is now the case on a great part of the globe; insomuch that the learned and judicious Dr. Prideaux, whose integrity is as well known as his ability, used to say, "That it was "a doubt with him, whether the benefit which the "world receives from government was sufficient to "make amends for tbe calamities which it suffers "from the follies, mistakes, and mal- administration "of those that manage it.'* •

When it is considered how little the most boasted governments have been able or. inclined to prevent the greatest calamity of the world, the frequent recurrence of war, it is natural to conclude, that there has been some radical defect or error in all govern-

ment, hitherto instituted on the face of the earth. *Violence* may be used where there is *no* government Governments pretend to direct human affairs by *reason;* but war is a dereliction of reason, a renunciation of all that refines and improves human nature, and an appeal to brute force. Man descends from the heights to which philosophers and legislators had raised him in society; takes the sword, and surpasses the beasts of the forest in ferocity. Yet so far from thinking himself culpable, he deems his destructive employment the most honourable of all human occupations, because governments have politically contrived to throw a glossy mantle, covered with tinsel and spangles, over the horrors of bloodshed and devastation. If governments, with all their riches and power, all their vaunted arts and sciences, all the mysterious policy of cabinets, all the wisdom and eloquence of deliberating senates, are *unable* to preserve the *blessing of peace,* uninterrupted, during the short space of twenty years together, they must be dreadfully faulty, either in their constitution or their administration. In what consists the fault ? I think in the selfish spirit of despotism, pursuing the sordid or vain-glorious purposes of the governors, with little regard to the real, substantial happiness of the governed. Despotism, in some mode or degree, has transformed the shepherds of the frock into wolves;.has ap innoxious animals, tore down the fences of the sheepfold, and laid waste the pasture.
the government that has distributed property so equitably, as that none to whom existence

OF DESPOTISM.

has been given should want the *necessaries* of existence; and where helpless age; and infirmity, as well as helpless infancy, should find a pillow to repose on, and plenty to nourish it, without supplicating a man, *equal* by nature, for the cold and scanty relief of eleemosynary charity ? The truth is, power gradually *engrosses* property; and the selfish spirit of despotism is ever striving to appropriate all tbe good, of every kind, which the earth is able to produce.

The truth is, *national glory*, the trappings of a court, tbe parade of armies, the finery of external appearance, have been the silly objects of *state* solicitude; while man was left to bewail, in the recesses of want and obscurity, that his mother had brought him into a world of woe, without means of comfort, or support, with little other prospect than to labour without ceasing, to fight those who never injured: him, and to die prematurely, unknown, and unlamen ted. All bis wretchedness has been aggravated by the *insults* of unfeeling pride; the *neglect* of aristocratic grandeur, which, under the spirit of despotism, mocked by the false pageantry of life, those who were doomed to feel its real misery. The vain pomp and glory of the world, held out the finger of. scorn to that wretchedness which itself contributed to create, and would not relieve. —*

Three score years and ten, and those often full of labour and sorrow, constitute the space allotted to the life of man in a venerable volume, fall of beauty as well as instruction, and worthy of great attention independently of the high authority.attributed to it by the religion established by the laws of this country. Few and evil are our days, even when they proceed to their natural extent, and are attended with the common portion of health and prosperity. Yet, as if a *superfluity* of years and happiness were lavished on men, the chief business of the greatest part of governments on the whole earth has been to abbreviate life, to poison and embitter its sweetest pleasures, and add new pungency to its anguish. Yet see the false *glitter* of happiness, the pomp and parade which such governments assume; observe the gravity and insolence of superiority which their ministers, their statesmen, and their warriors, assume, and you would imagine them a commissioned regency, lord lieutenants sent by Heaven to rule this lower world, and to rectify all disorders which had escaped the vigilance of the Deity. The time has been when they have actually claimed the title of God's vicegerents, and have been literally worshipped as gods by the servile crew of courtiers; men gradually bowed down by despotism from the erect port of native dignity, and driven by fear to crouch under the most degrading of all superstition, the political idolatry of a base fellow-creature.

After all the language of court adulation, the praises of poets and orators, the statues and monuments erected to their fame, the malignant consequences of their actions prove them to have been no other than conspirators against the improvement and happiness of the human race. What were their means of conducting their governments, of exercising this office of Heaven's vicegerents? Crafty, dishonest arts, oppression, extortion, and above all, fire and sword. They dared to ape the thunder and lightning of Heaven, and, assisted by the machinations of the Grand Adversary of man, rendered their imitative contrivances for destruction more terrible and deadly than the original. Their imperial robe derived its deep crimson colour from human blood; and the gold and diamonds of their diadems were' accumulated treasures wrung from the famished bowels of the *poor,* born only to toil for others, to be robbed, to be wounded, to be trodden under foot and forgotten in an early grave. How few, in comparison, have reached the age of threescore and ten, and yet, in the midst of youth and health, their days have been full of labour and sorrow. Heaven's vicegerents seldom bestowed a thought upon them, except when it was necessary either to inveigle or to force them to take the sword and march to slaughter. Where God caused the sun to shine gaily, and scattered plenty over the land, his vicegerents diffused famine and solitude. The valley which laughed with corn, they watered with the tear of artificial hunger and distress; the plain that was bright with verdure, and gay with flowrets, they dyed red with gore. They operated on the world as tbe blast of an east wind, as a pestilence, as a deluge, as a conflagration. And have they yet ceased from the earth? Cast your eyes over the plains of Russia, Poland, a great part of Europe, the wilds of Africa, and the gardens of Asia, European despotism has united with oriental, to unparadise the provinces of India.

Thus, if God, in his wisdom, has thought fit to

allot as a *few evils* for the purpose of discipline, the great ones of the world hare endeavoured to make the *whole* of life an evil to the despised and neglected million. The world is now old, and may profit by the lessons of Experience. She has decisively declared, that despotism is the grand source of human misfortune, the Pandora's box out of which every curse has issued, and scarcely left even Hope behind. Despotism, in its extreme, is fatal to human happiness, and, in all its degrees and modifications, injurious. The spirit of it ought therefore to be suppressed on the first and slightest appearance. It should be the endeavour of every good man, *pro virili,* as far as his best abilities will extend, to extirpate all arbitrary government from the globe. It should be swept from the earth, or trampled under foot, from China to Peru. But no power is Capable of crushing the Hydra, less than the Herculean arm of a whole people.

I lay it down as an incontrovertible axiom, that all who are born into the world have a right to be as happy in it as the unavoidable evils of nature, and their own disordered passions, will allow. The grand object of all good government, of all government that is not an usurpation, must be to promote this happiness* to assist every individual in its attainment and security. A government chiefly anxious about the emoluments of office, chiefly employed in augmenting its own power and aggrandizing its obsequious instruments, while it neglects the comfort and safety of individuals in middle or low life, is despotic and a nuisance. It is founded on folly as well as wickedness, and, like the freaks of insanity, deals mischief and misery around, without being able to ascertain or limit its extent and duration. If it should not be punished as criminal, let it be coerced as dangerous. Let tbe straight waistcoat be applied; but let men, judging fellow-men, *always* spare the axe.

For what rational purpose could we enter into life? To vex, torment, and slay each other with the sword? To be and to make miserable? No, by the sweet mercy of Heaven! I firmly believe, that the great King of Kiugs, intended every son and daughter of Adam to be as happy as the eternal laws of nature, under his control, permit them to be in this sublunary state. Execrated and exploded be all those politics, with Machiavel, or the Evil Being, their author, which introduce systems of government and manners among the great, inconsistent with the happiness of the majority. Must real tragedies be for ever acting on the stage of human life? Must men go on for ever to be tormentors and executioners of men ? Is the world never to profit by the experience of ages ? Must hot even *attempts* be made to improve the happiness of life, to improve government, though all arts and sciences are encouraged in their progress to perfection ? Must the grand art, the sublimest science, that of meliorating the condition of human nature, be stationary? No; forbid it reason, virtue, benevolence, religion! Let the world be made more and more comfortable to all who are allowed the glorious privilege of seemg the sun and breathing the liberal air. Our forefathere were duped by priests and despots, and, through the timidity of superstition and the blindness of ignorance, submitted to be made artificially miserable. Let us explode that folly which we *see;* and let every mortal under the cope of heaven, eiyoy ex. istence, as long as nature will allow the feast to continue, without any restraints on liberty but such as the majority of uncorrupted guests unite in agreeing to be salutary, and therefore conducive to the general festivity. Men are too *serious* in pursuing toys, money, titles, stare, ribands, triumphs, any thing that gives a momentary distinction, and gratifies an unmanly pride. They have emhraced a cloud for a goddess. Let them dispel the mist, raised by false policy and cruel despotism. Let them at last distinguish real good, from its delusive appearance. Let them value duly, and pursue diligently, solid comfort, health, cheerfulness, contentment, universal benevolence, and learn to relish the sweets of nature and simplicity. They will then see happiness in something besides the possession of *gold;* besides those *external* marks of superiority which raise them to notice, and distinguish them from their equals without a difference. Strife and wars will cease; when men perceive that their highest happiness is most easily attainable in a state of contented tranquillity; their guide, nature, and their guard, innocence.

The principal objects of all rational government, each as is intended to promote human happiness, are two; to preserve *peace,* and to diffuse *plenty.* Such government will seldom tax the necessaries of

OF DESPOTISM. 317

life. It will avoid wars; and, by such humane and wise policy, render taxes on *necessaries* totally superfluoiTS. Taxes on *necessaries* are usually caused by war. The poor, however, are not easily excited to insurrection. It is a base calumny which accuses them. They are naturally quiescent; inclined to submission by'their babits, and willing to reverence all their superiors who behave to them justly and kindly. They deserve to be used well. They de» serve confidence. But oppression and persecution may teach them to lift their gigantic arm, and then - vain will be resistance. Let not wars then be wantonly undertaken, which, besides their injustice and inhumanity, tend more than any thing else, by increasing taxes, to compel insurtvection. The poor mart hears great praises bestowed on the government he lives under, and perpetual panegyrics on the constitution. He knows little of general politics. He judges from the *ejects* he.FE$Lis He knows that malt,* leather, candles, soap, salt, and windows, without which he cannot exist in eomibrt, are ao heavily taxed **as** sometimes to exclude him from obtaining tbe scanty portion he would require. In return for the defalcations from malt, leather, candles, soap, salt, and windows; he sees pensions, places, rich contractors, disgraceful, ruinous, and bloody wars. Yet he rises up early, and goeth forth to his

* I heard a great borough-mooger of eleven or twelve thousand a-year assert, while he held a glass of Madeira in his hand to wash down a plentiful dinner, that *mult* codd not he reckoned among the *necessaries* of the poor labourer, because he might drink waiur, which is very *wholesome*.

work and his labour, with cheerfulness. Is he not a worthy, respectable member of society, and deserving of every indulgence? Ought he to be insulted by opprobrious appellations, considered as of no political consequence, as possessing no rights, and little removed from the cattle? Suppose millions of such men in a country, ought not their wishes to be consulted, and a regard for their comfort and security to stop the sword, while emerging from its scabbard at the command of a minister?

Great reforms usually come from the people. They are slow to anger, and submit in patience. But grievances may become intolerable; and then their energy displays itself like a torrent, that has long lain still and placid within the dam, which opposed its course to a certain point, but could resist no longer.

If ever any people should be roused to take their own affairs into their own hands, I hope they will refute the calumnies of the proud, by acting with justice and mercy. All human creatures are weak and fallible; kings' and ministers have exhibited remarkable instances of this common imbecility. Great allowances should therefore be made for their mors and even *crimes,* which, probably, originated in error. I wish to see the British government made as perfect as human ingenuity and virtue can render it; but I would effect reform in it, without injuring the person or destroying the life of the most obnoxious individual. I would pardon much to human infirmity. Not one drop of blood should be shed, nor a single mite of property violated. No injustice whatever should disgrace the wisdom of the people. Compensations should be made by the public to all individuals, of all parties and persuasions, when compelled to relinquish possessions or privileges lawdaily inherited, or honestly acquired. The most liberal, expanded generosity should vindicate the honour of human nature, too long insulted. Ministers and grandees, who form the aristocracy, either of opulence or nobility, however tyrannical and insolent in the day of their prosperity, should live out the little space allotted to man, in a state of ease and affluence adapted to. their habits and education. I would shew them how truly noble and glorious it is to forgive. And they could not be formidable against an united people. For how weak, how transitory is man! Death, *natural*, unprecipitated death, will soon tame the haughtiest spirit that ever swelled the fancied importance of a crown; and the infirmities attending the approach of death, the gradual decays of age, will usually teach a lesson of unfeigned humility.

The people, at present, appear to be sunk in a political lethargy. But let not ministers confide too much in the symptoms. A calm precedes a storm. Long continued abuses, heavy burdens, and severe grievances, without a dream of hope, may awaken the lion. Then, I think, those who have shown an inclination to set up a power unknown to constitutional freedom, and to render government hostile to the people, may justly fear.

And who, it may be asked, are they? I am happy

in the opportunity of declaring it my opinion, that the KING is not among them. They are men to whom neither the King nor the people are dear. They are, in a word, the *oligarchy of borougk-mongers,* whose power is founded on an usurpation; and whose assumed sovereignty is no less inconsistent with the real freedom of a king than of a people. A most respectable society, not long ago, asserted in a petition to the House of Commons, and offered to prove it at the bar, that *one hundred and fifty-four mm* nominate and appoint a majority of the House. Has it not been' suspected, that a war might have been made 4nd supported to prevent the annihilation of this oligarchy; by turning the attention of the people from a reform of parliament, and endeavouring to give a deadly stab to liberty. If the suspicion be well founded, this very circumstance is tbe strongest argument for reform which has ever been produced. Oceans of *blood,* and *treasure* enough to relieve all the poor in the nation for many years, lavished to establish a despotism, inimical to the King, tbe people, and to human nature J We have now reached the source of the evil, a source not so concealed as the fountain of the Nile, It is the corruption of boroughs, and the interference of ministers, peers, placemen, pensioners, and expectants, in parliamentary elections, which causes the *spirit of despotism* to increase; for nature, reason, and self-interest too, if they were not counteracted by corrupt influence, would revolt at it. The egg would be instantly crushed, if it were not constantly guarded and fostered in the warm, well-fortified nest of *borough-influence,* directing all measures and disposing of all patronage.

But they are all *honourable* men, who are concerned in this influence. They may not be morally worse or better than others in their situation. Their situation renders them politically iniquitous. The world is governed by men, and men by their passions, and their supposed interest. But it is the business of laws to restrain them. The people are bound to watch the conduct of all, whose conduct is influential on their welfare. Unlimited confidence should be given to no man, when the happiness of millions is concerned in the consequences of his actions or counsels.

"The conpnon people," says a sensible author, "generally think that *great* men have *great* minds, "and scorn *base* actions; which judgment is so false, "that the basest and worst of all actions have been "done by *great men.* They have often disturbed, "deceived, and pillaged the world; and he who is "capable of the *highest* mischief is capable of the "meanest. He who plunders a country of a million of money would, in suitable circumstances, "steal a silver spoon; and a conqueror, who steals "apd pillages a kingdom, would, in an humbler si-"tuation, rifle a portmanteau." I should not, therefore, choose to expese my watch or purse in a crowd, to those men who have plundered Poland, if, instead of possessing a crown of jewels, and the pocket of submissive nations, they had been in the circumstances of a *Barrington.* Nor, though men should be called *honourable*; will it be safe to trust our liberties to their honour, without some collateral security; especially when we see them interfering with and controlling elections, contrary to express laws, and contrary Hot only to the dictates of *honour,* but of common honesty. They *usurp* a power for the gratification of pride and avarice, which they cannot hold but to the injury of the lawful and right owners. How differs this, in a moral view, from robbery ? It differs, in a political view, indeed, inasmuch as it is infinitely more injurious to society.

The opposers of reform, the invaders of the people's rights, are no less blind and short-sighted than meanly selfish. Let them pour their venom on the people, and dispute popular claims to natural right, as much as they please; the people must at last triumph, and liberty will in time flourish all over Europe. Court parasites, and selfish grandees, will do right to use a little foresight; to consider what *revolutions* may be, by viewing what have been; and not to exasperate mankind too much, lest the irritation should produce, what God avert, a sanguinary, vengeance. [1]

I take my leave oh this occasion, recommending, from tbe bottom of my heart, to men in power, measures of conciliation. Let them come among us with *healing* in their wings. Letthem concede, with cheerfulness, whatever, cannot btf denied without injustice; Let them shew them selves, real friends to liberty and man. The English nation is remarkable for generosity and good-nature. All their mistakes will be forgiven. *There will be.no. leading, into cap-*

iivity, and no complaining in our streets. Mercy and truth shall meet together; and *righteousness and peace* kiss each other. In a word,—let parliament be reformed. This measure will remove all grievances, and satisfy all demands. It will at once give permanency to the throne, and happiness to the people. Kings will be republicans in the true sense of that term; and the Spirit of Despotism become the Spirit of Philanthropy.

THE END.

J. M'Creery, Tooks-Court,
Chancery-Lane, Loudon.

www.ingramcontent.com/pod-product-compliance
Lightning Source LLC
Chambersburg PA
CBHW030008240426
43672CB00007B/872